Literature and the Telephone

Literature and the Telephone

Conversations on Poetics, Politics and Place

Sarah Jackson

BLOOMSBURY ACADEMIC
LONDON • NEW YORK • OXFORD • NEW DELHI • SYDNEY

BLOOMSBURY ACADEMIC
Bloomsbury Publishing Plc
50 Bedford Square, London, WC1B 3DP, UK
1385 Broadway, New York, NY 10018, USA
29 Earlsfort Terrace, Dublin 2, Ireland

BLOOMSBURY, BLOOMSBURY ACADEMIC and the Diana logo
are trademarks of Bloomsbury Publishing Plc

First published in Great Britain 2023
This paperback edition published 2025

Copyright © Sarah Jackson, 2023

Sarah Jackson has asserted her right under the Copyright,
Designs and Patents Act, 1988, to be identified as Author of this work.

For legal purposes the Acknowledgements on pp. x–xii constitute
an extension of this copyright page.

Cover design by Rebecca Heselton
Cover image: Invasive Species 6/12 © Dillon Marsh

This work is published open access subject to a Creative Commons Attribution-NonCommercial-NoDerivatives 4.0 International licence (CC BY-NC-ND 4.0, https://creativecommons.org/licenses/by-nc-nd/4.0/). You may re-use, distribute, and reproduce this work in any medium for non-commercial purposes, provided you give attribution to the copyright holder and the publisher and provide a link to the Creative Commons licence.

Bloomsbury Publishing Plc does not have any control over, or responsibility for, any third-party websites referred to or in this book. All internet addresses given in this book were correct at the time of going to press. The author and publisher regret any inconvenience caused if addresses have changed or sites have ceased to exist, but can accept no responsibility for any such changes.

Any third party materials reproduced in part in this work are not licensed under this work's CC BY NC ND 4.0 license. They are reproduced with all rights reserved

A catalogue record for this book is available from the British Library.

Library of Congress Cataloging-in-Publication Data
Names: Jackson, Sarah, 1977- author.
Title: Literature and the telephone : conversations on poetics, politics
and place / Sarah Jackson.
Description: London ; New York : Bloomsbury Academic, 2023. | Includes
bibliographical references and index.
Identifiers: LCCN 2022060160 | ISBN 9781350259607 (hardback) |
ISBN 9781350269774 (paperback) | ISBN 9781350259614 (ebook) | ISBN 9781350259621 (epub)
Subjects: LCSH: Telephone in literature. | Technology in literature.
Classification: LCC PN56.T4426 J33 2023 | DDC 809/.9336–dc23/eng/20230330
LC record available at https://lccn.loc.gov/2022060160

ISBN:		
	HB:	978-1-3502-5960-7
	PB:	978-1-3502-6977-4
	ePDF:	978-1-3502-5961-4
	eBook:	978-1-3502-5962-1

Typeset by Integra Software Services Pvt. Ltd.

To find out more about our authors and books visit www.bloomsbury.com
and sign up for our newsletters.

Contents

Preface: Hello, yes?	vi
Acknowledgements	x
Introduction: The telephone – a question of literature	1
1 Interruption, interference and errancy	19
2 Secret communications	43
3 'WHR R U? XXX'	69
4 Calling without calling	95
5 Distress calls	117
6 Missiles and missives	145
7 Remains	173
Coda: A long goodbye	199
Bibliography	203
Index	226

Preface: Hello, yes?

In an essay on scientific treasures for the *New York Times*, Dennis Overbye describes a 'small white book, barely more than a pamphlet' that he discovered for sale at Christie's Auction House in 2008 and which he claims was the 'directory for [the] world's first commercial phone system, Volume 1, No. 1, published in New Haven by the Connecticut District Telephone Company in November 1878'.[1] Consisting of a list of fifty subscribers, the directory also incorporates operating instructions, including the statement that users 'should begin by saying, "Hulloa"'.[2] According to Ammon Shea, however, Alexander Graham Bell, the man who had in 1876 been granted the patent for the invention of the telephone, actually preferred the term 'ahoy' for answering a call – a nautical signal stemming from the Dutch 'hoi'.[3] Allen Koenigsberg claims that it was in fact Thomas Edison who insisted on answering the telephone with a 'hello'.[4] In a letter dated 15 August 1877 to T. B. A. David, President of the Central District and Printing Telegraph Company of Pittsburg, Edison writes: 'Friend David, I do not think we shall need a call bell as Hello! can be heard 10 to 20 feet away. What you think?'[5] Spelled with an 'e', as Edison did on this occasion, 'hello' was a relatively new word, its first published use dating back to 1827; it has since come to serve as a greeting, a means of attracting attention, or a way to express surprise.[6] But 'hello' is also related to 'halloo', which Koenigsberg tells us was the first word that Edison shouted into the strip phonograph on 18 July 1877: '"I shouted the word 'Halloo! Halloo!' into the mouthpiece, ran the paper back over the steel point and heard a faint Halloo! Halloo! in return!"'[7] These variations in spelling continued to cause consternation across the Atlantic into the twentieth century, where 'hullo' was thrown into the mix. In response to an article in the French press about their preference for "allo' over 'hello', the editors of the *National Telephone Journal* in May 1906 write: 'Is it not inflicting torture on a word to deprive it of its "H?"'[8] They continue:

> Why 'Hello!'? No Englishman ever uses the expression, unless he be one of a minority who form their manners on American comic journals. An Englishman always says 'Hallo!' or 'Hullo!' and it will be found that this is the only expression of the kind current in English literature.[9]

With a whole gamut of greetings at work in literature since the invention of the telephone, these variations and their implications continue to evolve even as its forms and format – from wired to WhatsApp – change beyond recognition.

The telephone greeting does not only register changes in language and etiquette; it also invokes questions of voice and address. '"Hello, Derby Derby Derby, this is Leeds Leeds Leeds"', says the narrator of Carol Lake's *Switchboard Operators*, explaining that 'when these are the only words you can utter you have to make them as wonderful as possible'.[10] This is not the attitude taken by Netta Longdon in Patrick Hamilton's *Hangover Square*, who responds with dismay to George Harvey Bone's telephone call: '"Hullo," she said. "Yes!"'[11] 'She was in a temper all right', George reflects: 'He could tell that because there was an exclamation mark, instead of a note of interrogation, after her "Yes"'.[12] The specificity of this punctuation mark is pointed, performing the destabilization of speech and writing in the literary phone call. In a move that threatens to overturn George's understanding of his exchange with Netta, Jacques Derrida argues that the telephonic 'yes' is in fact always haunted by a question mark: it is 'a *yes* that cannot necessarily be distinguished from the question or the request'.[13] For Derrida, even as the nature of the telephonic greeting continues to evolve – from the 'Hi darling' of Ariana Reines's *Telephone* to W. N. Herbert's 'Eh amna here tae tak yir caa' in 'Answerphone' – the literary telephone invariably invites (or demands) a response.[14] Discussing the '*yes phenomenon*' in James Joyce's *Ulysses*, Derrida goes on to point out that there is always another voice on the other end of the line: 'A yes never comes alone, and we never say this word alone'; it is always 'an address to an other'.[15] For Geoffrey Bennington, moreover, the 'alterity of the other' that structures the telephone call means that 'the other whom I am addressing is perhaps already on the telephone, fleeing me at the very moment I try to make sure of his or her precious "presence"'.[16] The uncanny effects of the telephone – the alterity of the call, the apparatus's double structure as both mouthpiece and receiver, and the indeterminable proximity and presence of the interlocutors – prompt a number of epistemological questions.

I open this book with a reflection on the telephone greeting because of the ways that it plays at the intersections between technology, language, voice and address. Thinking about the different ways that we pick up the receiver and communicate down the line, I propose, also provides a means of reframing the textual exchange. The literary call, in other words, invites us to reconceptualize the transmission and reception of the text, instigating new ways of thinking about the relationship between writing and telephony. My argument here draws on Maurice Blanchot's theorization of the space of the text. Echoing Derrida's interest in the 'yes' of the telephone call, Blanchot suggests that the essence of reading is a 'freedom that welcomes, consents, says yes, can say only yes, and, in the space opened by this yes, lets the work's overwhelming decisiveness affirm itself'.[17] In this way, the 'yes?' of the telephone call, I argue, is also the 'yes' of literature.[18] In uttering 'hello, yes?', the literary text always opens itself to reading.

But the telephone means different things to different people in different places and at different times. Given the alterity of the telephone exchange and its varied forms and formats, therefore, it is also important to open my reading to the multiplicity of voices on the line. Thus, even as it acknowledges the sometimes impossible exigency of a response as well as its own limitations, *Literature and the Telephone: Conversations on Poetics, Politics and Place* seeks to open itself to other voices. The readings that follow always hope to welcome, to consent, and to say yes to the ongoing conversations of which they are just one part.

Notes

1 Dennis Overbye, 'Among Scientific Treasures, a Gem', *New York Times* (10 June 2008), F3, available at: https://www.nytimes.com/2008/06/10/science/10auct.html (accessed 19 April 2022). Discussing this find, Ammon Shea remarks that this was in fact a slightly newer version of the 'ur-telephone directory', which appeared in February 1878 (Ammon Shea, *The Phone Book: The Curious History of the Book That Everyone Uses but No One Reads* (New York: Penguin, 2010), 16).
2 Overbye, 'Among Scientific Treasures', F3.
3 Shea, *The Phone Book*, 18.
4 Allen Koenigsberg, 'The First "Hello!" Thomas Edison, the Phonograph and the Telephone', *Antique Phonograph Monthly,* 8.6 (October 1987), 1, 3, 6–9 (1).
5 Ibid., 9.
6 'hello, int. and n.', *OED Online*, Oxford University Press (March 2022), available at: www.oed.com/view/Entry/85687 (accessed 19 April 2022).
7 James Baird McClure, *Edison and His Inventions* (Chicago: Rhodes and McClure, 1879), cited in Koenigsberg, 'The First "Hello!"', 9.
8 '"Allo!" "Hello!" and "Hullo!"', *The National Telephone Journal*, 1 (May 1906), 29.
9 Ibid.
10 Carol Lake, *Switchboard Operators* (London: Bloomsbury, 1994), 11.
11 Patrick Hamilton, *Hangover Square* (London: Abacus, 2016), 77.
12 Ibid.
13 Jacques Derrida, 'Ulysses Gramophone: Hear Say Yes in Joyce', in *Acts of Literature*, ed. Derek Attridge (London: Routledge, 1992), 253–309 (288–9).

14 Ariana Reines, *Telephone* (New York: Wonder, 2018), 122; W. N. Herbert, 'Answermachine', in *Cabaret McGonagall* (Northumberland: Bloodaxe, 1996), 128.
15 Derrida, 'Ulysses Gramophone', 288, 297, 299.
16 Geoffrey Bennington, 'Teleanalysis', *Paragraph*, 36.2 (2013), 270–85 (274).
17 Maurice Blanchot, *The Space of Literature*, trans. Ann Smock (Lincoln, NE: University of Nebraska Press, 1982), 194.
18 For further analysis of the telephonic 'yes', see Sarah Jackson, 'Derrida on the Line', *Derrida Today*, 10.2 (2017), 142–59.

Acknowledgements

Many people – both strangers and friends – have shared with me their own literary telephones during the course of my research (gifting me far more phones than could ever find their way into these pages), and this book is above all the product of an ongoing conversation with others. *Literature and the Telephone: Conversations on Poetics, Politics and Place* is indebted to all those who have kept me talking and listening on the telephone, and the list of people and networks to whom I owe my thanks is a long one.

First and foremost, my deepest thanks to the students, colleagues and friends who have inspired the writing of this book. In particular, I would like to express my gratitude to researchers in the English department at Nottingham Trent University, whose conversations, collegiality and connections have enabled it to take shape. Special thanks to Anna Ball, Daniel Cordle and Philip Leonard, who have offered invaluable feedback on draft chapters and whose insight and expertise make me a better reader and thinker, and to Sarah Carter, Cathy Clay, Becky Cullen, Sharon Monteith, Rory Waterman and Tim Youngs, all of whom have talked telephones, provided references, and otherwise offered advice and encouragement. I also wish to thank Angela Brown and Nahem Yousaf for their ongoing support for my research and for providing the funding that enabled this book to be available Open Access.

I am extremely grateful to UKRI who supported the development of this book through an AHRC Leadership Fellows grant. Huge thanks to Anne Archer, James Elder and David Hay at BT Heritage & Archives, to Tim Boon and Elizabeth Bruton at the Science Museum; and to Leah Gayer and Ebrahim Esmail at Compass Collective, all of whom, in different ways, kept me in touch with the telephone's varied histories and multiple users.

Thank you to Nicholas Royle, whose own writing on the telephone remains so influential to my work, to Sam Buchan-Watts for his work on the Dial-a-Poem initiative, and to all those – including Zayneb Allak, Joanne Dixon and Jack Thacker – who contributed to the wider events and activities that shaped this book. Special thanks to Delphine Grass, Hannah Van Hove, Helena Hunter and Maria Gil Ulldemolins, and to other members of the Critical Poetics Research Group who have written alongside me in recent months. I am also grateful to all the authors, editors, publishers and curators with whom I have worked during the course of my research; in particular, thank you to Ben Doyle and Laura Cope at Bloomsbury for their belief in and support for this project, as well as for their enduring patience in the final few weeks of preparing this manuscript.

My deepest thanks to Rachel, Beth, Lucy and Sarah for their friendship, and to Paul and Aoife for their endless love. And finally, my love and thanks to Mum, Dad and Anna, to whom I owe so much.

Literature and the Telephone: Conversations on Poetics, Politics and Place is dedicated to the young asylum seekers and refugees taking part in our 'Calling across Borders' project with Compass Collective (https://crossedlines.co.uk/calling-across-borders), with profound thanks to them all for sharing their own telephone calls with me.

A version of Chapter 4 was originally published Open Access as 'Calling without Calling: Barghouti, Derrida and "the international day of telephones"', *Textual Practice* 36.9 (2022), 1393–1412; I would like to thank the editors of *Textual Practice* and Taylor & Francis for granting permission to reproduce this article. Grateful acknowledgement is also made for permission to reprint the following material:

Excerpts from *Drift* by Caroline Bergvall, copyright © 2014 by Caroline Bergvall. Reprinted by permission of Nightboat Books (https://nightboat.org). All rights reserved.

Excerpt from *For What Tomorrow … A Dialogue* by Jacques Derrida and Élisabeth Roudinesco, translated by Jeff Fort (copyright © 2004 Jacques Derrida and Élisabeth Roudinesco). Reprinted by permission of Stanford University Press (www.sup.org). All rights reserved.

Excerpt from *De Quoi Demain … Dialogue* by Jacques Derrida and Élisabeth Roudinesco (copyright @ 2001 Jacques Derrida and Élisabeth Roudinesco). Reprinted by permission of Librairie Arthème Fayard (https://www.fayard.fr) and Éditions Galilée (www.editions-galilee.fr). All rights reserved.

Excerpts from 'Revolution Square', 'Iron Maiden', 'Bulb' and 'Textu' from *Textu* by Fady Joudah (copyright © 2014 by Fady Joudah). Reprinted by permission of the Permissions Company, LLC on behalf of Copper Canyon Press (https://www.coppercanyonpress.org). All rights reserved.

Excerpts from 'Electronic Necropolis' from *Oculus* by Sally Wen Mao (copyright © 2019 by Sally Wen Mao). Reprinted by permission of the Permissions Company, LLC on behalf of Graywolf Press (https://www.graywolfpress.org). All rights reserved.

Excerpts from '3 Poems about Kenneth Koch', 'Metaphysical Poem' and 'Nocturne' from *The Collected Poems of Frank O'Hara* by Frank O'Hara (copyright ©1971 by Maureen Granville-Smith, Administratrix of the Estate of Frank O'Hara, copyright renewed 1999 by Maureen O'Hara Granville-Smith and Donald Allen). Reprinted by permission of Alfred A. Knopf, an imprint of the Knopf Doubleday Publishing Group, a division of Penguin Random House LLC (https://www.penguinrandomhouse.com). All rights reserved.

Excerpts from 'But I Don' Love', 'There Are Lime-Trees in Leaf on the Promenade', 'The Wall', 'A Pressed Flower', '7/8 of the Real', 'Patch Patch Patch', 'Beautiful Habit', 'Ace', 'Writing', 'Catacoustics' and 'Nothing' from *Collected Poems* by Tom Raworth (copyright © 2003 by Tom Raworth). Reprinted by permission of Carcanet Press (www.carcanet.co.uk). All rights reserved.

Excerpts from 'Letters from Yaddo' from *Earn Your Milk: Collected Prose* by Tom Raworth (copyright © 2009 by the Estate of Tom Raworth). Reprinted by permission of the Estate of Tom Raworth and the Licensor through PLSclear on behalf of Salt Publishing Limited (www.saltpublishing.com). All rights reserved.

Excerpts from *Syncope* by Asiya Wadud, copyright © 2019 by Asiya Wadud. Reprinted by permission of Ugly Duckling Presse (https://uglyducklingpresse.org). All rights reserved.

Excerpts from 'sort by day, burn by night' and 'rise / riven / rice' from *Forage* by Rita Wong (copyright © 2007 by Rita Wong). Reprinted by permission of Nightwood Editions (www.nightwoodeditions.com). All rights reserved.

Excerpts from 'pollution dodged?' from *undercurrent* by Rita Wong (copyright © 2015 by Rita Wong). Reprinted by permission of Nightwood Editions (www.nightwoodeditions.com). All rights reserved.

Every effort has been made to trace copyright holders and to obtain their permission for the use of copyright material. The third-party copyrighted material displayed in the pages of this book are done so on the basis of fair dealing for the purposes of criticism and review in accordance with international copyright laws, and it is not my intention to infringe upon the ownership rights of the original owners. I apologize for any errors or omissions and would be grateful if notified of any corrections that should be incorporated in future reprints or editions of this book.

Introduction

The telephone – a question of literature

From the 'slender cry of the wire' in Elizabeth Stuart Phelps's 'The Chief Operator' to Will Self's 'five hundred-quid worry bead' in *Phone*, telephones have been ringing, buzzing, snapping and pinging across literature since Alexander Graham Bell and Thomas Watson first spoke on the line.[1] And yet the apparatus has long provoked anxiety for a number of writers and thinkers. Although Virginia Woolf famously remarks that 'the telephone, which interrupts the most serious conversations and cuts short the most weighty observations, has a romance of its own', she also privately admits to feeling 'some trepidation' about the apparatus.[2] This wariness extends to loathing for Franz Kafka. Writing from Prague in the margins of a letter to his fiancée Felice Bauer he begs: 'Don't worry. I definitely won't telephone. Don't you either; I couldn't bear it.'[3] But such concerns are not limited to the telephone's early decades; a century later, J. M. Coetzee confesses to Paul Auster a similar disdain, insisting that the telephone creates significant structural difficulties for the writer: 'If people [...] are continually going to be speaking to one another at a distance, then a whole gamut of interpersonal signs and signals, verbal and non-verbal, voluntary and involuntary, has to be given up. Dialogue [...] just isn't possible.'[4] Coetzee's reservations suggest that the telephone's disruptions to the mechanisms of narrative stifle the literary imagination. John Brooks agrees. Commenting on the frequent appearance of the telephone in twentieth-century literature, Brooks argues that 'close inspection in most literary uses shows that the telephone is only a conduit, a stage prop'.[5] In this way, Brooks's analysis speaks to Joseph Vogl's recognition of the 'invisible, nonperceptible, and anesthetic' nature of becoming-media or, in the words of Marshall McLuhan: '"If it works, it's obsolete."'[6] As the medium disappears into the message, so the telephone is rendered invisible by the call. In fact, Brooks goes on to conclude: 'My impression is that the great days of telephone literature are over: no matter how striking the changes in telephone uses that future technology may bring, the telephone as a subject for the creative imagination has been exhausted.'[7] For Brooks, as for Coetzee, the literary telephone is (in) trouble.

But while the effects of the telephone on narrative have long been acknowledged by writers such as Coetzee, the wider poetic, political, technological and epistemological implications of the literary telephone remain largely overlooked. In fact, as Nicholas Royle points out, 'really we have no idea what a telephone is, or what a voice is, or when or how. Least of all when it is linked up with the question of literature'.[8] Taking the 'question of literature' as its starting point, this book examines the telephone as a complex and mutating technology with literary and cultural effects yet to be explored. Certainly, far from operating simply as a conduit for the voice, the telephone for Jacques Derrida is embedded in a theory of literature: 'The telephone is a poetico-technical invention'.[9] Referring to Hélène Cixous's telepathic call in *H.C. For Life, That is to Say ...*, he remarks: 'this telephony, which nonetheless also literally invented the telephone, is thought itself'.[10] Drawing on Derrida's work on telepathy as a 'terrifying telephone', Avital Ronell also turns to the telephone's operations 'between science, poesy, and thinking'.[11] 'Why the telephone?' she asks in her seminal text *The Telephone Book: Technology, Schizophrenia, Electric Speech*.[12] Pointing out that it is 'unsure of its identity as object, thing, piece of equipment, perlocutionary intensity or artwork', she argues that the telephone overturns metaphysical certitudes: 'It destabilizes the identity of self and other, subject and thing, it abolishes the originariness of site; it undermines the authority of the Book and constantly menaces the existence of literature.'[13] In this way, Ronell draws attention to the ways that the telephone not only unsettles notions of proximity and distance, presence and absence, and self and other but also throws into question our understanding of writing and reading.

Royle, too, is interested in the writerly effects of the telephone and the ways in which it can 'structure' the text: 'Or rather, the extent to which the telephone structures and de-structures, orders and disorders, sets up and upsets.'[14] Arguing that the omniscient narrator appears able to operate according to 'telepathic transfer', he is concerned with a 'certain tele-logic in accordance with which the notions of telephone and telepathy are, however strangely, being put in touch'.[15] The conceptual link between telepathy and telephony in the cultural imagination has been addressed by a number of critics. Discussing the rise in the popularity of spiritualism in the nineteenth century, for instance, Pamela Thurschwell establishes a clear connection between telepathy and tele-technologies; for

Ned Schantz, moreover, 'telepathy is the telephone in a state of perfect dematerialization – no apparatus, no sound waves, no ear'.[16] But for Royle, this relationship is a specifically literary one. Turning to Frank O'Hara's claim that 'if I wanted to I could use the telephone instead of writing the poem' – a claim to which I will return in Chapter 1 – Royle sets out the possibility for a tele-logic in which 'literature would be a telephony. Linked up through a kind of intratextual exchange, literary texts would be telephone calls'.[17] Working to complicate the relations between telephony and telepathy, reader and writer, narrator and author, and text and call, these literary telephones are not merely the stage props to which Brooks refers; rather, they are wired up with the function of literature and of literary history, opening up our understanding of how, where and why literary communication takes place.

Many of the texts to which this volume refers (and the many more that are beyond the scope of my discussion) directly comment on and simultaneously perform the relationship between the telephone and the question of literature. Its potential for ordering and disordering the text is enacted, for instance, in Haruki Murakami's *Sputnik Sweetheart* – a novel that draws attention to its own operations as an intratextual exchange. When the narrator K reflects on Sumire's call from 'a totally semiotic telephone box', he wonders if 'the phone itself is some vital message, its very shape and colour containing hidden meaning'.[18] This study does not offer a straightforward literary history of the telephone, but, following K, it instead seeks to tease out some of its more cryptic resonances. In so doing, it argues that the uncanny logic of telephony – and its capacity for sparking new conversations between people, places, and ideas – is built into the very structure of reading and writing. This is of course played out in Holden Caulfield's famous statement in J. D. Salinger's *The Catcher in the Rye*: 'What really knocks me out is a book that, when you're all done reading it, you wish the author that wrote it was a terrific friend of yours and you could call him up on the phone whenever you felt like it.'[19] What sort of exchange takes place, this volume asks, between the reader and the writer, between different places and times, between different genders and genres, and between different cultural and critical perspectives? And if telephony is bound to a theory of writing, what happens when the network is down, when calls are intercepted, when they remain unanswered, or when the voice goes astray? In fact, although he wants to 'hook up' with the author, Holden, it turns out, has difficulty picking up and dialling the number: 'I couldn't think of anybody to call up. [...] So I ended up not calling anybody.'[20] Rather than facilitating connection and dialogue, the telephone in this text, as in many others, disorders and disconnects. This means that in addition to putting people in 'touch', as the AT&T slogan dictates, the telephone has the potential to transmit what Roland Barthes calls the *'wrong voice'*.[21]

The psychoanalytic telephone

Barthes's reference to the 'wrong voice' is taken from his discussion of Sigmund Freud, in which he describes the psychoanalyst's aversion to the telephone. It is true that Freud had a peculiar relationship with the device, describing the unconscious as an invisible telephone line and the psychoanalytic method as a telephone call, facts remarked upon by Friedrich Kittler, who states: 'Following the nationalization of the Vienna telephone exchange in 1895, [Freud] not only had a telephone installed in his study but also described the work that went on in that study in terms of telephony.'[22] Despite his apparent proficiency in listening, however, Barthes points out that Freud did not actually like using the telephone – a possibility that Peter Gay attributes not only to his 'cultural conservatism' but also to his superstitious fear of his own telephone number, 14362.[23] Despite his concern to stress the scientific rationalism of the psychoanalytic method, then, Freud's life and work cannot be detached from the strange and unnerving implications of the electric voice, and the various ways that the telephone is bound up with disorder and delusion. The relationship between psychoanalysis and the telephone is one that informs much of the existing scholarship in the field. Hannah Zeavin, for instance, contends that media technologies have always played a central role in the therapeutic encounter, with teletherapy offering just one form of 'distanced intimacy'.[24] It is central to the work of Ronell, for example, for whom the apparatus is a 'dual-functioning organ' with a 'split personality'.[25] Tracing the relationship between schizophrenia and the mechanized voice in the psychoanalytic work of Freud alongside Carl Jung and R. D. Laing, Ronell argues that the telephone is 'a privileged instrument of splitting for the schizophrenic'.[26] The literary telephone, it is clear, is haunted by its histories, delusions and disconnections. From Thurschwell's study of the relationship between the development of communication technologies and the 'real and fantasized connections' in the fin de siècle to Andrew Gaedtke's interest in the 'form and logic of a technological paranoia' in late-modernist culture, questions regarding telephony and madness have been in currency since the telephone's invention.[27]

The relationship between communication technologies and magical thinking has been discussed at length, and this book does not seek to replicate existing work in the field. To date, however, most of the scholarship on the representation of the telephone in literature has been restricted to its late Victorian and early- to mid-twentieth-century contexts.[28] For Richard Menke, for instance, the Victorian novelist's telephone operates as 'an imaginative switchboard' or 'device for representing an entire complex of media'.[29] For Thurschwell, this imaginative switchboard transforms metaphysical relations in the modernist text. Noting that developing tele-technologies appear to offer the annihilation of distance, she remarks that new media cultures enable previously unimaginable intimacies, ranging from speaking on the phone to contacting the dead.[30] David Trotter explains that the early twentieth-century phone was determined by its potential to malfunction: 'Modernist phones simply do not work, in the most basic sense; even when they do work, they don't, because their working is itself an estrangement, a disconnection.'[31] Whether this is the result of 'technological failure' or from a lapse in 'medium-specific-protocol', Trotter argues, 'a telephonic literature began when, and only when, the event ceased to function as the catalyst for ironies extraneous to its successful completion on its own terms'.[32] For Trotter, moreover, the advent of electronic digital computing during the late 1940s and early 1950s marked a 'watershed' moment in the history of telecommunications, bringing with it the notion of the human as an information-processing machine.[33] Suggesting that the rapid new developments in cybernetics and information theory after the Second World War led to the 'act of instantaneous or near-instantaneous, real-time communication at a distance, whatever its motive, method, or effect', Trotter argues that, in contrast to the previous decades, post-war literature appears to operate according to the 'principle of connectivity'.[34] This is a time, he suggests, that is marked not by a 'gradual change messily improvised with the help of whatever lies to hand' but by 'the sudden perfecting of a machine'.[35] In this way, Trotter identifies a perceived shift taking place in the second half of the twentieth century from estrangement and disconnection to connectivity and instantaneity.

Crossed lines

For Ned Schantz, this principle of connectivity feeds the fantasy of an ideal phone – one that transmits a 'singular meaning' and that 'always works smoothly, allowing its human masters to forge their bodies, their surroundings – indeed the apparatus itself – to engage in communication with perfect control'.[36] In a telling aside, however, Schantz admits that this version of the telephone 'never quite manages to exist', suggesting that 'as the phone ceases to behave itself, instead of delivering messages devoutly wished for, it unearths a repressed sense of isolation and chaos'.[37] Schantz alludes here to the ways that the telephone continues to disrupt and complicate experience, even as the technologies that facilitate the call grow ever more sophisticated. This is confirmed by Jean Baudrillard who argues in 'The Ecstasy of Communication' that the era of production and consumption has given way to a '"proteinic" era of networks' that operate to ensure that we always 'stay in contact' while also producing 'aleatory and dizzying' effects.[38] As a result, he says, we live 'in the ecstasy of communication' – an ecstasy that is obscene for its visibility.[39] Although he focuses primarily on the screen, Baudrillard also frames this condition in terms of the telephone: 'I pick up my telephone receiver and it's all there; the whole marginal network catches and harasses me with the insupportable good faith of everything that wants and claims to communicate.'[40] This 'delirium' of communication alters the limits of subjective experience. Thus, while its format and functionality – and the associated anxieties – have transformed the apparatus almost beyond recognition since its invention in 1876, the literary telephone remains haunted by disorder and undecidability.

Although, as I go on to discuss, considerable research on the smartphone has been undertaken in recent media and cultural studies, the specific relationship between telephony and literature after Trotter's watershed remains largely overlooked.[41] In fact, as this volume seeks to demonstrate, the ways in which the contemporary literary telephone is connected to technical, linguistic, social and political interference have ongoing significance. It is certainly clear that examples of wrong numbers, crossed lines and unanswered calls have continued to punctuate the literary imagination over the last seventy years, testifying to McLuhan's observation that media draw attention to themselves only when they cease to operate. It is evident, for instance, in Paul Auster's *City of Glass*, which opens with Daniel Quinn's observation: 'It was a wrong number that started it, the telephone ringing three times in the dead of night, and the voice on the other end asking for someone he was not.'[42] Picking up from the point at which Trotter departs, I am interested in precisely those moments in post-war literature when the phone and its users cease to behave. More than this, however, I am interested in the ways that these moments of disruption might be understood as attempts to reconceptualize the relationship between reading and writing. This productive interference is at work, for example, in Clarice Lispector's 'Correct Assumptions', in which she asserts: 'Let us assume that the telephone system has broken down throughout the city, which happens to be true.'[43] She goes on to assume that when she dials a number, it is engaged; when she finally makes a connection, no one answers; and when she does eventually get through, the line is 'crossed'.[44] But it is important to note that, for Lispector, these interruptions, interferences and disconnections open up the possibility for writing: 'I shall make no more assumptions. But simply say Yes to the world.'[45] In this way, the telephone's disconnective force marks not the end of literature but instead invites new ways of thinking and writing. This disconnective force structures her novel *Agua Viva*, for instance, in which Lispector conceives of 'the world' as 'a tangle of bristling telephone wires', suggesting that the literary text is 'crossed from end to end by a fragile connecting thread'.[46] The tangled and crossed wires of the telephone become a way of understanding intra- and intertextual relations. Thus, as Hélène Cixous remarks, Lispector's is a telephonic text, inviting the reader to 'imagine a telephone that lets fluid pass rather than words'.[47] Here, Cixous speaks to the specifically literary dimensions of telephony, a concept that her own writing explicitly explores: 'I owe books and books to the telephone', she admits in 'Writing Blind'.[48] With Cixous's words in mind, this volume not only examines the telephone's function as a disordering impulse in texts from the 1950s to the present but also seeks to explore the ways that its capacity to communicate at a distance contributes to and opens out a theory of writing.

Media and mobility

Building on work by Cixous, Derrida, Ronell and Royle, among others, and analysing the ways that the telephone informs an understanding of the ontological dimensions of the relationship between the human and the technological, this book is concerned with the possibilities for tele-technologies to destabilize logocentric assumptions, unsettling relations of presence and absence, near and far, mobility and stasis, the private and the public, and life and death. At the same time, however, it also examines the productive effects of the literary telephone, and the different ways that telephony and literature speak to each other. Of course, telephone technologies have transformed considerably over the last seventy years, and the form and function of the telephone in the literary text continue to evolve: from the push-button phone in the red booth of Wole Soyinka's 'Telephone Conversation' to the videophone hook-ups of David Foster Wallace's *Infinite Jest*, or from the text message in Imtiaz Dharker's 'Text' to the uploading of videos on Snapchat in Oyinkan Braithwaite's *My Sister, The Serial Killer*, the interactions between user, media and message remain mutable, multifarious and in flux.[49]

Since the 1990s, the development of cellular technologies has brought substantial change to telephoning practices. Giving rise to new ways of generating and sharing creative content, not only does this transform our experience of reading and writing, but it also shapes experiments with language and form. These changes have been worked through in many contemporary novels of the last two decades; Shari Benstock, for instance, notes the preponderance of phone calls, text messages and emails in contemporary 'chick lit', remarking that these function to convey the rapid pace of contemporary life.[50] Social media has also contributed to new ways of engaging with literature: Roddy Doyle's *Two Pints*, for example, first appeared as a series of Facebook posts before being collated and published in print and e-book formats.[51] The effects of digital media on the reading experience are further evidenced in novels such as Marisha Pessl's *Night Film*, in which 'interactive touch points buried throughout the text will unlock extra content on your smartphone or tablet'.[52] These effects are felt in poetry too: contemporary poets from Brian Bilston to Rupi Kaur have not only embraced the multimodality of Instagram but have generated new forms of 'twitterature', demonstrating that, as Kylie Jarrett and Janeen Naji point out, digitally mediated texts need to be reframed as an assemblage of 'interactions between technologies, human creative subjects, and the wider socioeconomic context'.[53] For Tore Rye Andersen, both the resurgence of serialization prompted by the digital revolution and its potential for interactivity are key to the appeal of twitterature – which he describes as 'situated in some undefined zone between marketing, individual work, transmedia storytelling, interaction with readers, text, paratext, poetry and narrative' – where 'the intervals between separate instalments can often be measured in minutes'.[54] The capacity for the mobile phone to operate as writing machine is further evidenced by the popularity of the cell phone novel, in which short chapters are written on a device and often distributed to readers via text message.[55] Moreover, the use of geospatial technologies to generate site-specific content enables readers to engage with multiple stories at and across different locations.[56] This is taken further still in ambient literary works such as Kate Pullinger's *Breathe*, which uses application programming interfaces to respond to location, weather and time in order to personalize the literary experience.[57] Reflecting on these changes and addressing the ways that mobile media facilitate our engagement with multiple platforms 'on the go', Bronwen Thomas remarks that the spatio-temporal effects of digital texts that engage with cross-platform, application programming interface, location-aware and multimodal technologies can be both 'exhilarating and unsettling'.[58]

The manner in which the computational capacities of the mobile phone transform the reading and writing experience continues to evolve. But while the medium-specificity of the mobile phone is important to my discussion, the histories and possibilities of both electronic literature, and literature that is specifically written on or for the phone, are beyond the scope of my analysis. Indeed, much of the current scholarship within media studies concerns precisely the generation, experience and distribution of creative content within an assemblage of human, technological, social and geospatial agents. But by bringing together the telephone and the question of literature, my aim is neither to offer a history of the telephone from the nineteenth-century apparatus to the digital devices of today, nor is it to provide a cultural, sociological or technical study of the phone's changing form and functions. These topics have been addressed at length, and in ways far better than I am able to offer, by the aforementioned writers and others. Rather, by foregrounding both the literariness of the telephone and the telephonic nature of the literary text, I hope instead to open up new conversations about the telephone's reciprocal relationship with print-based literatures from 1950 to the present, and the implications of this for how we understand the relationship between reading, writing, listening and calling.

Global networks

Of course, the telephone is not the same thing for all people at all times, and this study is sensitive to a range of cultural contexts. Telephone conversations take part in and constitute complex, heterogenous and unstable networks that are bound up with political, technological and linguistic forces. Of particular concern to this volume are the implications of literary telephony for rethinking questions of politics and place. Focusing on the early development of the apparatus, for instance, Stephen Kern points to a long-standing interest in the potential for the telephone to destabilize place: 'Telephones break down barriers of distance – horizontally across the face of the land and vertically across social strata. They make all places equidistant from the seat of power and hence of equal value.'[59] Far from overturning distance and flattening relations of power, however, I argue that telephones always remain bound up in and shape political and ideological relations. Claire Lynch notes, for instance, that digital technologies are not 'the same for any person in any place' and argues that 'cyberculture's primary function is to disrupt the authority of place'.[60] Joshua Meyrowitz, moreover, warns that even as media expand our perceptual field, experience remains place-bound: 'We are always in place, and place is always with us.'⁶¹ That these places are both embodied and ideological is evidenced, for example, in the front page image of the New York *Daily Graphic* on 15 March 1877.⁶² Captioned 'Terrors of the Telephone – the Orator of the Future', the graphic features what McLuhan calls 'a dishevelled Svengali' with a microphone connected by thousands of wires to receiving parties all around the world, including London, Boston, San Francisco and Fiji, as well as to what appears to be a lone Indigenous American in an unnamed location.⁶³ Far from obliterating local and global distinctions, then, the telephone operates within a confluence of geospatial, industrial, technological, infrastructural and political forces, and my analysis explores the aesthetic and political nature of telephoning practices, as well as the ways in which they speak to questions of both place and displacement.

The geopolitical dimensions of telephony are clearly at work, for instance, in Yuri Herrera's *Signs Preceding the End of the World*, a novel in which Makina runs the village switchboard housing 'the only phone for miles and miles around'.⁶⁴ When local calls are received, Makina is able to answer in the 'native tongue or latin tongue', and when she receives calls from the 'promised land' – which is increasingly the case – she responds 'in their own new tongue'.⁶⁵ Speaking to both gendered and racial telephoning practices, Makina's role as operator depends on her ability to translate and connect cultures: 'Makina spoke all three [languages], and knew how to keep quiet in all three too.'⁶⁶ When one of the first men to 'strike it rich after going north' returns to the village, he shows off to Makina by taking out two mobile phones and giving one to his mother: 'Here, jefecita, just press this button when you hear the briiiiiiing and you'll see, just step outside, and he brandished the other one.'⁶⁷ But the 'zzzz' of the dial tone 'didn't come' and the 'peep-peeps were followed only by silence', and eventually Makina says, 'Maybe you should have bought a few cell towers too?'⁶⁸ Herrera thus demonstrates that the telephone does not operate in isolation but functions as part of an always multiple and divided network – a network that is beset with both silence and noise.

Bearing in mind the fact that the telephone always speaks beyond its immediate interlocutors and is instead connected to a range of broader linguistic, theoretical, sociopolitical and technological concerns, it is critical that any analysis of the telephone must extend beyond a reading of its hardware to its assemblages and its formats as well as its participation in global, political and social structures. Thus, even as it focuses on the telephone and the question of literature, my discussion is informed by a sense of its wider effects and contexts. In addressing these concerns, and drawing on work by Sara Ahmed, Judith

Butler, Eyal Weizman and Jennifer Gabrys, among others, *Literature and the Telephone* prompts new ways of thinking about the poetic, political and geospatial implications of literary telephony from a range of national and cultural contexts. In so doing, it seeks to explore the telephone's propensity to mediate but also to interrupt communication, as well as the ways in which it taps into some of the most urgent concerns of our era, including warfare, surveillance, mobility, globalization, ecology and the ethics of answerability. Exploring its complex, multiple and mutating functions, the present volume thus examines the ways that the telephone ignites new conversations between different historical periods, global locations, theoretical perspectives, genres and voices. Addressing the reciprocal relationship between telephony and literary language and form, it considers both wired and wireless phones, and their capacity and failure to call across borders, languages and cultures.

Calling points

The structure of this book underscores its aims: rather than taking a chronological approach, I instead tap into a series of 'calling points' that operate within and between texts in order to tease out the telephonic effects of post-war writing. In so doing, these conversations produce moments of contradiction and tension, as well as both forward and backward movements. Chapter 1, my first calling point, returns to Frank O'Hara's claim in 'Personism' that 'if I wanted to I could use the telephone instead of writing the poem'. Troubling the relationship between poetry and calling by interrogating notions of address, sound, rhythm and silence, this chapter examines examples of interference and errancy in work by Tom Raworth and Fady Joudah. Setting out a theory of telephonic destinerrance, I argue that the principle of disconnection is simultaneously a disruptive and generative force in the text. In Chapter 2, I turn to the relationship between the telephone and the secret through a reading of (over)hearing in the work of Muriel Spark. Analysing the pattern of call and response in her writing, I read Spark's preoccupation with secrecy alongside the work of Frank Kermode, Jacques Derrida and Jean-Luc Nancy. Arguing that the telephone calls in Spark's writing are never fully determinable, I examine the ways in which the literary telephone speaks to a provisional and always incomplete definition of literature. Building on questions of undecidability and destabilizing the relationship between technology and epistemology, Chapter 3 addresses the impact of the mobile phone's locative technologies on how we understand the principle of orientation. Focusing on the work of Ali Smith, I consider the ways that contemporary smartphone technologies are linked to notions of (dis)location and displacement, prompting new questions regarding the relationship between disorientation and reading. In Chapter 4, I extend these questions of displacement by turning to the cultural and political implications of postcolonial telephony. Focusing in particular on telecommunications infrastructure in Israel-Palestine, I argue that the telephone in the work of Mourid Barghouti operates according to an impossible logic where picking up the phone means not getting through. Reading Barghouti alongside Jacques Derrida and Eyal Weizman, this chapter hopes to prompt a broader conversation regarding the possibilities for the literary telephone to intervene in debates regarding the relationship between telecommunication technologies, voice and power. Developing my concern with telephony and dislocation, Chapter 5 turns to the politics and poetics of the distress call. Discussing the ethics and aesthetics of 'answerability', this chapter focuses on the intersections between technology, politics, human rights and language in a reading of accounts of the 'left-to-die-boat' by Asiya Wadud and Caroline Bergvall. Questions of ethics and responsibility are picked up again in Chapter 6, where I consider the telephone call as both missive and missile in Cold War fiction. Focusing on a cluster of texts published around the time of the Cuban Missile Crisis, I investigate the role of the telephone in imagining nuclear catastrophe, exploring its capacity to communicate political and technological disruption, as well as the atomization of language. My final calling point engages with the role of the telephone in material culture and environmental justice by thinking through its contribution to human and ecological destruction. Focusing on mobile phone waste and the representation of Guiyu in China in work by Chen Qiufan, Sally Wen Mao and Rita Wong, Chapter 7 reflects on the implications of digital rubbish and the phone's interminable effects on the planet. Thus, this chapter's turn to the toxic potential of the telephone opens up wider questions regarding the telephone and the archive, as well as our possible telefutures.

By connecting different texts and themes, and offering a reading of the telephone through a series of calling points, this book acknowledges its own status as necessarily partial and incomplete. But in attempting to think through the crossed lines between literature and telephony – and the implications of this for notions of poetics, politics and place – it hopes to prompt new conversations regarding the relationship between writing and calling. In so doing, it seeks not only to challenge Brooks's claim that the great days of telephone literature are over but also to argue that literary telephone lines might offer new ways of conceiving ethical and creative technological futures, as well as different modes of talking and listening across cultures.

Notes

1. Elizabeth Stuart Phelps, 'The Chief Operator', in *The Oath of Allegiance and Other Stories* (Boston: Houghton Mifflin, 1909), 353–74 (357); Will Self, *Phone* (London: Penguin, 2017), 10.
2. Virginia Woolf, 'How It Strikes a Contemporary', *Times Literary Supplement* (5 April 1923), reprinted in *Virginia Woolf: Selected Essays*, ed. David Bradshaw (Oxford: Oxford University Press, 2009), 23–31 (27); Virginia Woolf, diary entry dated 27 December 1931, *The Diary of Virginia Woolf, Volume 4*, ed. Anne Olivier Bell and Andrew McNeillie (London: Hogarth Press, 1982), 56. See also Edward Allen, 'Romancing the Phone: Woolf's First Media Age', *Critical Quarterly*, 61.4 (2019), 100–15 (112).
3. Franz Kafka, letter dated 17 November 1912, *Letters to Felice*, ed. Erich Heller and Jürgen Born, trans. James Stern and Elisabeth Duckworth (New York: Schocken, 1973), 47. See also Franc Schuerewegen, 'A Telephone Conversation: Fragments', trans. Marvin N. Richards, *Diacritics*, 24.4 (1994), 30–40 (30).
4. Paul Auster and J. M. Coetzee, letter dated 7 April 2011, *Here and Now: Letters 2008–2011* (London: Vintage, 2014), 227.
5. John Brooks, 'The First and Only Century of Telephone Literature', in *The Social Impact of the Telephone*, ed. Ithiel de Sola Pool (Cambridge, MA: MIT Press, 1977), 208–24 (208).
6. Joseph Vogl, 'Becoming-Media: Galileo's Telescope', trans. Brian Hanrahan, *Grey Room* 29 (2007), 14–25 (22); Marshall McLuhan, *Understanding Media: The Extensions of Man* (London: Routledge, 2001), 13.
7. Brooks, 'The First and Only Century of Telephone Literature', 223.
8. Nicholas Royle, *Telepathy and Literature: Essays on the Reading Mind* (Oxford: Basil Blackwell, 1990), 164.
9. Jacques Derrida, *H.C. For Life, That Is to Say ...*, trans. Laurent Milesi and Stefan Herbrechter (Stanford, CA: Stanford University Press, 2006), 100.
10. Ibid.
11. Jacques Derrida, 'Telepathy', trans. Nicholas Royle, in *Deconstruction: A Reader*, ed. Martin McQuillan (Edinburgh: Edinburgh University Press, 2000), 496–526 (509); Avital Ronell, *The Telephone Book: Technology, Schizophrenia, Electric Speech* (Lincoln, NE: University of Nebraska Press, 1989), 84.
12. Ronell, *The Telephone Book*, 9.
13. Ibid.

14 Royle, *Telepathy and Literature*, 163.
15 Ibid., 89, 168.
16 Pamela Thurschwell, *Literature, Technology and Magical Thinking, 1880–1920* (Cambridge: Cambridge University Press, 2009), 14; Ned Schantz, *Gossip, Letters, Phones: The Scandal of Female Networks in Film and Literature* (Oxford: Oxford University Press, 2008), 80.
17 Frank O'Hara, 'Personism: A Manifesto', *Yugen*, 7 (1961), reprinted in *The Collected Poems of Frank O'Hara*, ed. Donald Allen (Berkeley: University of California Press, 1995), 499, cited in Royle, *Telepathy and Literature*, 178.
18 Haruki Murakami, *Sputnik Sweetheart*, trans. Philip Gabriel (London: Vintage, 2001), 227, 228.
19 J. D. Salinger, *The Catcher in the Rye* (London: Penguin, 1994), 16.
20 Ibid., 53.
21 Roland Barthes, *A Lover's Discourse: Fragments*, trans. Richard Howard (London: Jonathan Cape, 1979), 114.
22 Friedrich A. Kittler, *Gramophone, Film, Typewriter*, trans. Geoffrey Winthrop-Young and Michael Wutz (Stanford, CA: Stanford University Press, 1999), 89. In 'Recommendations to Physicians Practising Psycho-Analysis' published in 1912, Freud writes: 'To put it in a formula: [the doctor] must turn his own unconscious like a receptive organ towards the transmitting unconscious of the patient. He must adjust himself to the patient as a telephone receiver is adjusted to the transmitting microphone. Just as the receiver converts back into sound-waves the electric oscillations in the telephone line which were set up by sound waves, so the doctor's unconscious is able, from the derivatives of the unconscious which are communicated to him, to reconstruct that unconscious, which has determined the patient's free associations' (Sigmund Freud, 'Recommendations to Physicians Practising Psycho-Analysis', *Standard Edition*, vol. 12 (London: Vintage, 2001), 115–16).
23 Freud's seminal text, *The Interpretation of Dreams*, was published when he was forty-three, and it is reported that he took this as proof that the last two digits, sixty-two, signified the age at which he would die. See Peter Gay, *Freud: A Life for Our Time* (London: MAX, 2006), 507, 58.
24 Hannah Zeavin, *The Distance Cure: A History of Teletherapy* (Cambridge, MA: MIT Press, 2021), 25.
25 Ronell, *The Telephone Book*, 105.
26 Ibid., 252. See Carl G. Jung, *The Psychology of Dementia Praecox*, trans. Frederick Peterson and A. A. Brill (New York: The Journal of Nervous and Mental Disease Publishing, 1909), 99–153; R. D. Laing, *The Divided Self* (London: Penguin, 2010).
27 Thurschwell, *Literature, Technology and Magical Thinking*, 2; Andrew Gaedtke, *Modernism and the Machinery of Madness: Psychosis, Technology, and Narrative Worlds* (Cambridge: Cambridge University Press, 2017), 2. See also Jeffrey Sconce,

The Technical Delusion: Electronics, Power, Insanity (Durham, NC: Duke University Press, 2019).

28 Particular attention has been paid to telephoning practices in the work of writers including Marcel Proust, Ford Madox Ford, James Joyce, Virginia Woolf, Evelyn Waugh and Elizabeth Bowen. See, for instance: Allen, 'Romancing the Phone'; Andrew Bennett, 'Elizabeth Bowen on the Telephone', in *Elizabeth Bowen: Theory, Thought and Things*, ed. Jessica Gildersleeve and Patricia Juliana Smith (Edinburgh: Edinburgh University Press, 2019), 182–98; Jacques Derrida, 'Ulysses Gramophone: Hear Say Yes in Joyce', trans. Tina Kendall and Shari Benstock, in *Acts of Literature*, ed. Derek Attridge (London: Routledge, 1992), 253–309; Sara Danius, *The Senses of Modernism: Technology, Perception, and Aesthetics* (New York: Cornell University Press, 2002), 11–17, 180–2; Kate McLoughlin, 'Interruption Overload: Telephones in Ford Madox Ford's "4692 Padd"', *A Call* and *A Man Could Stand Up –*', *Journal of Modern Literature*, 36.3 (2013), 50–68; Richard Menke, *Literature, Print Culture, and Media Technologies, 1880-1900* (Cambridge: Cambridge University Press, 2019), 49–71; and David Trotter, *Literature in the First Media Age: Britain Between the Wars* (Cambridge, MA: Harvard University Press, 2013), 38–85.

29 Menke, *Literature, Print Culture, and Media Technologies*, 213, 214.

30 Thurschwell, *Literature, Technology and Magical Thinking*, 3.

31 Trotter, *Literature in the First Media Age*, 47.

32 Ibid., 47, 49.

33 David Trotter, *The Literature of Connection: Signal, Medium, Interface, 1850-1950* (Oxford: Oxford University Press, 2020), 2.

34 Ibid., 1.

35 Ibid., 3–4.

36 Schantz, *Gossip, Letters, Phones*, 8.

37 Ibid., 7.

38 Jean Baudrillard, 'The Ecstasy of Communication', trans. John Johnston, in *The Anti-Aesthetic: Essays on Postmodern Culture*, ed. Hal Foster (Port Townsend, WA: Bay Press, 1983), 126–33 (127–8, 132).

39 Ibid., 130.

40 Ibid., 131.

41 See, for instance: Gerard Goggin, *Cell Phone Culture: Mobile Technology in Everyday Life* (London: Routledge, 2006); Larissa Hjorth, Jean Burgess and Ingrid Richardson (eds), *Studying Mobile Media: Cultural Technologies, Mobile Communication, and the iPhone* (London: Routledge, 2012).

42 Paul Auster, *The New York Trilogy* (London: Faber, 1987), 3.

43 Clarice Lispector, 'Correct Assumptions' (15 January 1972), in *Discovering the World*, trans. Giovanni Pontiero (Manchester: Carcanet, 1992), 525–6 (525).

44 Ibid., 526.

45 Ibid.
46 Clarice Lispector, *Água Viva*, trans. Stefan Tobler (New York: New Directions, 2012), 18, 20.
47 Hélène Cixous, *Reading with Clarice Lispector*, trans. Verena Andermatt Conley (Minneapolis, MN: University of Minnesota Press, 1990), 77.
48 Hélène Cixous, 'Writing Blind: Conversation with the Donkey', trans. Eric Prenowitz, in *Stigmata: Escaping Texts* (London: Routledge 2005), 184–203 (189).
49 Wole Soyinka, 'Telephone Conversation', in *Modern Poetry from Africa*, ed. Gerald Moore and Ulli Beier (London: Penguin, 1963), 111; David Foster Wallace, *Infinite Jest* (London: Little, Brown and Company, 1996); Imtiaz Dharker, 'Text', in *The Terrorist at My Table* (Northumberland: Bloodaxe, 2006), 37; Oyinkan Braithwaite, *My Sister, The Serial Killer* (London: Atlantic, 2019).
50 Shari Benstock, 'Afterword: The New Woman's Fiction', in *Chick Lit: The New Woman's Fiction*, ed. Suzanne Ferris and Mallory Young (London: Routledge, 2006), 253–6 (256).
51 Roddy Doyle, *Two Pints* (London: Jonathan Cape, 2012).
52 Marisha Pessl, *Night Film* (New York: Random House, 2013), 10. See also Anna Weigel, 'New Reading Strategies in the Twenty First Century: Transmedia Storytelling via App in Marisha Pessl's *Night Film*', in *Reading Today*, ed. Heta Pyrhönen and Janna Kantola (London: UCL Press, 2018), 73–86.
53 Brian Bilston, *You Took the Last Bus Home* (London: Unbound, 2016); Brian Bilston (@brian_bilston) [Twitter]; Rupi Kaur, *Milk and Honey* (Kansas City, MO: Andrew McMeel, 2015); rupi kaur (@rupikaur_) [Instagram]; Kylie Jarrett and Janeen Naji, 'What Would Media Studies Do? Social Media Shakespeare as a Technosocial Process', *Borrowers and Lenders: The Journal of Shakespeare and Appropriation*, 10.1 (2016), 1–18 (20). See also, for instance: Alexander Aciman and Emmett Rensin, *Twitterature: The World's Greatest Books Retold Through Twitter* (London: Penguin, 2009); Mike Chasar, *Poetry Unbound: Poems and New Media from the Magic Lantern to Instagram* (New York: Columbia University Press, 2020), 175–94; Charlotte Cripps, 'Twihaiku? Micropoetry? The Rise of Twitter Poetry', *Independent*, 17 July 2013, available at: https://www.independent.co.uk/arts-entertainment/books/features/twihaiku-micropoetry-the-rise-of-twitter-poetry-8711637.html (accessed 15 October 2021); Janeen Naji, *Digital Poetry* (Basingstoke: Palgrave Macmillan, 2021), 20, 21.
54 Tore Rye Andersen, 'Staggered Transmissions: Twitter and the Return of Serialized Literature', Convergence, 23.1 (2017), 34–48 (46, 36). See also Bronwen Thomas, '140 Characters in Search of a Story: Twitter Fiction as an Emerging Narrative Form', in *Analysing Digital Fiction*, ed. Alice Bell, Astrid Ensslin and Hans Rustad (London: Routledge, 2014), 94–108.
55 Barry Yourgrau, 'Thumb Novels: Mobile Phone Fiction', *Independent* (29 July 2009), available at: https://www.independent.co.uk/tech/thumb-novels-mobile-

phone-fiction-1763849.html (accessed 15 October 2021). The rise of the 'mobile phone fiction' in the first decade of the twenty-first century was popularized in Japan as 'keitai shosetu' and brought to English-speaking audiences through Takatsu's *Secondhand Memories* (Hermitage, PA: Sakura, 2015). See also Matt Richtel, 'Introducing the Twiller', *New York Times* (29 August 2008), available at https://bits.blogs.nytimes.com/2008/08/29/introducing-the-twiller/ (accessed 15 March 2021).

56 Bronwen Thomas, *Literature and Social Media* (London: Routledge, 2020), 34. See also Jason Farman, 'Site-Specificity, Pervasive Computing, and the Reading Interface', in *The Mobile Story: Narrative Practices with Locative Technologies*, ed. Jason Farman (London: Routledge, 2015), 3–16; Jeremy Hight, 'Locative Narrative, Literature and Form', in *Beyond the Screen: Transformations of Literary Structures, Interfaces and Genres*, ed. Jörgen Schäffer and Peter Gendolia (New Brunswick, NJ: Transition, 2010), 317–30; Michael F. Miller, 'Why Hate the Internet?: Contemporary Fiction, Digital Culture, and the Politics of Social Media', *Arizona Quarterly: A Journal of American Literature, Culture, and Theory*, 75.3 (2019), 59–85; and Rita Raley, 'Walk This Way', in *Beyond the Screen*, ed. Schäffer and Gendolia, 299–316.

57 Kate Pullinger, *Breathe* (London: Editions at Play/Visual Editions, 2018), available at: https://www.breathe-story.com/ (accessed 13 November 2020). See also Tom Abba, Jonathan Dovey and Kate Pullinger (eds), *Ambient Literature: Towards a New Poetics of Situated Writing and Reading Practices* (Basingstoke: Palgrave Macmillan, 2021); Farman, 'Site-Specificity, Pervasive Computing, and the Reading Interface', 3–16; Hight, 'Locative Narrative, Literature and Form', 317–30; Miller, 'Why Hate the Internet?' 59–85; and Raley, 'Walk This Way', 299–316.

58 Thomas, *Literature and Social Media*, 34, 57.

59 Stephen Kern, *Culture of Time and Space, 1880–1918* (Cambridge, MA: Harvard University Press, 1983), 316.

60 Claire Lynch, *Cyber Ireland: Text, Image, Culture* (Basingstoke: Palgrave Macmillan, 2014), 6.

61 Joshua Meyrowitz, 'The Rise of Glocality: New Sense of Place and Identity in the Global Village', in *A Sense of Place: The Global and the Local in Mobile Communication*, ed. Kristóf Nyíri (Vienna: Passagen Verlag, 2005), 21–30 (21). For further discussion of the spatial geography of mobile media, see also Joshua Meyrowitz, *No Sense of Place: The Impact of Electronic Media on Social Behaviour* (Oxford: Oxford University Press, 1985); Nick Couldry and Anna McCarthy (eds), *MediaSpace: Place, Scale and Culture in a Media Age* (London: Routledge, 2004).

62 'Terrors of the Telephone', in *Daily Graphic* (15 March 1877), 1.

63 McLuhan, *Understanding Media*, 189–90.

64 Yuri Herrera, *Signs Preceding the End of the World*, trans. Lisa Dillman (Sheffield: And Other Stories, 2015), 7.

65 Ibid., 7, 33.
66 Ibid., 7. For a history of gender and race relations in telephoning practices, see Venus Green, *Race on the Line: Gender, Labor, and Technology in the Bell System, 1880–1980* (Durham, NC: Duke University Press, 2001).
67 Ibid., 20, 21.
68 Ibid., 21.

1

Interruption, interference and errancy

In 'Personism', a manifesto originally intended for Donald Allen's 1959 anthology *The New American Poetry* but eventually published in *Yugen* in 1961, Frank O'Hara responds to Allen Ginsberg's 'Abstraction in Poetry', in which Ginsberg advocates a 'freedom of composition' that 'avoid[s] personal considerations'.[1] Wanting to qualify Ginsberg's statement by indicating his opposition to this abstraction, O'Hara explains that 'Personism has nothing to do with philosophy, it's all art'.[2] In the manifesto, he also jokes that one 'vague idea' he had for Personism is the potential for the poem to 'address itself to one person'.[3] For Marjorie Perloff, this means 'the *illusion* of intimate talk between an "I" and a "you," giving us as readers the sense that we are eavesdropping on an ongoing conversation, that we are *present*'.[4] And it is by extending this analogy while reflecting on the process of writing a poem to a lover that O'Hara famously makes explicit the connection between the telephone and literature: 'While I was writing it I was realizing that if I wanted to I could use the telephone instead of writing the poem.'[5] On the surface, at least, O'Hara seems to suggest not only that there is an alliance between the poetic and telephonic address but also that there is a kinship between writing and calling. But although O'Hara's statement implies an easy hook-up between the poem and the call, the connection is beset with trouble. Subject to multiple forms of disruption and interference, O'Hara places poetic and telephonic lines into an uneasy but productive tension.

The telephone in O'Hara's manifesto has been discussed at length with critics variously describing it as 'tongue-in-cheek', a 'witticism', or a 'meaningful joke', but most often assuming an untroubled link between the poem and the call.[6] It was not an entirely new idea, of course – as early as 1877, Jones Very's poem 'The Telephone' suggests that with the telephone 'a new power be given to human speech' – but it is one that has endured, even as the telephone's mechanisms have shifted from the wired to the wireless and from the analogue to the digital.[7] Certainly, the relationship between technology and poetry is well established.

Writing in 1991, for instance, Perloff remarks on the ubiquity of electronic life: 'There is today no landscape uncontaminated by sound bytes or computer blips, no mountain peak or lonely valley beyond the reach of the cellular phone and the microcassette player. Increasingly, then, the poet's arena is the electronic world.'[8] And this 'contamination' – to use Perloff's term – has of course grown exponentially with the advance of digital technologies over the last three decades.

From William Carlos Williams's assertion that 'a poem is a small (or large) machine made of words' to Edward Hirsch's insistence that '[t]here must be something hardwired into [the sonnet's] machinery', poets and critics have long debated the relationship between the lyric and technology.[9] But the specific relationship between the poem and the telephone, and the reflexive relationship between the two, remains largely overlooked. In fact, Perloff goes on to argue that although 'the impact of electronic technology is now the object of intense study [...] what remains obscure is the role, if any, this technology has in shaping the ostensibly private language of poetry'.[10] Without delving into the problems of this statement, it is worth noting that Perloff responds to a perceived historical oversight that is in fact particularly pertinent to the telephone.[11] The reluctance to recognize the reciprocal relationship between telephony and poetics is evident, for instance, in Marshall McLuhan's seminal text, *Understanding Media*; while McLuhan identifies significant links between the use of the typewriter and the practice of poets such as Charles Olson – who, he writes, 'proclaim[s] the power of the typewriter to help the poet to indicate exactly the breath, the pauses, the suspension, even, of syllables' – he hardly mentions the impact of the telephone on the structure of the poem, a fact remarked upon by Michael Hennessey, who notes: 'When he turns his attention to the telephone, the poets are left behind.'[12] Despite the potency of the metaphor, then, the specific dialogue between the poem and the telephone, and the linguistic and structural connections between the two, remains critically neglected.[13] This is notwithstanding the recent turn to scholarship on poetry and new media by Christopher Funkhouser, Marjorie Perloff and Todd Tietchen, among others, who consider the ways that Anglo-American poets enact the immediacy and dynamics of the electronic age in poetic form.[14] For Seth Perlow, however, much of this work stresses the rational and informational functions of media and machines and the implications of this for the construction and reception of the poem. Such work, Perlow argues, 'elide[s] the persistent lyric norm of valorizing poetry's exemption from rational, informational purposes'.[15] Poetry, in other words, often exceeds the logical computational forms identified in some trends of digital writing. Moreover, this attention to machinic processes is clearly at odds with the number of poets – including O'Hara – who are drawn to the irrational, unsettling and disruptive potential of the telephone in their work.

In order to begin unpacking the relationship between literature and telephony – and in particular the ways that its disruptive potential endures across both wired and wireless technologies – this chapter considers the work of three post-war poets writing in English. Extending existing scholarship on Frank O'Hara through Jacques Derrida's concept of destinerrance, it offers new insights into the work of Tom Raworth and Fady Joudah in order to propose a poetics of interference that unfolds across the telephone's multiple and mutating forms. Building on work by Perlow, Angela Leighton and Nathan Jones, among others, the chapter not only explores the relationship between the telephone and the question of literature but also argues that the poetry of the telephone is bound up with the telephone's capacity for interruption, interference and errancy.

A fault on the line

The metaphor of the telephone in Frank O'Hara's 'Personism' is, perhaps, not particularly surprising given his apparent predilection for the apparatus. In fact, O'Hara's colleagues at the Museum of Modern Art in New York frequently describe him as on the phone, and it is worth noting the numerous photographs and films in which he appears at or beside it.[16] Reflecting on 'Personism', David Herd suggests:

> There is something very appealing, from the point of view of enthusiasm, of O'Hara's positioning of the telephone at the heart of his aesthetic, as if the 'call for' – what calls for poetry – can be found in the 'call to', where what the 'call to' stands for is a closeness of community in an otherwise technologically alienating world.[17]

O'Hara is quite serious, Herd goes on to suggest, in situating the poem as a form of communication that takes place between two people, and this is mirrored in the numerous references to telephones that recur in his oeuvre – for instance in '3 Poems about Kenneth Koch', 'Nocturne', 'Poem [Instant coffee with slightly sour cream]' or 'A Sonnet for Jane Freilicher' where the poet connects to the telephone operator via a long-distance line.[18] This interest in the telephone is often taken for sociability, gossip and easy communication. Referring to 'Music' as a poem 'framed as a series of cuts and dissolves, whether spatial, temporal, or referential', for instance, Perloff notes: 'The repetition of definite articles and demonstratives reenforces this sense of intimate conversation and invites the reader's participation.'[19] This view is extended by Hazel Smith, who describes the social networks and spoken modes within O'Hara's work as contributing to the 'talkscapes' that structure his verse.[20] Drawing on Walter Ong's work on secondary orality produced by a technological society, Smith suggests that O'Hara's social milieu 'was marked out by talk', and although he is not an oral or performance poet, his poems 'engage numerous different types of recontextualised talk'.[21] His asides, digressions, interjections, questions and exclamations, Smith remarks, create the 'ambivalence of live talk', leading to what she calls a 'polylogue' of multiple voices, each of which is superimposed on the voice of the poet.[22] This is evident in '3 Poems about Kenneth Koch', a sequence that veers from addressing 'Kenneth' in the second to the third person; the final poem in the sequence, 'The Inca Mystery', closes with the start of a call: 'And now the telephone. "Hello Kenneth?"'[23] The phone call from Koch simultaneously interrupts and transports the poet, and at the same time challenges the reader to participate in the call either as eavesdropper or as interlocutor: the reader's precise position in the poem remains always undecidable. Here, the telephone call interrupts the poem, but at the same time it sets it in motion elsewhere, down the long-distance wire.

Although the reference to the telephone in 'Personism' offers a convenient way of reading the alliance between poetry and calling, O'Hara's poetics are haunted by interference and disconnection – destabilizing forces that are addressed by Perloff in her reading of his 'verse telephone call'.[24] On the surface, she points out, 'Metaphysical Poem' performs a telephonic dialogue between two interlocutors as they discuss arrangements to meet. But using lineation to distinguish between the two speakers, O'Hara's poem is in fact characterized by miscommunication and distance rather than the intimacy of a lover's phone call. The poem ends when the interlocutors agree not to get together, deferring their meeting to the next exchange: 'okay I'll call you / yes call me'.[25] The resolution of the present conversation is thus extended to a future call – one that is always suspended. But however familiar this dialogue may feel to readers, Perloff admits that critics are mistaken in assuming that the poem is a simple transcription of a conversation, arguing:

> There is, I would conclude, a real difference between the 'verse letter' or 'verse telephone call' we find in the *Collected Poems* and an actual letter or phone call. The letter moves from one item to another just as we all talk (even if we don't all write such charming and amusing letters); the poem *looks* improvisatory but doesn't introduce elements it can't somehow pick up later, thus exploiting what we might call, following O'Hara, the *esthetic of culmination*.[26]

Although she focuses here on the letter, her point remains: while 'Metaphysical Poem' appears to play out a spontaneous telephone call, its economy of expression and sense of culmination give it a structure far from the open-ended and often digressive conversations of the social world. By the same token, rather than depicting the easy social exchange and intimacy proffered by the telephone, the voices in this poem are fractured and awkward, emphasizing the distance and miscommunication between interlocutors. The alliance between the telephone and the poem, then, is subject to different and multiple forms of textual static.

Returning here to O'Hara's manifesto and his claim that he could call his lover on the telephone instead of writing the poem, it is evident that there is interference on the line from the very beginning. Oren Izenberg rightly points out: 'The realization that the poet could simply call his beloved on the telephone does not lead him *in fact* to call his beloved on the telephone.'[27] He does not pick up and dial the number; he writes the poem instead. Here, the poem is thus facilitated by the act of *not* calling. Perlow explains: 'Many read this famous sentence as equating poems and telephone calls, but O'Hara writes a poem to his lover "instead of" calling him.'[28] In fact, Perlow suggests, the ordinariness of the telephone 'contrasts with the difficulties of social exchange'.[29] As a result:

> Contrary to such claims, the telephone for O'Hara does not provide a simple metonym for the chattiness, triviality, ordinariness, or indeed the social connectivity of a poem, but quite the opposite: he defines the social potentialities and technical conditions of poetry by distinguishing these from his use of the telephone.[30]

Whereas the ready connections facilitated by the telephone suggest an inherent sociability and ease of communication, O'Hara's poetic address provides, Perlow argues, a 'negative analogy', calling attention to the social distance and anonymity in his work.[31] Building on this, Perlow points to O'Hara's use of apostrophe, which is directed not only to the reader but also to 'someone or something that cannot hear the call'.[32] In 'Nocturne', for instance, O'Hara addresses a 'you' that both is and is not the poem's audience, lamenting the space that separates the poet and the second-person addressee and decrying his inability to tell them how he feels. Except, of course, as Perlow points out, he *is* telling you, creating 'an enunciative impasse paradoxically resolved by its own enunciation'.[33] As the poem concludes, O'Hara writes that this failure of communication comes about because 'you have / no telephone'.[34] Here, poetry and calling could not be further apart: one depends upon the absence of the other.

O'Hara's frequent use of the nameless 'you', Perlow argues, neither evokes intimacy nor affirms social experience but rather demonstrates the ways that our calls 'interrupt and defer contact'.[35] Far from Jones Very's account of the 'human voice [that] speaks through the electric wire', this is an apparatus that always exposes the potential for communication to falter, regardless of the sophistication of its media.[36] In fact, for Perlow, O'Hara's poems 'unfold the indefinite spatial and temporal distances across which such a call seems never quite to reach its addressee, even as it does span those same distances to reach its reader'.[37] While Perlow makes an important point about the deferral of contact here, he appears to assume that even if the call never quite reaches its addressee, it does nevertheless reach its reader: the telephone, according to this logic, performs the potential failure of telecommunication, while ensuring that the poem itself still arrives at its destination. But this perspective fails to take into account the telephonic structure of all (literary) communication – a fluid and often indeterminable force that is extended in the poetic act. Rather than suggesting that direct communication (without any form of electronic mediation) is full, smooth and without interruption, I propose that O'Hara's work instead enacts the possibility for the telephone to heighten our awareness of the possibilities of miscommunication in every speech act. This draws on Jacques Derrida's conceptualization in *The Post Card* of the letter's potential failure to arrive as 'destinerrance' – from 'destination' and 'errancy': 'Not that the letter never arrives at its destination, but it belongs to the structure of the letter to be capable, always, of not arriving.'[38] Might the same not be said of the telephone? Certainly, for Derrida's correspondent(s) in *The Post Card*, the telephone is haunted by a fault on the line. In an entry dated 28 August 1977, for instance, he writes: 'You just called. You asked me if I had heard you call me? Is that a question? I stayed silent. The idea that you might "call" me and that I might not answer overwhelms me. All this telephone between us.'[39] Rather than enabling one person to speak to another, Derrida illustrates the telephone's potential to come between interlocutors. Like the letter, then, the telephone call is subject to the possibility of destinerrance. Crucially, however, this is not simply the condition of the postal principle; it is the condition of all writing, where signification is always at risk of going astray. David Wills explains:

> Not only are there any number of examples of letters, signs, senses, going astray, but that possibility must exist as soon as and as long as the sign, the message, the sense, is defined as involving even the smallest displacement, distance, difference.[40]

In other words, O'Hara is not simply demonstrating the potential failure for telephonic communication to reach its destination; instead, he exposes the ways in which the poem itself is subject to the principle of destinerrance. Far from offering a clear and simple connective between poetry and calling in his manifesto, then, O'Hara's statement – 'While I was writing it I was realizing that if I wanted to I could use the telephone instead of writing the poem' – exposes the potential but necessary fault on every line.

An over-plugged switchboard

Thinking further about the necessary but productive disconnections between writing and calling, this chapter turns to the work of Tom Raworth, whose poems, according to Brian Reed, are 'radical experiments that rigorously unsettle conventional reading practices'.[41] I propose that Raworth's resistance to sense-making, enacted through the proliferating disconnections and the telephonic rhythms of his work, can be further developed through Derrida's theory of destinerrance. In fact, as with O'Hara, telephones appear throughout his poems – from the 'drops of sweat / / on the receiver' in 'But I Don' *Love*', to the phone that 'keeps ringing' in 'Reverse in Through Driving'.[42] In 'Patch Patch Patch' there is another call, where 'in one part of the ship a phone rings / a message from another part of the ship', and in 'There Are Lime-Trees in Leaf on the Promenade', the poet notes: 'we heard the phone ringing in the empty house then went to bed / later that morning we spoke for the first time'.[43] The recurrence of the telephone is particularly marked in his early collections including *The Relation Ship* and *The Big Green Day*, but Raworth's fascination with the phone continues throughout his oeuvre, returning for example in *Eternal Sections* and his contribution to *Etruscan Reader V*.[44]

Throughout these works, the telephone does not operate merely as a medium for speaking at a distance; instead, Raworth repeatedly demonstrates its capacity to unsettle presence, agency, embodiment and sense. In 'The Wall', for instance, the poet suggests that although 'through black / bakelite and wire we were connected', he later admits 'the connection is broken'.[45] This sense of disconnection is also played out in 'A Pressed Flower', where the telephone disrupts rather than facilitates domesticity. Here, the poet contemplates the isolation that he feels from his family and describes an evening when 'your grandfather whom i also love is perhaps dying'.[46] In the face of this grief, the speaker is 'at the other end of the line' where 'i say / there is no answer'; only 'the room there / is filled with people looking at the phone'.⁴⁷ Looking at the apparatus rather than picking up the receiver, this telephone symbolizes loss, paralysis and silence. This sense of disconnection features repeatedly in Raworth's work: in 'Nothing', for example, the poet has 'nothing to write'; his mind is 'sleepy jelly' and he is 'too tired to phone'; there is 'a / cross / connection' in 'Ace'; and in the long poem *Writing*, a voice says: '"that number / is out of service"'.⁴⁸

Raworth's telephonic address can be read in the context of his brief employment as a telephone operator.⁴⁹ Simon Perril, Marjorie Perloff and Gavin Selerie have all remarked on the fitting nature of this occupation in light of the connections and disconnections that make up his writing, and in 'Letters from Yaddo' Raworth himself directly addresses this role.⁵⁰ 'Letters from Yaddo' is structured, according to Perloff, as an intricate collage consisting of poems, found texts, letters and documentary fragments.⁵¹ But within this collage, there is one letter in particular that highlights his experience of working as an operator. Addressing the letter 'Dear Ed' (this is the poet Ed Dorn), the location of his poem is the exchange in London: 'It is two in the morning, one day in 1964. I am sitting in the fluorescent glare of the canteen at the top of the Faraday Building, near St. Paul's Cathedral, where the Continental and International Telephone exchanges are'.⁵² This is an environment, Raworth explains, that at peak times is filled with voices rattling down the wires: 'At eight the previous night, when the exchange was ablaze with lights from incoming calls, a subscriber would have had to wait perhaps ten minutes for an answer'.⁵³ Now, however, in the early hours of the morning, the exchange is quiet:

> Plugging in my headset I lean on my left elbow, hold an answering cord ready in my right hand, and try to doze. A supervisor shouts 'One up!' I look at the multiple and a white light glows for a second or two, then vanishes. I hear an operator down the room say sleepily 'Continentalservicenumberplease'.⁵⁴

Despite the exhaustion, Raworth enjoys the job. His pleasure is derived not from putting people in touch, however, but from generating disconnections, interferences and crossed lines: 'I would "accidentally" disconnect people whose tone I didn't like or who were rude to me. [...] One Christmas I linked the East Berlin operator to the West Berlin operator (there was no direct link then) and left them connected all evening'.⁵⁵ His role, then, is more scrambler than connector. He explains:

> We invented games to pass the time. A telephone number picked at random would be handed round, and in turn, at one hour intervals, we'd call the number and ask for Joe. At eight in the morning, whoever made the last call

would say 'This is Joe ... any messages?' For a month, every time I worked all night I'd ring the British Embassy in Paris on one line, Orly airport on the other, then pull back the monitor key and listen to them argue about who'd called whom. At four in the morning. Or we'd find a number with a tape-recorder connected (like Westminster Abbey at night) and fill the tape with scraps of conversation, the weather forecast in French, the time signal from Norway, and pop records you could dial on certain German numbers.[56]

What is remarkable about this passage is the multiple ways that it links to the telephonic economy of Raworth's own poetry, which is filled with overheard conversations, over-plugged circuits, numbers picked at random, scraps of conversation and accidental connections: these spliced voices echo the material and form of a number of Raworth's works. Rather than setting the poem up as a direct line, then, this is a far more complex operation, with Raworth at the switchboard making unexpected (dis)connections in the text. In fact, 'Letters from Yaddo' itself operates as a long-distance exchange; within the collection, Raworth scrambles passages of reportage, correspondence, memory and dream to create a switchboard of intersecting voices. In Perloff's words: 'Here Tom is already practicing what will be his poetic mode, the accidental "connect" and "disconnect" between overheard utterances that comes together to "fill the space with trace."'[57]

This sense of scrambling is evident in poems such as 'Catacoustics' which, even as it does not refer directly to the telephone, remains haunted by the apparatus. Explaining that 'catacoustics is the part of acoustics that studies echoes or reflected sounds', Robert Sheppard points out that 'the poem contains numerous patterns of, and references to, echoes, mirrorings, reflections, inversions, reversals, refractions, distortions, peripheral visions and barely caught memories'.[58] These echoes and refracted sounds not only unsettle traditional conceptions of the lyric voice, but also disconnect this voice from identity and presence. Here, Raworth scrambles different voices without providing a context for any of them, mixing, for instance, 'I catch to memory a car / seen from the back seat / moving past stone walled fields' with 'bell rings / so a current / is running through the circuit / up a stair'.[59] A page later, the poet encounters 'a mint policewoman / saying / "have you been drinking? / is there something wrong?"' while proclaiming 'o come o come o come / no sounds but words' sounds'.[60] And a few lines later, he splices '"birds must have a hard ...." / he tapped the milktop / with his nose' with 'their inflexions / dovetail / entropy capital / issue / reissue / search / research / (taking gravity /

as a function of time / itself a memory / of almost there)'.[61] This intermingling of times, places and contexts is heightened by the incongruity of the different conversations taking place at once. This 'talkscape', to use Smith's phrase, not only mixes multiple voices but also splices together different languages and species; the poem creates a world in which 'english / is mandarin', 'in gaelic / cloud is skye', where 'la rosée' moves seamlessly towards 'o relàmpago', and where 'dramas of songbirds / chaffinch' converse directly with 'algebra / the relative sizes of fractions'.[62] Interweaving scientific, mechanical, political, domestic, maternal, authoritarian and more-than-human voices, it is as if Raworth is back at the exchange, plugging in different calls, and then 'pull[ing] back the monitor key and listening to them argue about who'd called whom'. The result is a poem in which the reader is forced to tune into multiple and proliferating voices, often talking at cross-purposes, without ever being fully present to the conversation.

The disruptive potential of Raworth's telephonic economy is perhaps most explicit in *Writing*, a poem in which the different voices, Perloff writes, 'crowd the mental field with all the momentum of a television set that is tuned to three channels at the same time or one telephone conversation that crosses another'.[63] But while the possibilities of voice are central to this poem, Raworth stresses that 'voice / prints / are not / identity'.[64] Disrupting the perceived connection between the voice and the subject, this poem emphasizes its material qualities; it is worth noting that the frontispiece of the first (and only) edition of *Writing*, which was printed by The Figures, features Raworth's own voice print or sonogram which was recorded at the Exploratorium in San Francisco. Discussing this sonogram, Colin MacCabe remarks: 'This image of the voice serves as an emblem for the book, for it dissolves the unity of the personal voice into differentiated bands of sound'.[65] This is made explicit when Raworth writes: 'screech / rattle / rumble / hum / whir / buzz / throb / voice: she hands him / new colours'.[66] *Writing* thus operates as an echo chamber, drawing attention to the ways in which, disconnected from the subject, the voice becomes throb, and speech becomes sound. Following Ferdinand de Saussure's statement that 'it is impossible for sound alone, a material element, to belong to language', Michel Chion points out that language does not have sounds but phonemes and that when the phoneme is separated from its signifier, it becomes 'sonic matter, voice, noise, what have you'.[67] Raworth's attention to the screech, rattle and hum in *Writing* demonstrates this blurring between sound and language, recalling Claude Shannon and Warren Weaver's theory of noise as sounds that are 'added to the signal which were not intended by the information source'.⁶⁸ But for Perloff and Craig Dworkin:

> The relation of sound to poetry has always been triangulated, implicitly or explicitly, by an equally nebulous third term: sense. The relation is ambiguous, and shifting, because sound – especially in the context of poetry – is of that species of homographs which produce their own antonyms.⁶⁹

Here, Perloff and Dworkin put forward a theory of poetic language in which the acoustic resonance has the potential to interrupt the signifying chain in a move that Garrett Stewart describes as the '*challenge* of sound to sense'.⁷⁰ In this way, Raworth's screech, rattle and hum participate in the poem's potential for destinerrance – in other words, the potential for signification to go astray. Thus, by drawing out the potential for sonic errancy, Raworth's switchboard enacts a collision not only between language and sound but also between sense and non-sense.

Composed of short, breathy fragments, where noise, information, languages and tones are intermingled, the reader of *Writing* is on the receiving end of a stream of overlapping voice prints – a rapid network of signals and sounds. Raworth's performances of *Writing*, moreover, are characteristically fast-paced and breathless.⁷¹ In fact, as John Barrell notes:

> His readings are extraordinarily charged, tense occasions which leave the audience as breathless as the poet. He reads at high speed and in a tone which is not exactly uninflected, but which has the effect of being so, because it gives almost the same inflection, and an almost equal emphasis, to every line.⁷²

This urgency taps into the poem's telephonic economy: writing in 'A Letter from London', Gavin Selerie recalls attending a Miners' Benefit Reading, where he observes: 'The thing is that Raworth's voice is very special – it comes out layered like crossed lines on the telephone.'⁷³ The speed of Raworth's delivery also relates in important ways to the speed of contemporary telecommunications – where the voice appears to travel the world in an instant. From a perceived synonymy with enlightenment to a fear of excessive accelerated processes, speed is inevitably associated with modernity. For Bob Hanke, real-time telecommunication technologies mean that we have entered a 'new digital age of speed' in which time is measured in nanoseconds.⁷⁴ This shift from a spatial to a temporal phenomenon, he suggests, indicates that 'technology is now on the verge of conquering time'.⁷⁵ Following this, Raworth's writing, I propose, interrupts spatio-temporal dimensions, exposing not only the ways that the telephone constricts space but also the ways that it restructures time. This is played out in '7/8 of the Real', for instance, where Raworth writes:

> all ways show
> a little speed
>
> you can't stop any thing
> that's in the air
>
> all ways things coming
> to where you are[76]

As if to recall his experience at the intercontinental exchange, Raworth stresses the speed at which the voices in the air appear to travel. This instantaneity is played out through the operation of syntax in poems such as *Writing*, where semi-clauses and minimal lines cut across each other in quick succession in a manner that enacts Paul Virilio's argument that velocity is the basis of the technological society. Using the term 'dromology' – from the Greek *dromos* for race course – to explore the 'logic of speed', Virilio traces the continuum between technologies of representation and speed and argues that the ways that images reach us – across screens, down the wires, and through the ether – reshape our cultural lives.[77] By confronting us with impermanence, ephemerality, and rapidly appearing and disappearing voices, Raworth's dromological poetics forces the reader to accept the text's resistance to totalization and control. This logic of speed, moreover, heightens the reader's own sense of his or her failure to fully comprehend the poem. Thus, Raworth reinforces the structure of destinerrance that interrupts the poetic switchboard, opening up the possibility that, as he says in 'Beautiful Habit', we are listening to 'the wrong / voice print'.[78]

The text message

My analysis of the relationship between poetry and calling has so far concerned the age of the landline, where voices and sounds travel down wires. But how does telephone usage in the twenty-first century – and in particular the mobile phone's capacity to function as a portable text messaging service – play into contemporary poetics? The text message emerged in 1992, but by the end of the decade, as Gerard Goggin and Caroline Hamilton note, it was ubiquitous.[79] Not only did the popularity of texting transform communication, but it also impacted the shape of the poem. Speaking to the interest in text message poetry in the first decade of the twenty-first century, for instance, Carol Ann Duffy draws attention to the productive limitations of character constraint: 'The poem is a form of texting … it's the original text. […] It's a perfecting of a feeling in language – it's a way of saying more with less, just as texting is.'[80] For Michael Rudin, short-form content is key: 'In this age of texting', he writes, 'the littlest texts may matter most'.[81] But neither of these claims fully acknowledge the potential for the text message to disrupt received notions of poetic communication. Extending my discussion of speed and the possibilities for the telephone to compress both time and space, the chapter now turns to the work of Palestinian-American physician and poet Fady Joudah and the impact of the text message on the shape and direction of his writing. In so doing, and moving away from poetry that is voiced to a live audience, it also draws on Angela Leighton's interest in writing that 'stays silent on the page while shaping the labor of the ear through which it might, nevertheless, be heard'.[82] Developing our understanding of sound in poetry, I seek to complicate the ways in which telephony intervenes in debates regarding voice, presence and language.

Each poem, or each part within each poem, is exactly 160 characters, which is designed, Joudah explains in his introduction, to be 'specific to text-message parameters'.[83] First published as an e-book available for download on a mobile device, the printed copy of *Textu* is small and slim, not much larger than the smartphone of 2014; the layout, the use of white space, the lack of punctuation, and the fragmentary style, all contribute to the sense that Joudah is playing with the ways that new and rapid media, as well as our apparently insatiable appetite for ever smaller and lighter smartphone technologies, inform the generation, experience and distribution of the poetic artefact.[84] But rather than focus on writing that is produced specifically on or for the telephone, I am interested in the ways that telephoning practices change and are changed by print-based literature.

In a 2015 interview with Kaveh Akbar, Joudah describes his process of writing *Textu*, during which he found himself paying a different kind of attention to 'sounds and sentences and ideas that came floating through my mind or through the mouths of others'.[85] In a way, then, he is both receiver and mouthpiece, scrambling the words and rendering them as a text message – a medium whose capacity for swiftness of dispatch is at odds with the complex processes of signification at work within each poem. In fact, although they do not directly broach the telephone as a thematic concern – engaging largely with humanitarian issues, anti-capitalist politics, the body, global conflict and spirituality – the poems in *Textu* demonstrate a density and concision appropriate to the text-message character count. The collection incorporates traces of contemporary smartphone speak, including the 'at sign' in 'Revolution 3', where the poet, with 'so many middle names', utters 'meet me tonight @five'.[86] Referring both to a commercial symbol and to a location, '@' now also links with the 'handle' on a social media platform, refiguring the possibilities of naming in the Twitter age. This recalls Maurizio Ferraris's argument:

> Mobile phones are not only machines for speaking, they are also writing machines. E-mails and mobile phones today are virtually identical, and they do not only convey phonetic writing but also ideograms –:):-):-(;-) – that is, the kind of writing furthest from speech that you can think of.[87]

As a writing machine, Joudah's 'textu' is generated not only by phonetic writing and character count but also by immediacy of language and address. In 'Revolution 3', the second person of the poem collides with the reader, playing on the possibilities for the reader to receive the message on their own device, complete with GPS navigational tools and instructions for meeting face to face. The poem continues:

> Rush Hour Libation Square
> leave your car on the highway
>
> walk out walk slowly
> start there![88]

But the text message constraint is not simply an aesthetic choice. Joudah explains to Akbar that using character count for metre is 'an inescapable reality' given that 'our language [is] governed by scientific and market forces'.[89] Here, he refers to the way that contemporary communication is shaped – even compressed – according to consumer forces. Although he goes on to admit that most people in the West now have unlimited texting and therefore do not need to worry about getting billed for a message over 160 characters, Joudah reminds us that in other parts of the world, many people still pay per text: 'So to use character count is also a reflection of this sort of market economy translation of life in our time, the differences between those who have and those who don't.'[90] *Textu* thus makes a political and an economic statement, as well as an aesthetic one. This is perhaps most evident in 'Luke Cool Hand I'm Your Father', where 'Nurturing people into junkies' is 'par for the course', and where 'pills & fear / & salt & sugar & grease

// @the dollar store' are offered as if 'they did have a choice'.[91] Condensed form, chopped syntax, technological constraint and the compression of language operate hand in hand with the indeterminacy and errancy of the message. In this way, *Textu* exposes the ways in which aesthetic form is also political, insisting on the co-implication of the technological and the literary, and the possibilities for this to shape, and be shaped by, a range of material, socio-economic and environmental concerns.

In her discussion of Joudah's collection alongside Twitter poems by Elizabeth Alexander, Claire Schwartz suggests: 'It's at once, as you say, this chatty language, but with profound spatial constraints.'[92] But the poems in *Textu* far exceed the assumed ease of social media 'chat'; in fact, Joudah is at pains to point out the difference between text message and Twitter post, recalling for instance, that some readers questioned his character count: 'I have to correct them and say, "No, Twitter is 140 characters including the hashtag."'[93] He also claims that whereas the public nature of Twitter feels 'sort of like spitting something out in the wind', the text message 'is more private for poetry'. At odds with Schwartz's account of 'chatty language', and perhaps recalling Perloff's problematic assumption regarding the ostensibly private nature of poetry, Joudah insists: 'I chose to do something that emphasized the intimacy and privacy of the matter or medium, which is also a reflection of the contemporary poem and its limitation as well.'[94] The intimacy to which Joudah refers is certainly evident in poems such as 'Iron Maiden', where 'in the no reply zone', the poet and his lover are 'touching jamming / silence with our breaths'.[95] The double spondee here adds to the poem's tactility, feeling thumbed out on the screen and page. Continuing, 'Still I will bang my body // into your body's rhythms', Joudah's repetition of 'b' contributes to the architecture of sound. In 'Bulb', for instance, the 'cyanide' in the first line echoes with the 'vibe' of the third but also sets up a contrast with the shorter sound in 'pit', 'dermis', 'ninja' and 'tulip', which combine to create a heterogeneous literary texture. In so doing, Joudah plays out Leighton's assertion that 'sound is also a physical object which literally touches the ear when heard'.[96] Here, Leighton draws on R. Murray Schafer's argument that 'hearing is a way of touching at a distance', going on to point out that although Schafer stresses 'distance' here, 'actual soundwaves touch the ear literally, at no distance, and thus set its mechanisms for hearing in motion'.[97] Thus, sound dissolves into touch, just as connection tends towards disconnection, and text becomes voice.

The final lines of 'Iron Maiden' consist of contrasting long and short vowel sounds in 'I am wave you are kelp', anticipating and providing a contrast to the metrical pattern of the closing line: 'We are gardener & tulip'. Although these poems have a touching rhythm of their own, their call provides a contrast to Raworth's often lengthy and breathless operations. Rather than accelerating communication, the character limitation in fact shapes the poem's pace. 'Reading', Virilio writes, 'implies time for reflection, a slowing down that destroys the mass's dynamic efficiency'.[98] But in an accelerated culture, we are subject to 'mediatization', and thus deprived of the freedom to reflect. Honing the sound bites that make up each poem forces the reader to pause and results in moments of controlled tension at odds with the apparent speed of a text message. In their silent and understated manner, Joudah's poems thus encourage us to read 'with the ears', which, Leighton says, means 'going slower, no longer following the lines to the end in order to discover what is meant, but attending instead to any number of incidental rhythmic effects and sound combinations'.[99] In fact, in the age of instant messaging, Joudah describes the collection as 'an elegy of sorts', and its precise, measured metre is one that celebrates and commemorates an attentiveness to detail.[100]

And yet these poems resist the temptation to offer the reader a straightforward message as such but rather play with the text message's parameters in order to deconstruct the possibility of signification, where sender and receiver are both subject to slippage. As a result, Joudah's *Textu* poems frustrate the relationship between sound, matter and sense. This resistance is at work in the first of the two title poems, in which the poet insists on a networked imagination where 'No idea is an island'.[101] Parodying textspeak but including a pointed 'g' at the end of 'talking', he continues: 'Whoview bin talking 2?', highlighting through the homonym 'two / to' that this is written communication.[102] In this way, Joudah's poem resonates with Ferraris's claim that 'despite the appearances, *the mobile phone is a writing machine*'.[103] At the same time, however, the poem draws attention to its own phonotext, thus playing on the aural overlaps inherent in language characteristic of the text message. For Adelaide Morris, this kind of wordplay 'foregrounds sound's generative aspect: its capacity to make or unmake meaning'.[104] Discussing this in the context of modernism, Morris notes that 'this capacity is most perceptible through breached word boundaries and puns that complicate and confuse the process of meaning-making'.[105] Transposed to the twenty-first century, Joudah's 'textspeak', like modernist wordplay, embodies the triangulation between poetry, sound and sense, demonstrating the ways that the poem draws attention to its errancy and its capacity to be heard in the ear of the mind.

The acoustic possibilities of the poem are further developed by Joudah's assertion that 'a fistula is an isthmus'; here, he not only yokes together through a series of linguistic traces the signifier of being, 'is', but he also links the abnormal connection between two body parts in a 'fistula' with the 'isthmus', a narrow portion of land enclosed on both sides by bodies of water. 'Heavenchew an app for it?' the poem continues, reminding the reader not only of the prevalence of new app technologies ostensibly designed to make life quicker and easier but also the potential for punning to complicate sense. Concluding 'We shed light then leave its husk behind' – hinting at the electronic waste caused by the planned obsolescence of the mobile – Joudah demonstrates that far from shedding light on the poem, the reader is left with the 'husk' of signification. His use of the @ symbol, homonyms, abbreviations and textspeak, therefore, draw attention not only to Ferraris's theory of writing but also to what Morris refers to as 'textualised sound' and, in so doing, highlight the aurality of the poem.[106] Through rhythm, homonym, wordplay and symbol, then, the poems in *Textu* invite the reader to translate text into sound, causing what Leighton refers to as a 'kind of aural distraction', which, rather than conveying the instantaneity of the telephone, 'might even hold us up forever in its reverberating halls'.[107]

But Joudah's work does more than this: in highlighting the aurality of its form, the poem also stresses its materiality. This is significant given the seeming immateriality of mobile media. It does so not through direct reference to the hardware which frames its composition but through the staging of interference and errancy that signal the potential failure of its software. In this way, Joudah's work can be read alongside Nathan Jones's analysis of glitch poetics. Discussing the origins of the term 'glitch' and its possible etymological link to the Yiddish *glitchen*, for slip, Jones explains that 'by definition a "glitch" is momentary, an error that is trivial enough to be overcome', linking its usage to 'forms of interference in media – the traces or artifacts that instabilities, edits, mistakes leave behind'.[108] These 'messy media moments' are integral to its aesthetics, instigating what Jones (after Rosa Menkman) calls 'an authentic "critical sensory" encounter with language'.[109] Although not limited to the digital age, the propensity of the glitch, Jones argues, exposes the entanglement of human and machine, the technical and the material, and the depth and the surface of media. Discussing this errancy in the age of the Anthropocene, Jones argues that we need to find new strategies for language. Our current geological epoch, combined with unprecedented advances in electronic media, has resulted, he suggests, in 'the preponderance of neologisms and ephemeral slang in contemporary discourse'.[110] Although Joudah does not, in *Textu*, open up the kind of linguistic, typographical and technical disordering and misplacement that Jones attributes to the work of poets such as Caroline Bergvall, his attention to language as technology intersects with the productive significance of errors in communication. Exposing the disruptive encounters between poem and message, between materiality and media, and between sound and sense, Joudah's 'Whoview bin talking 2?' and 'Heavenchew an app for it?' enact the kind of linguistic anomaly that Jones suggests is 'best understood as the response to a series of gaps and faults opened in the "interoperability" of the English language by a new sense of the world'.[111] By incorporating errancy – for instance 'bin' for 'been' – into the poem at the level of language, Joudah enacts the 'interoperability' of literature, technology and politics. Moreover, this glitchy, scrambled and overworked textspeak performs the disruptive encounter between poetry and the mobile phone, highlighting the telephone's creative capacity for (mis)communication and its potential for finding new ways of making sense in and of the world.

In different ways, then, O'Hara, Raworth and Joudah each show us that although there is a tangible connection between poetry and calling, this hook-up involves multiple, divergent and often tangled lines. Exchanging different voices, languages and forms, and marking the collision between registers that are variously intimate, sociable, informal, detached and awkward, work by these poets opens up the aesthetic and the political nature of the poetry of the telephone. Perhaps most of all, however, it is by playing with the productive qualities of disconnection that these poets complicate the relationship between sound and sense and demonstrate that rather than immediacy and connection, destinerrance is always at work in the text. Indeed, for Leighton, the literary text offers us 'a threshold rather than a destination, and makes us pause there, to hear all the summoned sounds that words can make or bring to the ear. It stops us going straight over into sense and comprehension'.[112] For Garret Stewart, the challenge of sound to sense can be read as 'the errand of meaning versus the errancy and hazard of signifying', which, Leighton remarks, 'reminds us to listen against the grain of running meaningful errands and to wander (or err) among noises that may seem no more than a distraction, but a distraction that could be the whole point'.[113] Although neither Stewart nor Leighton refers directly to Derrida's concept of destinerrance here, their turn to the 'errant' forces at work in poetry suggests that the telephone is simultaneously a disruptive and generative force in the text – a force that crosses the lines between meaningful errands and the errancy of meaning.

Notes

1 Frank O'Hara, 'Personism: A Manifesto', *Yugen*, 7 (1961), reprinted in *The Collected Poems of Frank O'Hara*, ed. Donald Allen (Berkeley: University of California Press, 1995), 498–9; Allen Ginsberg, 'Abstraction in Poetry', *It Is*, 3 (Winter-Spring 1959), 75, cited in Marjorie Perloff, 'Frank O'Hara and the Aesthetics of Attention', *boundary, 2*, 4.3 (1976), 779–806 (798).
2 O'Hara, 'Personism', 498–9.
3 Ibid., 499.
4 Perloff, 'Frank O'Hara and the Aesthetics of Attention', 799.
5 O'Hara, 'Personism', 499.
6 Perloff, 'Frank O'Hara', 798; Todd Tietchen, 'Frank O'Hara and the Poetics of the Digital', *Criticism*, 56.1 (2014), 45–62 (46); Hazel Smith, *Hyperscapes in the Poetry of Frank O'Hara: Difference, Homosexuality, Topography* (Liverpool: Liverpool University Press, 2000), 143.
7 Jones Very, 'The Telephone', in *The Complete Poems*, ed. Helen R. Deese (Athens: The University of Georgia Press, 1993), 503.
8 Marjorie Perloff, *Radical Artifice: Writing Poetry in the Age of Media* (Chicago: University of Chicago Press, 1991), xiii.
9 William Carlos Williams, 'Author's Introduction to The Wedge', in *Selected Essays of William Carlos Williams* (New York: New Directions, 1954), 256; Edward Hirsch, 'My Own Acquaintance', in *The Making of a Sonnet: A Norton Anthology*, ed. Edward Hirsch and Eavan Boland (New York: Norton, 2009), 39. Scholarship on the relationship between poetry and technology includes, for example, Horace J. McNeil and Clarence Stratton (eds), *Poems for a Machine Age* (New York: McGraw-Hill, 1941); Friedrich Kittler, *Gramophone, Film, Typewriter*, trans. Geoffrey Winthrop-Young and Michael Wutz (Stanford, CA: Stanford University Press, 1999); and Carrie Noland, *Poetry at Stake: Lyric Aesthetics and the Challenge of Technology* (Princeton, NJ: Princeton University Press, 1999).
10 Perloff, *Radical Artifice*, 2–3.
11 Edward Allen discusses Perloff's use of the term 'private', noting: 'The suspect word – "ostensibly" – is made to do some serious work in Perloff's formulation, such that we might begin to wonder how "private" the language of poetry has *ever* been, or ever could be, or why it might be important to find another term for "private" altogether and thus dispense with the caginess of ostensibility' (Edward Allen, *Modernist Inventions: Media Technology and American Poetry* (Cambridge: Cambridge University Press, 2007), 27).
12 Marshall McLuhan, *Understanding Media: The Extensions of Man* (London: Routledge, 2001), 282; Michael S. Hennessey, 'Poetry by Phone and Phonograph: Tracing the

Influence of Giorno Poetry Systems', in *Audiobooks, Literature, and Sound Studies*, ed. Matthew Rubery (London: Routledge, 2011), 76–91 (82).

13 Discussions of the specific relationship between poetry and the telephone most often focus on a single author and are limited to single chapters in book-length studies. See, for instance, Allen, 'Robert Frost on the Telephone' in *Modernist Invention*, 37–79; Hennessey, 'Poetry by Phone and Phonograph'; and Seth Perlow, *The Poem Electric: Technology and the American Lyric* (Minneapolis, MN: University of Minnesota Press, 2018), 135–78.

14 Christopher T. Funkhouser, *Prehistoric Digital Poetry: An Archaeology of Forms, 1959–1995* (Tuscaloosa: University of Alabama Press, 2007); Christopher T. Funkhouser, *New Directions in Digital Poetry* (London: Continuum, 2012); Marjorie Perloff, *Unoriginal Genius: Poetry by Other Means in the New Century* (Chicago: University of Chicago Press, 2010); Todd Tietchen, *Technomodern Poetics: The American Literary Avant-Garde at the Start of the Information Age* (Iowa: University of Iowa Press, 2018). See also Lori Emerson, *Reading Writing Interfaces: From the Digital to the Bookbound* (Minneapolis, MN: University of Minnesota Press, 2014); Nathan Jones, 'Glitch Poetics: The Posthumanities of Error', in *The Bloomsbury Handbook of Electronic Literature*, ed. Joseph Tabbi (London: Bloomsbury, 2017), 237–52; Brian Kim Stefans, *Word Toys: Poetry and Technics* (Tuscaloosa: University of Alabama Press, 2017); Adelaide Morris and Thomas Swiss, *New Media Poetics* (Cambridge, MA: MIT Press, 2006); Paul Stephen, *The Poetics of Information Overload: From Gertrude Stein to Conceptual Writing* (Minneapolis, MN: University of Minnesota Press, 2015).

15 Perlow, *The Poem Electric*, 2.

16 See David Herd, *Enthusiast! Essays on Modern American Literature* (Manchester: Manchester University Press, 2007), 160. See also Perlow, *The Poem Electric*, 144–5.

17 Herd, *Enthusiast!*, 160.

18 O'Hara, *Collected Poems*, 61, 151, 224, 244.

19 Perloff, 'Frank O'Hara', 283.

20 Smith, *Hyperscapes*, 136.

21 Walter Ong, *Orality and Literacy: The Technologizing of the Word* (London: Methuen, 1982); Smith, *Hyperscapes*, 137, 143.

22 Smith, *Hyperscapes*, 143, 146.

23 O'Hara, *Collected Poems*, 151–2.

24 Marjorie Perloff, *Frank O'Hara: Poet among Painters* (Chicago: University of Chicago Press, 1977), 29.

25 O'Hara, *Collected Poems*, 434–5.

26 Perloff, 'Frank O'Hara', 801.

27 Oren Izenberg, *Being Numerous: Poetry and the Ground of Social Life* (Princeton, NJ: Princeton University Press, 2011), 136.

28 Perlow, *The Poem Electric*, 140–1.
29 Ibid., 140.
30 Ibid., 139.
31 Ibid., 140.
32 Ibid., 141.
33 Ibid., 142.
34 O'Hara, *Collected Poems*, 225.
35 Perlow, *The Poem Electric*, 152.
36 Very, 'The Telephone', 503.
37 Perlow, *The Poem Electric*, 152.
38 Jacques Derrida, *The Post Card: From Socrates to Freud and Beyond*, trans. Alan Bass (Chicago: The University of Chicago Press, 1987), 444.
39 Ibid., 41.
40 David Wills, 'Post/Card/Match/Book/Envois/Derrida', *SubStance*, 43 (1984), 19–38 (21–2).
41 Brian M. Reed, *Phenomenal Reading: Essays on Modern and Contemporary Poetics* (Tuscaloosa: University of Alabama Press, 2012), 56.
42 Tom Raworth, *Collected Poems* (Manchester: Carcanet, 2003), 9–10, 50.
43 Ibid., 110, 17.
44 Tom Raworth, *The Relation Ship* (London: Goliard Press, 1967); Tom Raworth, *The Big Green Day* (London: Trigram, 1968); Tom Raworth, *Eternal Sections* (Los Angeles: Sun & Moon Press, 1993); Tom Raworth, Bill Griffiths and Tom Leonard, *Etruscan Reader V* (Wilkes-Barre: Etruscan Books, 1997).
45 Raworth, *Collected Poems*, 26.
46 Ibid., 27.
47 Ibid.
48 Ibid., 385, 209, 306.
49 Raworth writes: 'Between leaving school in 1954 and going to the University of Essex in 1967 I had a variety of jobs, including Insurance Clerk, Builders' Labourer, Packer, Assistant Transport Manager, and Continental Telephonist' (Tom Raworth, 'Curriculum Vitae', last updated 1 August 2016; available at: https://web.archive.org/web/20161110063408/ and http://tomraworth.com/cvweb.html (accessed 18 March 2022)).
50 Marjorie Perloff, 'Filling the Space with Trace: Tom Raworth's "Letters from Yaddo"' in *Removed for Further Study*, ed. Nate Dorward, *The Gig* 13/14 (2003), 130–44; Simon Perril, '"What Rhymes with Cow / and Starts with an N": Tom Raworth's Time and Motion Studies', in *Removed for Further Study*, ed. Dorward, 108–29; Gavin Selerie, 'A Letter from London', *North Dakota Quarterly* (11 May 1985), 115–34 (117). See Tom Raworth, 'Letters from Yaddo', in *Earn Your Milk: Collected Prose* (Cambridge: Salt, 2009), 79–134.
51 Perloff, 'Filling the Space', 17–18.

52 Raworth, 'Letters from Yaddo', 115.
53 Ibid., 116–17.
54 Ibid., 116.
55 Ibid., 117.
56 Ibid., 117–18.
57 Perloff, 'Filling the Space', 6.
58 Robert Sheppard, *The Poetry of Saying: British Poetry and Its Discontents, 1950–2000* (Liverpool: Liverpool University Press, 2005), 176.
59 Raworth, *Collected Poems*, 321.
60 Ibid., 322.
61 Ibid., 323.
62 Ibid., 325, 326, 339, 330, 340.
63 Marjorie Perloff, 'The Word as Such: L=A=N=G=U=A=G=E Poetry in the Eighties', *The American Poetry Review*, 13.3 (1984), 15–22 (22).
64 Raworth, *Collected Poems*, 269.
65 Colin MacCabe, 'Dissolving the Voice: Tom Raworth's *Writing*', first published in *Times Literary Supplement* (30 December 1983), reprinted in *Critical Quarterly*, 59.2 (2017), 83–6 (83).
66 Raworth, *Collected Poems*, 308.
67 Ferdinand de Saussure, *Course in General Linguistics*, trans. Wade Baskin (New York: Columbia University Press, 2011), 118, cited in Michel Chion, *Sound: An Acoulogical Treatise*, trans. James A. Steintrager (Durham, NC: Duke University Press, 2016), 45.
68 Claude E. Shannon and Warren Weaver, *The Mathematical Theory of Communication* (Urbana: The University of Illinois Press, 1964), 7; see also Tietchen, *Technomodern Poetics*, 37–51.
69 Marjorie Perloff and Craig Dworkin, 'The Sound of Poetry/The Poetry of Sound: The 2006 MLA Presidential Forum', *PMLA*, 123.3 (2008), 749–61 (755). For a brief history of sound poetry, see Steve McCaffery, 'From Phonic to Sonic: The Emergence of the Audio-Poem', in *Sound States: Innovative Poetics and Acoustical Technologies*, ed. Adelaide Morris (Chapel Hill, NC: University of North Carolina Press, 1998), 149–68.
70 Garrett Stewart, *Reading Voices: Literature and the Phonotext* (Berkeley: University of California Press, 1990), 25.
71 For an example, listen to Raworth reading *Writing*, Rockdrill #5 (Contemporary Poetics Research Centre, Optic Nerve for Birkbeck College, 2004), available at: https://media.sas.upenn.edu/pennsound/authors/Raworth/Rockdrill-5/Raworth-Tom_01_Writing_Writing_Rockdrill-5_2004.mp3 (accessed 15 March 2019).
72 John Barrell, 'Subject and Sentence: The Poetry of Tom Raworth', *Critical Inquiry*, 17.2 (1991), 386–410 (393).
73 Selerie, 'A Letter from London', 117.

74 Bob Hanke, 'McLuhan, Virilio and Speed', in *Transforming McLuhan: Cultural, Critical, and Postmodern Perspectives*, ed. Paul Grosswiler (New York: Peter Lang, 2010), 203–26 (205).
75 Ibid., 205.
76 Raworth, *Collected Poems*, 103.
77 Paul Virilio, *Speed and Politics*, trans. Marc Polizzotti (Los Angeles: Semiotext(e), 2007), 69.
78 Ibid., 177.
79 Gerrard Goggin and Caroline Hamilton, 'Narrative Fiction and Mobile Media after the Text-Message Novel', in *The Mobile Story : Narrative Practices with Locative Technologies*, ed. Jason Farman (London: Routledge, 2014), 223–37 (225).
80 Carol Ann Duffy, cited in Joanna Morehead, 'Poems Are a Form of Texting', *The Guardian*, 5 September 2011, available at: https://www.theguardian.com/education/2011/sep/05/carol-ann-duffy-poetry-texting-competition (accessed 12 November 2021).
81 Michael Rudin, 'From Hemingway to Twitterature: The Short and Shorter of It', *The Journal of Electronic Publishing*, 14.2 (2011), n.p.
82 Angela Leighton, *Hearing Things: The Work of Sound in Literature* (Cambridge, MA: Harvard University Press, 2018), 18.
83 Fady Joudah, *Textu* (Washington: Copper Canyon Press, 2014), xi.
84 Given the existing work on both digital poetry (see n. 14) and the mobile phone in media studies – see, for instance, Gerard Goggin, *Cell Phone Culture: Mobile Technology in Everyday Life* (London: Routledge, 2006); Gerard Goggin and Larissa Hjorth (eds), *The Routledge Companion to Mobile Media* (London: Routledge, 2014) – the present study does not address works that are created only for the phone and instead seeks to examine what Perlow describes as 'the implicit, unintended ways that electronics alter poetry cultures' (Perlow, *The Poem Electric*, 248 n. 49).
85 Fady Joudah, 'Interview' with Kaveh Akbar, 2 February 2015, available at: https://www.divedapper.com/interview/fady-joudah/ (accessed 15 March 2019).
86 Joudah, *Textu*, 22.
87 Maurizio Ferraris, *Where Are You? An Ontology of the Cell Phone*, trans. Sarah De Sanctis (New York: Fordham University Press, 2014), 10.
88 Joudah, *Textu*, 22.
89 Joudah, 'Interview' with Akbar.
90 Ibid.
91 Joudah, *Textu*, 39–41 (39).
92 Claire Schwartz, 'An Interview with Rita Dove', *The Virginia Quarterly Review*, 92.1 (2016), 164–71 (168).
93 Joudah, 'Interview' with Akbar. In 2017, Twitter increased the limit from 140 to 280 characters.
94 Ibid.

95   Joudah, *Textu*, 4.
96   Leighton, *Hearing Things*, 4.
97   R. Murray Schafer, *The Soundscape: Our Sonic Environment and the Tuning of the World* (Rochester, VT: Destiny Books, 1993), 11; Leighton, *Hearing Things*, 4.
98   Virilio, *Speed and Politics*, 31.
99   Leighton, *Hearing Things*, 2.
100 Joudah, 'Interview' with Akbar.
101 Joudah, *Textu*, 34.
102 Ibid.
103 Ferraris, *Where Are You?*, 10.
104 Adelaide Morris, 'Sound Technologies and the Modernist Epic: H.D. On The Air', in *Sound States: Innovative Poetics and Acoustical Technologies*, ed. Adeline Morris (Chapel Hill, NC: University of North Carolina Press, 1998), 32–55 (43).
105 Ibid., 43.
106 Morris, 'Introduction', in *Sound States,* ed. Morris, 1–14 (2).
107 Leighton, *Hearing Things*, 5.
108 Jones, 'Glitch Poetics', 237–52 (237).
109 Ibid., 238. See Rosa Menkman, *The Glitch Moment(um)* (Amsterdam: Institute of Network Cultures, 2011), 33.
110 Jones, 'Glitch Poetics', 248.
111 Ibid., 248.
112 Leighton, *Hearing Things*, 38.
113 Stewart, *Reading Voices*, 27; Leighton, *Hearing Things*, 30.

2

Secret communications

On 22 January 1966, *The Bookseller* ran an announcement entitled 'Speed' under 'Points from Publishers':

> On Tuesday evening this week Macmillan reported that a children's book which Muriel Spark had started to write in a London hotel at 5.30 that morning had been completed by her, delivered to her publishers by 3 p.m. and formally accepted by them by telephone at 3.30 p.m. Lines were at once put out for a possible illustrator and, very enthusiastic indeed about the book, Macmillan say quite definitely that it will be illustrated in full colour and published in the early autumn. The title is *The Small Telephone*.[1]

Reportedly written at great speed and confirmed down the line, 'The Small Telephone' was not published that autumn; in fact, it did not materialize for almost thirty years, eventually appearing in print in 1993 alongside 'The French Window'. But although the text is neglected by critics, the story introduces some of the complex ways in which the crossed lines of Muriel Spark's literary telephone are plugged into the writing ear.

The story features a small and lonely telephone named Doctor Downie who, because he was 'never being spoken into', starts 'to talk to himself'.[2] During such exchanges, he tells himself jokes and laments the fact that he has not yet met his wife, Miranda Judith. Realizing that it is unlikely that he will ever meet Miranda, he sinks into silence and 'brood[s] quietly on his table with his receiver resting on his neck'.[3] One day, however, he receives a call from an elegant pink telephone named Snowdrop Bentley Fergusson, who is dismayed at the hook-up: '"You are just someone who has crossed my line by mistake. [...] I shall get through to the Telephone Exchange and tell them our wires have been muddled."'[4] Although he is rejected by Snowdrop for being 'too old-fashioned and small and poor', Downie does not give up, and when he eventually finds himself on the line with Miranda, who claims to be Snowdrop's current owner, the two make a connection.[5] In a rapid turn of events, Miranda moves into Downie's residence, bringing many friends with her who 'all spoke into Doctor Downie, one after the other, every day, morning, noon and night, and they all lived happily ever after'.[6]

Despite its deceptive simplicity, this story presents a series of epistemological knots. For Avital Ronell, the telephone always 'presupposes the existence of another telephone, somewhere'; in Spark's story, however, the apparatus that talks to itself creates a rupture in the signifying chain.[7] Moreover, the poor telephone appears able to read the future – or at least, to have some knowledge of his future wife, knowing her name before he has even heard of her; how this has come about remains, in the text, a secret. In this way, Spark's uncanny telephone taps into the relationship between telepathy, the auditory imagination and literary secrecy. In so doing, it also enacts what Martin McQuillan describes as Spark's 'redistribution of narrative possibilities' by introducing impossible questions regarding telecommunications, narrative knowledge and the undecidable.[8]

A preoccupation with the telephone is of course pervasive throughout Spark's works, with Spark herself admitting to an 'addiction to the telephone', which she claims in her autobiography *Curriculum Vitae* began during the years following the end of the Second World War.[9] Certainly, more than any other writer featured in this book, Spark's interest in the telephone has received the most scholarly attention. Critics have addressed her fraught relationship with media culture, the apparent connections between hearing voices and Catholicism, and the link between Spark's own work in the Political Warfare Executive (PWE) and the operation of auditory surveillance.[10] Noting that her writing exposes 'the problems and the possibilities of technological advances of the twentieth century through their engagement with the telephone and telephonic networks', for instance, Amy Woodbury-Tease argues that the repeated technical difficulties that Spark's characters encounter down the line are symptomatic of the political and cultural instability of post-war Britain.[11] More than this, though, as Patricia Waugh points out, emphasizing the association with Spark's own self-proclaimed possession of a 'writing ear', Spark's telephone connects the reader with aesthetic and metaphysical questions regarding the relationship between technology, listening and writing.[12] Despite this research, the specific relationship between Spark's telephone and what Martin McQuillan calls the 'forms of intelligibility' at work in her writing remains neglected. Pursuing these connections, I am interested in the ways that Spark's facility for 'overhearing' stretches to its limits our own capacity to listen down – or rather between – the lines, and the potential of this for thinking through the relationship between literature, the undecidable and the secret.[13]

Building on my discussion in Chapter 1 of the manner in which the telephonic address is disrupted by interruption, interference and errancy, and extending criticism by Martin McQuillan, Patricia Waugh and Amy Woodbury-Tease, among others, this chapter reads the relationship between auditory imagination and the undecidable through the figure of the telephone. Arguing that the aesthetics and politics of telephone tapping in Spark's work are connected to both the possibilities and limitations of reading as a mode of listening in, it focuses on the connections between telephony and the aporetic condition of the secret. Drawing on work by Frank Kermode, Jacques Derrida and Jean-Luc Nancy, and exploring novels including *The Girls of Slender Means*, *Memento Mori*, *The Hothouse by the East River* and *The Abbess of Crewe*, the chapter argues that Spark's telephone taps into secret communications that always remain suspended at the edge of meaning.

'Heaps to tell'

Spark's 1963 novel *The Girls of Slender Means* opens to a 'bomb-ripped' London, one week after Victory in Europe Day. Home to a group of 'poor' but 'nice' girls, where its windows were shattered by nearby blasts three times during the war, the May of Teck Club seems to have escaped a direct hit.[14] Spark immediately immerses the reader in the world of the Club, which is situated between the Albert Memorial and the Kensington Gardens, but only three pages in, this 1945 narrative is interrupted by the first of a series of telephone conversations set in the novel's present. Jane Wright, a former member of the Club and now 'woman columnist', calls another former member: '"I've got something to tell you,"' she says.[15] 'At the other end of the telephone', writes Spark, 'the voice of Dorothy Markham, owner of the flourishing model agency, said, "Darling, where have you been?"'[16] Jane is calling with regard to the death of Nicholas Farringdon, missionary and former poet. '"I've got something to tell you"', she repeats, highlighting the gaps in the connection: '"Do you remember Nicholas Farringdon? Remember he used to come to the old May of Teck just after the war, he was an anarchist and poet sort of thing".'[17] Nicholas is known best among the Teck girls as the man who slept with Selina on the roof of the Club but, following a mysterious 'conversion' to Catholicism, it now turns out that he has been 'martyred' in Haiti, and Jane is calling all her contacts to find out as much as she can. '"You'll have to find out more through your grapevine"', Dorothy tells her, alluding to Jane's current occupation as gossip columnist. '"I'm shattered"', Dorothy continues, '"I've got heaps to tell you".'[18] Abruptly switching back to the narrative set in 1945, Spark cuts the phone call here – before any revelations between the women can take place.

The primary narrative of *The Girls of Slender Means* recounts the fire at the May of Teck Club on 27 July 1945, triggered by the blast of a previously undetonated bomb in the garden, and the subsequent death of Club member Joanna Childe, the daughter of a country rector, and a teacher of elocution. But this narrative is interrupted by a further six calls from Jane to Anne, Rudi (twice), Pauline, Lady Julia and Nancy in turn, to convey or to receive as much information about Nicholas's mysterious demise as possible. Discussing the 'double narrative' structure of Spark's novel as it switches between 1945 flashbacks and the 1963 telephone conversations, Woodbury-Tease argues that the calls 'produce a temporal divide that forces the reader to negotiate between two different diegetic spaces'; as a result, she writes, drawing on Ronell's *The Telephone Book*, these calls 'interfere with the "normally functioning text" and turn it into a mediated one, reconfiguring the way the reader experiences the novel'.[19] Dividing the text both temporally and spatially, Spark's telephone simultaneously structures and deconstructs the text. Moreover, the fact that these calls are perpetually thwarted generates further textual instability; no matter how much the interlocutors have to tell each other, they manage to say nothing much at all. When Jane calls Anne, for instance, Anne asks her to hold on while she shuts the door because her children are making a 'row'.[20] Later, when she tries to call Pauline, Jane finds that her interlocutor is 'resting' following an appointment with a psychiatrist.[21] The conversation that follows is fragmented, and Jane cannot be sure that Pauline is even on the other end of the line, let alone capable of talking or listening:

> 'Well, I just wanted to tell you something, can you listen? Do you remember Nicholas Farringdon?'
> 'No, I don't think so. Who's he?'
> 'Nicholas ... remember that last time on the roof at the May of Teck ... Haiti, in a hut ... among some palms, it was market day, everyone had gone to the market centre. Are you listening?'[22]

The call ends here, and with no response from Pauline, the text also withholds knowledge from the reader. In light of these interrupted telephone conversations, Woodbury-Tease describes the structuring principle of the novel as a 'pattern of call and answer', arguing that it 'forces the reader to move back and forth between the narrative present and an undisclosed future, marked by the fragments of conversations taking place over the telephone'.[23] But although Woodbury-Tease makes an important point here, the motif of 'call and answer' does not fully acknowledge the failure of these connections and, moreover, their central relationship to Spark's narrative technique. In fact, not only are Jane's calls continually thwarted, but Spark's telephone ensures that narrative knowledge can only ever be experienced in terms of interruption, distance and deferral: the full 'answer' is always withheld. As a result, and in line with a principle of telephonic destinerrance, the text only ever offers an incomplete answer to the call.

Across the numerous other phone calls that punctuate the novel, the reader is promised – in the words of Dorothy – 'heaps' of telling, while only ever receiving fragments of the conversation. The telephone in the text thus holds out a promise of knowledge that is never fully delivered. Instead, Spark uses the mechanism of the telephone to enact a pattern of interruption and interference. If the problem does not lie with the recipient of the call, then Jane finds that the line itself is unreliable. "'I've got something to tell you, Rudi," said Jane', to which Rudi responds: "'I can't hear you, it's a rotten line …'", followed by Jane's own "'I say I can't hear, Rudi …'".[24] Jane is keen to maximize the potential value of Nicholas's manuscript, which is in Rudi's possession, but the conversation proceeds through exaggerated interruption and ellipsis:

> 'This line is bad by the way, can you hear me? How has he died … ?'
> '… a hut …'
> 'I can't hear …'
> '… in a valley …'
> 'Speak loud.'[25]

This call, like so many others, is characterized by miscommunication and misunderstanding with the obscured speech only heightening the sense that something is missing from the conversation. Woodbury-Tease notes that the repetition of the question 'how has he died … ?' is crucial because of the way that the collapse in communication is enacted through the 'breaking up of the text'; the 'ruptures' are made material in the text through the ellipses that represent the 'lost information'.[26] The ellipses, this suggests, enact the inevitable unknowability at the heart of the novel. But while Woodbury-Tease remarks on these ruptures, the telephonic structure of the text – and its specific relationship to the indeterminable – needs to be further unpacked.

Secret calls

When Spark's telephone rings, it signals the presence of the text's secret. In other words, the call operates not simply to communicate a message (a message that, more often than not, concerns death) but to put the undecidable on the line. Moreover, the narrative disconnections that rupture Spark's text are neither merely the result of the malfunctioning telephone of the early twentieth century nor the lapse in media specific protocol of the 1930s to which David Trotter refers in *Literature in the First Media Age*.[27] Instead, I suggest, the interrupting and interrupted telephone calls are inextricably connected to Spark's conceptualization of the form and structure of the novel and the ways in which narrative is bound to the undecidable. In this manner, the telephone simultaneously exposes multiple disconnections between interlocutors and holds in suspension the very possibility of narrative knowledge.

My argument here builds on Martin McQuillan's work on the ways that Spark's writing questions the forms of intelligibility available in the realist tradition. McQuillan reads Spark in terms of the *nouveau roman*, which, he argues, offers 'a redistribution of narrative possibilities':

> It is a reaction to a certain use of narrative form in the novel, associated with the power of the middle class, and certain ideologically charged conceptions of the self and world. In as much as narrative is the mode by which we understand the world, to disrupt the hegemony of a certain narrative form is to introduce the possibility of a different way of understanding.[28]

McQuillan goes on to locate these alternative narrative possibilities in moments of contrapuntality – the tendency, for instance, for her narrative to interrupt itself with a seemingly incongruent aside.[29] Such moments, he suggests, enact a narrative impasse, their significance remaining opaque: 'they say what they say and no more, they remain as secrets in Spark's text'.[30] In the same way, I suggest that Jane's thwarted telephone calls present the reader with a narrative impasse – or, in other words, they 'say what they say and no more'. Jane's aporetic calls are thus bound up with the secret.

The stress on the secret is deliberate here, for Spark's fascination with secrecy operates at multiple levels in her work. In *The Girls of Slender Means*, for instance, the three kinds of 'brain-work' in which Jane is absorbed are all connected to the secret:

> First, and secretly, she wrote poetry of a strictly non-rational order [...]. Secondly, also secretly, she wrote letters of a friendly tone but with a business intention, under the auspices of the pale foreigner. Thirdly, and more openly, she sometimes did a little work in her room which overlapped from her day's duties at the small publisher's office.[31]

It transpires that in addition to her 'secret' writing, Jane's work as the assistant to the publisher Huy Throvis-Mew (whom she knows as George) also involves a good deal of 'secret' as well as 'secretarial' work.³² Accordingly, her vocation as a writer and her involvement in publishing – both in 1945 and during her later work as a newspaper columnist – are always in some way tied to the secret. But for McQuillan, the relationship between secrecy and the text is an epistemological problem:

> Secrecy is the very condition of responsibility for the writer. The formulation of a response to the urgency of today requires that this response be thought through in all its infinite complexity and singularity. In the event, however, the writer must write and so cut short the process of formulating a response. Their response will always be inadequate, compromised, not thought enough, and so be irresponsible. A truly responsible response must remain in thinking: undecidable, unknowable and thus a secret.³³

McQuillan argues that the necessary impossibility for a text to say it all is bound to the condition of secrecy. But by bringing together secrecy and what he calls 'a truly responsible response', McQuillan's repeated use of the term 'response' draws attention once again to the potential failure of the model of call and answer to which Woodbury-Tease refers. The suspension of the full answer or response is, I propose, enacted through Jane's thwarted telephone calls, which play out the ways in which signification in the text is always undecidable, unknowable and endlessly deferred. With the interrupted call serving as synecdoche for writing's secret, Jane's failed telephone conversations perform the productive breakdown of the text.

Frank Kermode touches on the operation of secrecy and its relation to the unknown in Spark's work in his essay 'To *The Girls of Slender Means*', noting that the novel would appeal to any reader 'who takes an interest in the ways fiction can body forth the shape of things unknown'.³⁴ Whereas McQuillan focuses on the necessary failure of the writer to provide answers, Kermode approaches it from the perspective of the reader, arguing that Spark's 'obscure figurations' of the world 'assume the reader's participation in muddle'.³⁵ This can be read alongside Kermode's interest in the displacement of the mastery of structuralist interpretation in *The Genesis of Secrecy*, in which he turns his attention to 'the forces' that make interpretation both 'necessary' and 'virtually impossible'.³⁶ Focusing largely on Biblical interpretation, and acknowledging the irreducible complexity of both world and book, he argues that the narrative 'always entails a measure of opacity'.³⁷ As critics, he suggests, we are unwilling to accept this mystery, and so our interpretative acts can be understood as attempts to 'satisfy ourselves with explanations of the unfollowable world'.³⁸ The interpretation, however, is always and 'endlessly disappointing'; it is, he says, always 'bound to fail; it is an intrusion always, and always unsuccessful'.[39] What we find instead, he insists, is 'something irreducible, therefore perpetually to be interpreted; not secrets to be found out one by one, but Secrecy'.[40] Although, for Kermode, the text's refusal to give up its secret is framed largely in terms of disappointment, Jonathan Arac points out that 'the text's secrecy is what prevents its being consumed, for secrecy is *potential* for interpretation, an available reserve'.[41] As such, secrecy is thus bound up with the literary, and with the possibilities of re-reading.

The literariness of the secret is extended by Jacques Derrida in *Literature in Secret*, in which he discusses the phrase '"*Pardon de ne pas vouoir dire*"', translated by David Wills as 'Pardon for not meaning (to say) … '.[42] This phrase, Derrida argues, is an example of 'nonknowledge' because although we can understand the words, the statement's origin and end can never be fully determined.[43] According to Derrida, however, it is the very fact of its nonknowledge that opens the phrase up to the literary: 'the absence of a fully determinate context predisposes this phrase to secrecy and at the same time, conjointly, according to the conjunction that concerns us here, to its becoming-literary'.[44] Derrida argues:

> Every text that is consigned to public space, that is relatively legible or intelligible, but whose content, sense, referent, signatory, and addressee are not fully determinable realities – realities that are at the same time non-fictive or immune from all fiction, realities that are delivered as such by some intuition, to a determinate judgement – can become a literary object.[45]

Such literary objects, Derrida writes, are not and can never be fully determinable; instead, they remain 'suspended' or 'up in the air', hovering between the legible and the secret.[46] Crucial to this is the fact that the text's origin, addressee and signatory remain always undecidable and in suspension.

Bringing this to bear on Spark's work, we can read the ways in which secrecy operates through the telephone exchange in *The Girls of Slender Means* where any sense of an answer remains perpetually up in the air. This indeterminability, moreover, operates across her oeuvre. Spark's third novel, *Memento Mori*, for instance, holds the origin of the telephone call always in suspension. In this novel, twelve elderly residents of Kensington receive mysterious phone calls insisting 'Remember you must die'.[47] Various theories are put forward, including the possibility of hoax callers and mass hysteria, but it is Jean Taylor – claiming 'I did once know something about the telephone system' – who deduces that 'the author of the anonymous telephone calls is Death himself'.[48] The fact that Jean describes the caller as the 'author' introduces an implicit connection between writing and calling. But even the possibility of Death on the line is never confirmed. Nicholas Royle notes that despite setting itself up as a 'whodunnit', Spark's novel refuses to reveal the identity of the caller; it ends, he writes, in a 'suspension and dissemination' of the source of the call:

> No answer is given. Likewise the identity of the recipient or addressee. It may be one or other character in the novel. It may be the reader, any reader, you or me, alive or dead, alive *and* dead. And of course it may also be the novel addressing itself, addressing the genre of the novel itself, metafiction (a word first used only in 1960 according to the *OED*) already in a dead language: *memento mori*.[49]

Both the call and the novel's secret remain in suspension. 'No answer is given', Royle stresses, frustrating the finality implied by Woodbury-Tease's model of 'call and answer'. Moreover, by referring here to the novel's self-referentiality, Royle draws attention not only to the structure of the telephone exchange but also to the ways in which Spark's writing addresses itself, rather like Doctor Downie's autocommunication in 'The Small Telephone'. For Martin Stannard, too, the anonymous telephone voices in *Memento Mori* shake up both narrative and metaphysical securities; ultimately, he writes, the telephone 'becomes a literary question'.[50] Tracing the connection between the telephonic voice and the question of literature, he echoes Derrida in suggesting that this literariness is part of the text's refusal to confirm either the origin of the call or the security of an answer. The indeterminable nature of Spark's telephone is thus bound up with the very possibilities and limits of writing.

The undecidability of the telephone is a motif to which Spark returns in her later work. An absurd and wildly comic novel full of phone calls, *The Hothouse by the East River* follows the lives (and deaths) of Elsa and Paul Hazlett. Elsa is reportedly a schizophrenic socialite who made her money in real estate and who spends her time either sitting at the window and gazing out at the river or on the telephone. Moreover, it transpires that Elsa and Paul are dead, having been killed when a V2 bomb demolished the carriage of a train in which they were travelling in the autumn of 1944. Noticing that Elsa's shadow falls the wrong way, both Elsa and Paul are at some level aware of their own deaths, and at one point, Elsa attempts to use the telephone line as a means of ascertaining her existence. Having spoken to her daughter Katerina, she asks Paul and her analyst Garven Bey if they had overheard her conversations, explaining: 'I just wondered if I was real, that's all. Imaginary people can't very well have telephone calls outside of their owners' imagination'.[51] Rather than confirming her existence one way or another, however, the telephone instead calls up the undecidable: when Paul says 'Be careful on the phone. I don't know what to believe, Elsa', his words emphasize the indeterminability of the narrative.[52] What becomes clear is only that this is a text in which 'loose ends are destined to float in the vague cosmos'; resisting narrative closure, it concludes with a protagonist who 'trails her faithful and lithe cloud of unknowing across the pavement'.[53] But by reading this 'cloud of unknowing' in light of Derrida's theory of the secret, it is apparent that the narrative knowledge that remains forever 'up in the air' in Spark's text is also that which is most literary.[54] Prefiguring Derrida's argument, Spark does not hide the spectral nature of Elsa and Paul's condition; rather, opening the text up to the absurd, she ensures that the telephone call hovers between the legible and the secret. The unknowability of the text and its connection to the telephone line, then, provide the structuring force of Spark's novel, leaving both characters and readers always suspended and listening out for an answer that is forever deferred.

Intelligence networks

If Spark demands a listening reader, she invites us not only to listen out for more but also to listen in between the lines – a form of overhearing that is heightened through her multiple references to espionage across her works. Following this, a number of critics including Barbara Keyser, Lewis MacLeod, and Sheryl Stevenson have pointed to Spark's preoccupation with intelligence networks.[55] Marina Mackay, for instance, remarks that her interest in 'the illicit acquisition and deployment of information is the central obsession of Spark's early work'.[56] Her fascination with espionage is also evident in Laurence Mander's conviction that his grandmother Louisa runs a gang of 'communist spies' in her first novel *The Comforters* as well as in Miss Brodie's declaration that 'Sandy will make an excellent Secret Service agent, a great spy' in *The Prime of Miss Jean Brodie*.[57] This interest is apparent in *The Girls of Slender Means* too, where the work being undertaken in the 'American-occupied attic of the hotel next door' to the club is related to international intelligence networks.[58] Spark repeatedly stresses the clandestine nature of Nicholas's work 'for the Intelligence', remarking: 'At this time Nicholas still worked for one of those left-hand departments of the Foreign Office, the doings of which the right-hand did not know. It came under Intelligence.'[59] The pervasive sense of not knowing in her work is thus tied to the secret intelligence networks that maintain Nicholas's undecidable position in the text.

The anxieties regarding the relationship between developing communication technologies and new opportunities for surveillance are magnified in Spark's later fiction. The plot of *The Hothouse by the East River*, for example, is bound up with Elsa and Paul's wartime work in British Intelligence. Living in New York in the early 1970s, Elsa tells Paul that a shoe salesman going by the name of Mueller is actually a former German prisoner-of-war called Helmut Kiel. She claims that they first met this double-agent in 1944 while working at 'the Compound', a 'small outpost of British Intelligence in the heart of the countryside' which specializes in black propaganda and psychological warfare and is thus 'reputed to be the most intelligent outfit of the war'.[60] Working at the heart of this 'world of wartime secrets', Elsa's role at the Compound 'consists of taking messages and reports from military intelligence personnel on a special green telephone used everywhere during the war for secret communications'.[61] For Woodbury-Tease, this green line is tied to cultural anxieties regarding technology's threat to individual subjectivity, as well as Cold War paranoia around technological surveillance.[62] In the novel, the green telephone thus connects wartime secrets with ways of listening between the lines.

Along with Patricia Waugh and Beatriz Lopez, Woodbury-Tease unpacks the significance of the green telephone by arguing that it can be contextualized in light of Spark's own war work.[63] In her autobiography *Curriculum Vitae*, Spark recounts her return from Africa towards the end of the war. Applying for secretarial work in London, she attends an interview during which she finds herself discussing the literary merits of Ivy Compton-Burnett. Obviously impressed, her interviewer asks if she would 'like to do secret work for the Foreign Office', warning her to 'Tell no one'.[64] She is sent to Bush House where she meets Sefton Delmer, the Austrian-born British propagandist and former correspondent of the *Daily Express* who led 'the dark field of Black Propaganda or Psychological Warfare'.[65] Black propagandists, Spark goes on to explain, present themselves as Germans loyal to the Führer; pretending to broadcast from a German station, they offer 'detailed truth with believable lies'.[66] Eventually she is employed in the Political Intelligence department of MI6, working at 'Delmer's Compound at Milton Bryan, near Woburn'.[67] Her job is that of 'Duty Secretary' to the unit, 'an opaque definition which somehow fitted in with the untransparent nature of the work'.[68] As part of her secret role, she recalls in *Curriculum Vitae*, she 'learned to use the "scrambler" which was a green-painted telephone on which a continual jangling noise made interception difficult'.[69] Involved in receiving and passing on information regarding the location of bombs dropped by the Allied forces, Spark recalls: 'I would wait for the right code-name when I answered the phone, then I would say, or the Air Force spokesman would say, "Shall we go over?" We then went on to the scrambler.'[70] The workings of this scrambler and its potential to simultaneously convey and disrupt communication are explained in *The Hothouse by the East River*:

> It is known as a scrambler because the connection is heavily jammed with jangling caterwauls to protect the conversation against eavesdropping; this harrowing noise all but prevents the speakers from hearing each other, but once the knack is mastered it is easy to hear the voice at the other end giving such information as flight details from newly-returned bomber missions, the numbers sent, the numbers lost, the numbers of enemy planes felled.[71]

Playing out the structure of what Elsa describes as 'secret communications', the scrambler simultaneously facilitates and muddles the call, mirroring the operations of the narrative as it remains suspended between the legible and the secret. And although Spark's narrator claims that once the knack is mastered, the voice is easily discernible, it is evident that any answers remain 'heavily jammed' in the text.

The green line makes a reappearance just a year later in *The Abbess of Crewe*, where its role in secrecy and encryption is tied not to international politics but to domestic affairs. Following the death of the former abbess Hildegarde, Sister Alexandra has been elected the new Abbess of Crewe. She tells the nuns: 'The sooner we perfect the green line system the better. We should have in our laboratory a green line to everywhere; it would be convenient to consult Gertrude.'[72] The Abbey's green line system functions as part of an all-pervasive network of auditory espionage, the presence of which is signalled in the novel's opening pages. With two nuns walking through an avenue of poplars, the novel begins with a question: '"What is wrong, Sister Winifrede," says the Abbess, clear and loud to the receptive air, "with the traditional keyhole method?"'[73] Commanding Winifrede to silence, she confirms when they are out on the lawn that 'whatever is spoken in the avenue of meditation goes on the record'; it transpires that even the trees are listening: it is a 'corridor of meditation lined by the secret police of poplars':

> 'The trees of course are bugged', says the Abbess. 'How else can we operate now that the scandal rages outside the walls? And now that you know this you do not know it so to speak. We have our security to consider, and I'm the only arbiter of what it consists of, witness the Rule of St Benedict. I'm your conscience and your authority. You perform my will and finish.'[74]

Creating an impasse for Winifrede with her statement that 'now that you know this you do not know it so to speak', the Abbess refers to the scandal that has emerged in the Abbey following the recent elections for the new head of Order. It becomes evident that during the campaign, Alexandra suspected that not only was her rival Felicity getting the younger novices on side, but she was also involved in a liaison with a Jesuit priest. Working with her co-conspirators Walburga and Mildred, and always covering her own tracks, Alexandra has bugged the convent, listening out for any information that will put her at an advantage. The nuns are recruited both knowingly and unknowingly into her scheme, and Alexandra's methods ensure that they learn about modern electronics and recording systems alongside their religious instruction. Co-ordinating a plan that will expose Felicity's improper behaviour, she arranges for two local Jesuits to break into the abbey and steal Felicity's correspondence. The police are called and Felicity is forced to flee the abbey, moving in with her Jesuit lover. Soon after, Felicity makes public her conviction that there are 'eavesdropping devices' placed throughout the Abbey.[75]

Writing in the years immediately following the publication of Spark's novel, Barbara Keyser draws a direct connection between the scandal at the Abbey and the Watergate affair of the 1970s, during which Nixon's administration attempted to cover up their involvement in a number of illegal surveillance activities.[76] But Keyser goes on to stress that beyond the simple analogy of Watergate, 'Spark's real target is the mass media and its all-pervasive influence on contemporary life'.[77] Here, she draws attention to Spark's 'collage of communication images' which include references to a range of electronic devices, including the bugging of telephones.[78] When Alexandra's superiors in Rome write to her to demand an explanation, for instance, the Abbess argues that 'electronic surveillance (even if a convent were one day to practise it) does not differ from any other type of watchfulness, the which is necessary for any Religious Community'.[79] Walburga, however, disagrees, suggesting that Rome might 'object that telephone-tapping and bugging are not simply an extension of listening to hearsay and inviting confidences, the steaming open of letters and the regulation search of the novices' closets'.[80] It seems that for Walburga, the introduction of new technologies and electronic devices goes far beyond the 'watchfulness' deemed necessary to a religious community; telephone tapping, she suggests, marks a new and more obtrusive turn in the operation of surveillance.

Notwithstanding her comments on electronic surveillance, it is also worth noting Walburga's somewhat ironic stress on 'watchfulness'. This comes as no surprise given the translation of the French *'surveillance'* as 'to watch over'. Walburga is of course not especially watchful but, despite her lack of foresight, she is described instead as having a 'mind all ears'.[81] This attention to the auditory imagination – a preoccupation that runs throughout Spark's work – suggests that an aesthetics of 'listening-in' deserves particular analysis.⁸² Challenging the Western tradition of ocularcentrism in his *All Ears: The Aesthetics of Espionage* – a title that inadvertently recalls Spark's description of Walburga – Peter Szendy argues that although spies watch over things, their role is also to listen, insisting that spies are, 'above all, attentive listeners to what is afoot. They are hearing devices deployed to capture what is coming or what is hiding, or what is secretly coming'.⁸³ Remarking that there is always a 'basic structural affinity between listening and espionage', Szendy points out that the French word for 'listen' does not refer to a neutral action. It also means hearing without being seen and can be used to refer to a guard who monitors the enemy's progress; as a result, he says, 'every listener is perhaps primarily and above all a spy'.⁸⁴ In fact, Szendy argues that historical accounts of a number of auditory chambers can actually be read as precursors to Jeremy Bentham's famous inspection house and Foucault's model of the panopticon in *Discipline and Punish*.⁸⁵ To demonstrate this, he points to the ancient 'Ear of Dionysus' described by travellers visiting Syracuse. In the mid-seventeenth century, for example, a Jesuit preacher referred to Dionysus's mythical grotto as a form of '"echotechtonics" (an architecture of echoes) used for the purposes of auditory surveillance'.⁸⁶ A century later, around 1780, Henry Swinburne also recorded in his travel journals an encounter with 'a groove or a channel, which served, as is supposed, to collect the sounds that rose from the speakers below, and to convey them to a pipe in a small double cell above, where they were heard with the greatest distinctness'.⁸⁷ Swinburne goes on to argue that it was 'constructed intentionally for a prison, and a listening place'.⁸⁸ Arguing that such architectural devices might be read as 'precursors in the acoustic domain' to Foucault's panopticon, Szendy puts forward a theory of the panacousticon. This theory of 'panacoustic telelistening' offers a way of conceptualizing the relationship between the telephone and Spark's 'secret communications'.⁸⁹

Sister Alexandra's Abbey, it transpires, is constructed as an architecture of echoes. Notwithstanding Rome's presence in the novel as an ineffectual panopticon, the Abbess's private rooms function as a central – albeit flawed – 'listening place'. Gathering together her spies in her inner cloisters, the Abbess tells the sisters that they must wait for Sister Gertrude, the Abbey's peripatetic nun, to call:

> The telephone in the adjoining room rings so suddenly that surely, if it is Gertrude, she must have sensed her sisters' want from the other field of the

earth. Mildred treads softly over the green carpet to the adjoining room and answers the phone. It is Gertrude.
'Amazing', says Walburga. 'Dear Gertrude has an uncanny knowledge of what is needed where and when.'
The Abbess moves in her fresh white robes to the next room, followed by Walburga. Electronics control-room as it is, here, too, everything gleams. The Abbess sits at the long steel desk and takes the telephone.[90]

Taking centre stage in the electronics control-room is of course the green telephone – an apparatus that inevitably fails to operate as required:

> 'Where is Sister Gertrude at this hour?'
> 'In the Congo', Walburga says.
> 'Then get her on the green line.'
> 'We have no green line to the Congo', Walburga says. 'She travels day and night by rail and river. She should have arrived at a capital some hours ago. It's difficult to keep track of her whereabouts.'[91]

When they do eventually get Gertrude on the line, it is made clear that she does not want to talk, and the telephone conversations are, as in both *The Girls of Slender Means* and *The Hothouse by the East River*, perpetually cut short with Gertrude hanging up mid-conversation. On one occasion, when Alexandra attempts at length to entreat the Sister to return to Crewe, she finds: 'Something crackles on the line. "Gertrude, are you there?" says Alexandra.'[92] After further crackles, Gertrude says: 'Sorry, I missed all that. I was tying my shoelace.'[93] The Abbess's efforts to construct her own architecture of echoes fail as Gertrude once again thwarts the possibility of full communication down the line. In many ways, then, the Abbess's preoccupation with auditory surveillance works both ways: the novel signals a capacity both to listen too much and to hear nothing at all.

Overhearing

Notwithstanding her characters' frequent failure to listen, Spark's writing remains always open to the possibilities of hearing more. In *All Ears*, Szendy examines the term 'overhearing', drawing attention to its potential to refer not only to something overheard but also to a surplus of hearing or intensified listening. In this way, overhearing or close-listening coalesce and the distinction between listening and spying begins to fray. Szendy's work here is indebted to Jean-Luc Nancy's *Listening*, in which Nancy points out that 'after it had designated a person who listens (who spies), the word *écoute* came to designate a place where one could listen in secret'.[94] He goes on to remark that '*Être à l'écoute*, "to be tuned in, to be listening," was in the vocabulary of military espionage before it returned, through broadcasting, to the public space, while still remaining, in the context of the telephone, an affair of confidences or stolen secrets'.[95] Spark's particular interest in 'overhearing' is evident in *Curriculum Vitae*, in which she describes herself as 'an avid listener'.[96] Opportunities for listening colour her recollections of childhood: 'I liked to listen. Not only did I feel at home with the immense list of characters who peopled our lives, and who largely ignored me, but there was also those whom I knew by hearsay, and often I touched people who had touched real history'.[97] In fact, Spark's lived history of listening is also one of listening-in; she remarks, for instance, that 'a table covered by a long cloth is a good hiding place and listening post for children'.[98] The development of Spark's writing voice can thus be traced back to Nancy's notion of overhearing, which operates simultaneously as a way of listening without being heard and as a means to hear more than is said.

For Waugh, Spark's propensity for listening is bound up with her writing voice. Not only challenging social constraints to comedic effect, she suggests that 'listening in' operates in Spark's work as a figure for connecting memory and the imagination.[99] Waugh discusses this in terms of Spark's hallucinations, explaining that Spark's conversion to Catholicism and transition from poetry to fiction coincided with her belief that she was the recipient of secret messages.[100] Also commenting on this episode, Martin Stannard notes:

> T. S. Eliot, she insisted, was sending her threatening messages. His play was full of them. Some were in the theatre programme. Obsessively she began to seek them out, covering sheet after sheet of paper with anagrams and cryptographic experiments.[101]

According to Spark's own letter to the Ministry of National Insurance which she composed upon her recovery, she had started to 'imagine secret codes in everything [she] read'; although she claims that these hallucinations were 'due to overwork and insufficient rest', it is widely reported that her condition was impacted by her use of Dexedrine alongside malnutrition.[102] It is also suggested that these hallucinatory experiences inform her fiction, with Spark explaining in *Curriculum Vitae* that she 'made' the protagonist Caroline Rose from *The Comforters* '"hear" a typewriter with voices composing the novel itself'.[103] This listening, Waugh argues, 'might take the form of inward self-meditation, aural mind-wandering, absorbed listening, or the intent eavesdropping that follows the sudden awareness of salient vocalization in the midst of noise'.[104] Her capacity for intensified listening is also evident in her autobiography when she reflects on her time working for the *European Affairs* magazine run by Elma Dangerfield and Monty Radulovitch:

> I kept an ear out for her voice and her terms of expression, as I always do with people. Monty's way of speech was a treasure-house to me. I was not yet writing stories and novels, but I was working towards the narrative art, and saved up 'Voices' in my memory-file.[105]

For Waugh, Spark's aptitude for 'aural mind-wandering' is central to the development of her own writing voice; its 'radical alterity', she argues, is 'facilitated not through vision but through cultivation of the discipline of attentive listening'.[106] Overhearing, as a form of intensified listening or surplus of hearing, is deeply embedded in Spark's literary imagination; as a result, her writing invites a mode of reading as listening down, or between, the lines.

But Spark's interest in listening extends beyond the voice to a larger preoccupation with auditory culture and nonhuman language. On multiple occasions in *The Girls of Slender Means*, for instance, Spark sets the scene by drawing attention to its aural qualities:

> The number and variety of muted noises-off were considerable. Laughter went on behind the folded doors of the first-floor dormitory. Someone was shovelling coal in the cellar, having left open the green baize door which led to those quarters. The telephone desk within the office rang distantly shrill with boyfriends, and various corresponding buzzes on the landings summoned the girls to talk.[107]

Further, on VE day, the members of the club, accompanied by Nicholas, head to Buckingham Palace to join in the celebrations. Seeing the royal family, the narrator observes 'the huge organic murmur of the crowd', which was 'different from anything like the voice of animate matter but rather more a cataract or a geological disturbance' – a sound that 'spread through the parks and along the Mall'.[108] Nicholas, it transpires, has especially sensitive hearing that befits his work in Intelligence, where he must keep his ear to the ground: 'The sights and sounds impinging on him from the hall of the club intensified themselves, whenever he called, into one sensation, as if with a will of their own'.[109] Sound thus takes on a peculiar agency in the novel, where it invites an engagement with the sensorial. This is also at work in Spark's telephone calls, in which interlocutors exchange not only words but noises too. The calls in *The Abbess of Crewe*, for instance, are interrupted by unexpected sounds: first 'something crackles on the line' and 'the telephone then roars like a wild beast'.[110] In *The Hothouse by the East River*, moreover, Paul's attention is described as being 'eared to the voice at the other end', but often all he can hear is the 'sound of the receiver being placed on its side'.[111] This also recalls Elsa's work on the scrambler, listening through the 'jangling caterwauls' and 'harrowing noise' in an attempt, in the terms of Claude Shannon and Warren Weaver, to remove the 'spurious and undesirable' sounds from the signal.[112] But rather than signifying what Shannon and Weaver class as unwanted distortions or errors in transmission, I propose that these noises are integral to the text's secret.

Nancy's account of the word *écoute* as the place in which one can listen in secret directly links overhearing with the undecidable. In the context of the telephone, Nancy writes, *écoute* remains 'an affair of confidences or stolen secrets'.[113] He continues: 'What secret is at stake when one truly listens, that is, when one tries to capture or surprise the sonority rather than the message?'[114] Tying together the two strands of this discussion – the auditory and the unknowable – Nancy points to the difference in French between *écouter* (listening) and *entendre* (to both hear and to understand). Relating philosophy's prioritization of hearing as understanding, he argues for a new attention to the sensorial in listening: 'Isn't the philosopher someone who always hears (and who hears everything) but who cannot listen, or who, more precisely, neutralizes listening within himself, so that he can philosophize?'[115] Thinking through the ear, then, Nancy asks: 'What does it mean for a being to be immersed entirely in listening, formed by listening or in listening, listening with all his being?'[116] Although he focuses primarily on the force of music and its inclination to the sensory, the possibility that meaning can be 'formed by listening or in listening' enables us to rethink the noise transmitted in Spark's literary phone calls. If hearing is understanding, then to listen, he argues, 'is to be straining toward a possible meaning, and consequently one that is not immediately accessible'.[117] Accordingly, listening to the sounds of the telephone in Spark's work means listening beyond hearing – an intensified listening to the secret communications that remain always suspended or up in the air.

In 'The Small Telephone', Doctor Downie's conversations with himself and with his future interlocutor not only raise a series of questions regarding listening and narrative knowledge but also put forward the possibility of a telephone that listens in to itself and in so doing opens up the possibilities for the undecidable. Indeed, the relationship between listening and secrecy recurs throughout Spark's oeuvre, in which her numerous telephone calls are always bound up with not saying enough and hearing too much. This chapter suggests that reading the surplus ruptures and noises engendered by the literary telephone offers a different way of thinking about the relationship between telephony, writing and listening. Arguing that Spark's strategy of interrupting communication and suspending signification is bound up with the literariness of her work, I propose that the telephone call's refusal to be fully known can be read as part of the narrative's aporetic condition. Spark's secret communication thus demands a certain overhearing – a mode of reading that is always 'eared' to the text, even as its secrets remain always suspended, or up in the air.

Notes

1. 'Points from Publishers: Speed', *The Bookseller* (22 January 1966), 210–11.
2. Muriel Spark, 'The Small Telephone', in *The French Window and The Small Telephone* (London: Colophon Press, 1993), 37–44 (37).
3. Ibid., 38.
4. Ibid., 40.
5. Ibid., 41.
6. Ibid., 44.
7. Avital Ronell, *The Telephone Book: Technology, Schizophrenia, Electric Speech* (Lincoln, NE: University of Nebraska Press, 1989), 3.
8. Martin McQuillan, 'Introduction – "I Don't Know Anything about Freud": Muriel Spark Meets Contemporary Criticism', in *Theorising Muriel Spark: Gender, Race, Deconstruction*, ed. Martin McQuillan (Basingstoke: Palgrave Macmillan, 2001), 1–31 (20).
9. Muriel Spark, *Curriculum Vitae* (London: Penguin, 1993), 163.
10. See, for instance, Barbara Y. Keyser, 'Muriel Spark, Watergate, and the Mass Media', *The Arizona Quarterly*, 32.2 (1976), 146–53; Beatriz Lopez, 'Muriel Spark and the Scrambler Telephone', *Telepoetics Symposium*, 27 May 2020, available at: https://crossedlines.co.uk/conversation2 (accessed 12 January 2022); Marina MacKay, 'Muriel Spark and the Meaning of Treason', in *Muriel Spark: Twenty-First-Century Perspectives*, ed. David Herman (Baltimore, MD: Johns Hopkins University Press, 2010), 94–111; Lewis MacLeod, 'Matters of Care and Control: Surveillance, Omniscience, and Narrative Power in *The Abbess of Crewe* and *Loitering with Intent*', *Modern Fiction Studies*, 54.3 (2008), 574–94; Patricia Waugh, 'Muriel Spark's "Informed Air": The Auditory Imagination and the Voices of Fiction', *Textual Practice*, 32.9 (2018), 1633–58; and Amy Woodbury-Tease, 'Call and Answer: Muriel Spark and Media Culture', *Modern Fiction Studies*, 62.1 (2016), 70–91.
11. Woodbury-Tease, 'Call and Answer', 86–7.

12 Waugh, 'Muriel Spark's "Informed Air"', 1639. In her preface to the revised edition of her biography of Mary Shelley, Spark reflects: 'On first reading through my work after so many years, I was amused to perceive that my prose style had taken on a touch of Mary Shelley's. Through my experience as a writer of fiction I know now that I have a "writing ear," that is the act of imaginatively getting under the skin of a character that produces the individual character's diction' (Muriel Spark, *Mary Shelley: A Biography* (Manchester: Carcanet, 2013), xvi). Spark's biography of Shelley was originally published as *Child of Light* (1951) but was later revised as *Mary Shelley* (1987).
13 McQuillan, 'Introduction', 15.
14 Muriel Spark, *The Girls of Slender Means* (London: Penguin, 2013), 7.
15 Ibid., 9.
16 Ibid., 10.
17 Ibid.
18 Ibid.
19 Woodbury-Tease, 'Call and Answer', 80, 81. Woodbury-Tease is citing from Ronell's 'The User's Manual': 'Our problem was how to maintain an open switchboard, one that disrupts a normally functioning text equipped with proper shock absorbers' (Ronell, *The Telephone Book*, xv).
20 Spark, *The Girls of Slender Means*, 18.
21 Ibid., 85.
22 Ibid.
23 Woodbury-Tease, 'Call and Answer', 81.
24 Spark, *The Girls of Slender Means*, 60, 69.
25 Ibid., 69.
26 Woodbury-Tease, 'Call and Answer', 83.
27 David Trotter, *Literature in the First Media Age: Britain Between the Wars* (Cambridge, MA: Harvard University Press, 2013), 47–9.
28 McQuillan, 'Introduction', 10. See also Martin McQuillan and Muriel Spark, 'The Same Informed Air', in *Theorising Muriel Spark: Gender, Race, Deconstruction*, ed. Martin McQuillan (Basingstoke: Palgrave Macmillan, 2001), 210–29 (215–16); Ian Rankin, 'Introduction', in *The Hothouse by the East River* by Muriel Spark (Edinburgh: Polygon, 2018), ix–xvi (xii). Also related to this is Spark's position at the intersection of modernism and postmodernism which has informed the subject of much scholarly work; although it is beyond the scope of this chapter to rehearse this debate, it is useful to note this as another instance of the refusal of Spark's work to give up its terms. Woodbury-Tease, for instance, argues that while her 'preoccupation with and anxieties about media and mediated spaces anticipates the unstable landscape of our postmodern digital age', her novels at the same time 'expose a pervasive anxiety about the status of the individual in relation to the machine, as well as a palpable paranoia about surveillance, that positions her

fiction within a modernist framework' (Woodbury-Tease, 'Call and Answer', 71, 72). Moreover, when asked by McQuillan during an interview in 1998, 'Would you say you were a modernist writer?' Spark herself responds: 'Maybe Post-modernist; I don't know about Modernist. I think so, probably. They say postmodernist, mostly, whatever that means' (Spark and McQuillan, 'The Same Informed Air', 216).

29 McQuillan cites as an example a passage in *The Abbess of Crewe* in which the Abbess interrupts her intimate discussion with Walburga and Mildred with a comment on the 1973 oil crisis: 'The motorway from London to Crewe is jammed with reporters, according to the news. The A51 is a solid mass of vehicles. In the midst of the strikes and the oil crises' (Muriel Spark, *The Abbess of Crewe* (New York: New Directions 1995), 18; McQuillan, 'Introduction', 18).
30 McQuillan, 'Introduction', 20.
31 Spark, *The Girls of Slender Means*, 37.
32 Discussing the relationship between secretaryship and secrecy, Richard Rambuss turns to Angel Day's letter-writing manual *The English Secretary*, in which he insists that a secretary is always 'a keeper or conserver of the secret unto him committed'; drawing attention to the etymological root of the Latin term '*secretarius*', meaning secret, Day states that it is 'by the verie etimologie of the worde it selfe, both Name and Office in one, doe conclude uppon secrecie' (Angel Day, *The English Secretary* (London: Printed by Peter Short for C. Burbie, 1599), Part 2, 103, cited in Richard Rambuss, 'The Secretary's Study: The Secret Designs of the Shepeardes Calendar', *ELH*, 59.2 (1992), 313–35 (314)).
33 McQuillan, 'Introduction', 20.
34 Frank Kermode, 'To *The Girls of Slender Means*', *New Statesman*, 66 (September 1964), 397–8, reprinted in *Critical Essays on Muriel Spark*, ed. Joseph Hynes (New York: G. K. Hall Co., 1992), 174–8 (174).
35 Ibid., 175, 178.
36 Frank Kermode, *The Genesis of Secrecy: On the Interpretation of Narrative* (Cambridge, MA: Harvard University Press, 1979), 125.
37 Ibid., 25.
38 Ibid., 145.
39 Ibid., 145, 27.
40 Ibid., 143. Kermode develops this focus on secrecy in 'Secrets and Narrative Sequence', where he cites Conrad as an example of an author for whom the 'nonsequential elements' of their works 'may grow unruly enough to be disturbing', pointing out that models of the world 'always have their secrets' (Frank Kermode, 'Secrets and Narrative Sequence', *Critical Inquiry*, 7.1 (1980), 83–101 (86, 87)).
41 Jonathan Arac, 'History and Mystery: The Criticism of Frank Kermode', *Salmagundi*, 55 (1982), 135–55 (153).
42 Jacques Derrida, *The Gift of Death and Literature in Secret*, trans. David Wills (Chicago: University of Chicago Press, 2008), 119.

43 Ibid., 130.
44 Ibid., 131.
45 Ibid.
46 Ibid., 133.
47 Muriel Spark, *Memento Mori* (New York: New Directions, 2000). For further discussion of the telephone in *Memento Mori*, see Marilyn Reizbaum, 'The Stranger Spark', in *The Edinburgh Companion to Muriel Spark*, ed. Michael Gardiner and Willy Maley (Edinburgh: Edinburgh University Press, 2010), 40–51; Nicholas Royle, 'Memento Mori', in *Theorising Muriel Spark: Gender, Race, Deconstruction* (Basingstoke: Palgrave Macmillan, 2001), 189–203.
48 Spark, *Memento Mori*, 39, 179.
49 Royle, 'Memento Mori', 202.
50 Martin Stannard, *Muriel Spark: The Biography* (London: Weidenfeld & Nicolson, 2009), 206–7.
51 Spark, *The Hothouse by the East River*, 97.
52 Ibid., 71.
53 Ibid., 94, 112, 136. It is worth noting that Spark's early plans for *The Hothouse by the East River* included a character electrocuted down the telephone line – an idea later abandoned. See Stannard, *Muriel Spark*, 336.
54 Derrida, *The Gift of Death and Literature in Secret*, 133.
55 See Keyser, 'Muriel Spark, Watergate, and the Mass Media'; MacLeod, 'Matters of Care and Control'; and Sheryl Stevenson, '"Poetry Deleted," Parody Added: Watergate, Spark's Style, and Bakhtin's Stylistics', *Ariel* 24.4 (1993), 71–85.
56 MacKay, 'Muriel Spark and the Meaning of Treason', 96. Focusing on the recurring motif of treason in Spark's novels – 'a matter of pressing urgency in the middle of the twentieth century, during the years when the end of the Second World War shaded into the first half of the Cold War' – Mackay makes an intervention in Spark criticism that usually focuses on theology and Spark's conversion to Catholicism, stressing instead the historical and literary-historical complexes in her work (97).
57 Muriel Spark, *The Comforters* (London: Virago, 2009), 18; Muriel Spark, *The Prime of Miss Jean Brodie* (London: Penguin, 2012), 109. See further MacKay, 'Muriel Spark and the Meaning of Treason', 96–7.
58 Spark, *The Girls of Slender Means*, 60.
59 Ibid., 53, 60.
60 Spark, *The Hothouse by the East River*, 18, 48.
61 Ibid., 31, 49–50.
62 Woodbury Tease, 'Call and Answer', 72.
63 Ibid., 73–4. See also Waugh, 'Muriel Spark's "Informed Air"' and Lopez, 'Muriel Spark and the Scrambler Telephone'.
64 Spark, *Curriculum Vitae*, 146.
65 Ibid., 146, 147.

66 Ibid., 148.
67 Ibid.
68 Ibid., 152.
69 Ibid.
70 Ibid.
71 Spark, *The Hothouse by the East River*, 50.
72 Spark, *The Abbess of Crewe*, 23.
73 Ibid., 7.
74 Ibid., 8.
75 Ibid., 16.
76 Keyser describes, for instance, the Abbess Alexandra as 'a delightfully incongruous Nixon', noting that she has a 'familiar taste for luxury, using her nuns' dowry money to satisfy her taste for pâté and fine wine' (Keyser, 'Muriel Spark, Watergate, and the Mass Media', 149, 150). Offering a detailed comparison between the key players in the Watergate scandal and the structure of the abbey, Keyser also points out that the repetition of phrases such as 'in it up to the neck' is taken directly from the Watergate tapes, which revealed that Nixon had attempted to cover up his own role in the conspiracy (150).
77 Ibid., 147.
78 Ibid., 149.
79 Spark, *The Abbess of Crewe*, 26. The relationship between Christianity and surveillance has drawn the attention of critics. Offering a playful reading of Genesis, in which the Tree of Knowledge is a database and Eve the first hacker, for instance, Peter Marks points out that '[a]ccepting God's mind as perfect, and therefore omniscient, takes us back to Genesis and the eutopian Garden of Eden' (Peter Marks, *Imagining Surveillance: Eutopian and Dystopian Literature and Film* (Edinburgh: Edinburgh University Press, 2015), 142–3). Similarly, Peter Szendy asks: 'Could we go as far as thinking, for example, that the very first listeners, Adam and Eve, were not far from adopting the role of spies when, after having sinned by tasting the fruit of the "tree of knowledge of good and evil," they hide and seem to listen anxiously for the "sound" of the footsteps (or the voice, according to some other versions) of the Eternal who walks in the garden at the fall of night? (Gen. 3:8)' (Peter Szendy, *All Ears: The Aesthetics of Espionage*, trans. Roland Vésgő (New York: Fordham University Press, 2017), 10).
80 Spark, *The Abbess of Crewe*, 27.
81 Ibid., 79.
82 It is worth noting that although Sandy in *The Prime of Miss Jean Brodie* is 'notorious for her small, almost non-existent, eyes', she also has remarkable hearing, learning to listen to Miss Brodie 'with double ears' (Spark, *The Prime of Miss Jean Brodie*, 7, 72).

83   Szendy, *All Ears*, 9.
84   Ibid., 6.
85   Tracing the movement from spectacle to rehabilitation, Foucault argues that crucial to this new disciplinary regime is the possibility of continuous surveillance. To conceptualize this, he outlines Jeremy Bentham's 1787 plans for an inspection house. Describing it as a Panopticon, Foucault explains: '[A]t the periphery, an annular building; at the centre, a tower; this tower is pierced with wide windows that open onto the inner side of the ring' (Michel Foucault, *Discipline and Punish: The Birth of the Prison*, trans. Alan Sheridan (London: Vintage, 1979), 191). He continues: 'All that is needed, then, is to place a supervisor in a central tower and to shut up in each cell a madman, a patient, a condemned man, a worker or a schoolboy. By the effect of backlighting, one can observe from the tower, standing out precisely against the light, the small captive shadows in the cells of the periphery. They are like so many cages, so many small theatres, in which each actor is alone, perfectly individualized and constantly visible' (191). Foucault explains that this design ensures that many can be watched by the invisible few. While he or she can never be sure that they are being observed, the inmate internalizes the possibility of continuous surveillance, ensuring, says Foucault, that 'surveillance is permanent in its effects, even if it is discontinuous in its action' (192). Amplifying power structures, he insists, 'The Panopticon is a machine for dissociating the see/being seen dyad' and is thus 'a guarantee of order' (192).
86   Althanasius Kircher, *Musurgia Universalis* (Rome: Francesco Corbelletti, 1650) 2: 291, cited in Szendy, *All Ears*, 17.
87   Henry Swinburne, *Travels in Two Sicilies, in the Years 1777, 1778, 1779, and 1780* (London: T. Cadell & P. Elmsky, 1790), 105, cited in Szendy, *All Ears*, 17.
88   Ibid. Szendy also gives Italo Calvino's story 'A King Listens' as an example of this 'architectural vocabulary' (Italo Calvino, *Under the Jaguar Sun*, trans. William Weaver (New York: Harcourt Brace, 1990), 38, cited in Szendy, *All Ears*, 18).
89   Szendy, *All Ears*, 116.
90   Spark, *The Abbess of Crewe*, 24.
91   Ibid., 22.
92   Ibid., 43.
93   Ibid.
94   Jean-Luc Nancy, *Listening*, trans. Charlotte Mandell (New York: Fordham University Press, 2007), 4. See also Mladen Dolar's discussion in *A Voice and Nothing More*, where he argues: '[H]earing is after meaning, the signification which can be linguistically spelled out; listening is, rather, being on the lookout for sense, something that announces itself in the voice beyond meaning. We could

say that hearing is entwined with understanding [...] while listening implies an opening toward a sense which is undecidable, precarious, elusive, and which sticks to the voice' (Mladen Dolar, *A Voice and Nothing More* (Cambridge, MA: MIT Press, 2005), 148).
95 Nancy, *Listening*, 4.
96 Spark, *Curriculum Vitae*, 25. See also Waugh, 'Muriel Spark's "Informed Air"', 1637.
97 Spark, *Curriculum Vitae*, 27.
98 Ibid., 41.
99 Waugh, 'Muriel Spark's "Informed Air"', 1638.
100 Spark's well-documented relation to Catholicism is beyond the scope of this chapter; see further, for instance, Gerard Caruthers, 'Muriel Spark as Catholic Novelist', in *The Edinburgh Companion to Muriel Spark*, ed. Michael Gardiner and Willy Maley (Edinburgh: Edinburgh University Press, 2010), 74–84. Given my focus on the unknowable, however, it is useful to cite McQuillan's claim in this context: 'My argument is not that Spark is not a writer who happens to be a Catholic (although Cardinal Winning might have got his cassock in a twist over what is promoted in Jean Brodie's classroom). Rather, if she is a "Catholic", or "religious", writer then this question of religion has yet to be thought. What does it mean to be a "Catholic writer"? Surely, the term is an oxymoron. Writing is not a theological activity, it purposely undermines essential and stable meanings, which presuppose and seek a single and authoritative centre. Meaning is always plural, writing is always cut adrift from its source and origin' (McQuillan, 'Introduction', 4).
101 Stannard, *Muriel Spark*, 151.
102 Typed carbon copy of letter, 21 May 1954, Spark to Ministry of National Insurance, from 8 Sussex Mansions, 65 Old Brompton Road, London SW7 NLS, cited in Stannard, *Muriel Spark*, 52.
103 See, for instance, Stannard, *Muriel Spark*, 52; Spark, *Curriculum Vitae*, 207.
104 Waugh, 'Muriel Spark's "Informed Air"', 1638.
105 Spark, *Curriculum Vitae*, 193.
106 Waugh, 'Muriel Spark's "Informed Air"', 1642.
107 Spark, *The Girls of Slender Means*, 81.
108 Ibid., 17.
109 Ibid., 84.
110 Spark, *The Abbess of Crewe*, 43, 49.
111 Spark, *The Hothouse by the East River*, 46, 49.
112 Ibid., 50; Claude E. Shannon and Warren Weaver, *The Mathematical Theory of Communication* (Urbana, IL: University of Illinois Press, 1964), 19.
113 Nancy, *Listening*, 4.

114 Ibid., 4–5.
115 Ibid., 1.
116 Ibid., 4.
117 Ibid., 6.

3

'WHR R U? XXX'

Based on a series of telephone calls, Ali Smith's short story 'Being Quick' opens with a first-person narrator discussing onion bhajis on a mobile while crossing the concourse at King's Cross station. The conversation is interrupted when the narrator stumbles into Death. The narrator apologizes for the near collision, but the telephone interlocutor misinterprets the exchange, thereby enacting the play of linguistic, technical and ontological disconnections that operate across Smith's oeuvre:

> I'm sorry, I said.
> Sorry for what? you said in my ear. He smiled and stepped back and stood to one side as if waiting.
> I can't stop now, I said, I'm on the phone.
> Who are you talking to? you said.[1]

When Death smiles, the narrator's screen goes 'dead'.[2] In response, the narrator gives the phone a shake, as if the object itself might utter a cry in response: 'I put it against my ear but there was only the sound of an off phone, the sound of plastic and nothing. I pressed the on button. Nothing happened.'[3] This sense of disconnection is extended when the narrator boards the train, selecting the only empty seat available, which is next to a girl who is coughing into her mobile. Early in the journey, the reception is severed:

> She looked at her phone as the train went through a tunnel. So did all the other people who had been in the middle of conversations up and down the train, which was packed with people behind me and ahead of me shouting their hellos forlornly, like lost or blind people. The stray hellos reached nobody. They hung unanswered above our heads in the air and cancelled out everybody they weren't for, then as soon as we were out of the tunnel the phones began again by themselves in a high-pitched spiralling, the signature tunes of TV shows, the simplified Beethoven symphonies.[4]

Dismantling the communicative capacity of the phone – and with answers remaining suspended or up in the air – Smith's high-pitched spiralling unsettles the promise of contemporary technologies to facilitate connection from afar: 'I got my mobile out but it was still dead.'[5] Providing only suspended answers and with death on the line, 'Being Quick' thus extends my account in the previous chapter of thanatographical secrecy in relation to Muriel Spark's telephone. In Smith's fiction, however, we move beyond the apparent fixity of the landline to the portability of wireless communications, where mobile technologies operate according to the principle of telephonic destinerrance to disrupt the politics of place.

Certainly, disconnected and disconnecting calls recur throughout Smith's fiction, where subjects can no longer be sure who or where they are. In 'The Unthinkable Happens to People Every Day' published in *Free Love and Other Stories*, for instance, an anonymous man repeatedly calls the same number only to be told 'I'm sorry son but there's no one of that name lives here'.[6] In 'Cold Iron', included in the same collection, the narrator's last telephone conversation with her ailing mother is on 'a portable phone, one of those that crackle so you can't hear anything if they're held a certain way, and my mother spoke to me but I couldn't hear'.[7] And in 'Blank Card', published in *Other Stories and Other Stories*, the interlocutor of an erotic phone call realizes: 'It was only after I hung up that I wondered if the you you believed you were talking to on the phone was definitely me after all.'[8] Discussing what he describes as the 'postal effects' of Smith's short fiction, Ben Davies observes 'an overwhelming sense that these short stories are concerned with missed messages, non-reception and unintended destinations'.[9] Although he does not specifically address the relationship between the postal economy and the telephone, Davies connects the motif of misdelivery to the structure of short stories such as 'Being Quick', a form that uses what Smith describes as her 'you-me' device, in which she combines first- and second-person narratives to offer two different accounts of the same events. Although, as Davies remarks, the 'second persons' or 'yous' in the stories are at times identifiable as a character in the story, there are also times when the addressee remains 'unidentified, ambiguous, enigmatic'.[10] Drawing on Derrida's work in *The Post Card*, he argues that with the identity of the second person remaining 'open and unanswered', there is always the possibility that the message fails to reach its final destination.[11] Suggesting that the 'you' also operates as the text's addressee, receiver and interceptor, he proposes that the reader is 'at once addressed and not addressed, the you and not-you of the story', resulting in what he terms their 'uncertain positionality'.[12] But although Davies's reading of Smith's short fiction touches on a range of telecommunication methods, he neither unpacks the specific relationship between this you-me structure and the 'open and unanswered' nature of her telephonic address nor examines the implications of this for the disorienting effects of the mobile phone.

The relationship between the literary telephone and this uncertain positionality is at work in 'Being Quick' where Smith combines the you-me structure with the troubling implications of a text message that is neither sent nor delivered. The second part of the story is narrated from the perspective of the character on the other end of the line who is growing increasingly concerned at the lack of news: 'I get my own mobile out and text you. WHR R U? XXX. I press send. Message fails. I press send again. Message fails again. I phone 453 and an automaton tells me I have 6p left on my phonecard.'[13] The misdelivery of this text message 'WHR R U?' – and its ensuing kisses 'XXX' – operates crosswise throughout Smith's works, where the you-me structure prompts questions regarding the position and place of both interlocutor and reader. With Death also on the line, the effects of this displacement stretch beyond the earthly, further destabilizing the reader's own position in the text. In this way, Smith moves beyond considerations of orientation that relate only to physical space towards what Marcella Schmidt di Friedberg calls 'orientation/disorientation in relation to thought'.[14] As Schmidt di Friedberg points out, disorientation is a useful metaphor for understanding the contemporary moment and our sense of dislocation from long-established points of reference. 'Our orientation', she argues, 'is thus constructed around the question, both material and metaphorical, "Where am I?" and around its multiple and heterogenous answers'.[15] Engaging with both material and metaphorical mobile ontologies, Smith's own question – 'WHR R U? XXX' – thus explores the textuality of contemporary disorientation and, in so doing, enacts its queer and plural possibilities.

Centred on the text message in 'Being Quick', this chapter builds on my earlier discussions of destinerrance and the relationship between the telephone and literary secrecy in order to explore the connection between the mobile phone and dislocation. Extending Davies's discussion to Smith's novels, it considers the ways in which Smith's uncertain positionality is enacted through the smartphone, arguing that her queer ontology prompts new questions regarding the relationship between disorientation and reading. Indeed, across much of her fiction, Smith finds ways not only to ask 'WHR R U?' but also to trouble the possibility of any single or fixed answer. Focusing primarily on Smith's novel *How to Be Both* and her seasonal quartet *Autumn*, *Winter*, *Spring* and *Summer*, and drawing on work by Sara Ahmed and Philip Leonard, among others, this chapter interrogates the uncertain positionalities and queer possibilities invoked by a phone communicating crosswise.

'A mighty twisting thing'

Smith's novel *How to Be Both* is presented in two parts. One part is set in Italy in the 1460s and features the artist Francesco del Cossa. Inspired by an Italian Renaissance painter of the same name, Smith's Francesco was born a girl, but in order to ensure the recognition of her artistic talent she has been raised as a boy. In the novel Francesco manifests as a disembodied spirit; unable to remember her own death, she is searching across the centuries for a grave. The other part is set in Cambridge in 2014, following sixteen-year-old Georgia (known as George), who is struggling in the aftermath of her mother's death, attempting to preserve the memory of her mother intact and survive her grief while also exploring her own queer identity. Both parts are labelled 'One', with half of the published copies printed with Francesco's narrative first, and half beginning with George.[16] From the very start, then, the twisted structure of Smith's novel makes the reader's position in relation to the text an uncertain one: approaching the conclusion of George's narrative, for instance, the reader may either be halfway through or at the end of the story: *where* the reader is in relation to the text remains always in question.

The two narratives twist around each other, converging and pulling apart at intervals as the lives of George and Francesco touch. But despite the fifteenth-century setting in one half, the phone plays a prominent part in both sections of the novel. Early in her narrative, for instance, Francesco spots George gazing up at one of her own paintings in the gallery of the Palazzo Schifanoia in Ferrera. Mistaking George for a 'poor boy', Francesco observes that she holds up 'as if to heaven' what she perceives to be a 'holy votive tablet'.[17] In fact, George is holding up her phone to take a picture of the painting; moreover, this is not the only occasion that Francesco spots George looking at or through her phone, which she describes as a 'too-small window'.[18] Francesco observes:

> [T]his place is full of people who have eyes and choose to see nothing, who all talk into their hands as they peripatate and all carry these votives, some the size of a hand, some the size of a face or a whole head, dedicated to saints perhaps or holy folk, and they look or talk to or pray to these tablets or icons all the while by holding them next to their heads or stroking them with fingers and staring only

at them, signifying they must be heavy in their despairs to be so consistently looking away from their world and so devoted to their icons.[19]

Here, Francesco draws attention to what Jessica Oliver calls the 'Grail-like' nature of the phone for the twenty-first-century subject.[20] But Smith's comparison between the mobile phone and the religious icon does more than simply highlight the phone as commodity fetish.[21] Rather, Smith interrogates the phone's capacity to simultaneously facilitate and twist the narrative trajectory. Her treatment of telecommunications is one that refuses either reification or reduction. Instead, it complicates the technicity of the human condition.

In an interview with Gillian Beer, who comments on 'all these different modes of communication that you use', Smith addresses 'the overflow of information which is around us all of the time', explaining that she resists the 'fixing of information which has happened over the last hundred years'.[22] Challenging the capitalist structures that tell us 'the things we should be and the things we should be buying and the things we should be being and the ways we should be living', she remarks that 'we are fluid creatures' and that we need to avoid the promise of 'great safety in fixity' and instead open up to this uncertainty and flux.[23] Rather than merely providing a pessimistic view of the commodification of communication, however, she also challenges recent representations of the phone, remarking: '[I]t's always tragic; there's always someone lying on the side of the road holding a mobile phone in their hands, and they're dead, but they're holding their phone.'[24] Instead, she is interested in the potential for new smartphone technologies to 'hold' stories, noting that from the pencil to the telephone 'they are just, all the same, modes of communication':

> I think the exciting thing about all the new ways that we have to communicate, all of them, there are new ways every day ... they have 140 characters or they have email shape or they take text shape, and whatever shape the future will take, we don't know ... but stories, they hold them all, and that's exciting.[25]

Even as she critiques the notion of technology as a form of mastery, then, Smith celebrates the kinds of stories that telecommunication devices offer, exploring the potential for the telephone to simultaneously contain and open up new spaces for queer and fluid narrative modes.

My use of the term 'queer' here recalls Eve Kosofsky Sedgwick's focus on the 'relational' and the 'strange'.[26] Following Sedgwick's reminder that 'the word "queer" itself means *across* – it comes from the Indo-European root – *twerkw*, which also yields the German *quer* (transverse), Latin *torquere* (to twist),

English *athwart*, I am interested in the 'twisting' and 'transverse' orientations evoked by Smith's writing.[27] At the same time, however, the queer orientations of this chapter move beyond its challenge to heteronormativity towards its role in rethinking political, social and spatial concerns.[28] Picking up on the spatiality of the term 'queer', Sara Ahmed notes: 'If the sexual involves the contingency of bodies coming into contact with other bodies, then sexual disorientation slides quickly into social disorientation, *as a disorientation in how things are arranged.*'[29] While recognizing the need to acknowledge what she describes as the 'specificity of queer as a commitment to a life of sexual deviation', the twist thus moves beyond the sexual to the social, spatial and textual registers, without, as Ahmed says, 'flattening them or reducing them to a single line'.[30] Smith's novel appears concerned with the sexual, spatial and textual orientations of queer phenomenology, where her use of the phone twists narrative and disorients the reading process.

In *How to Be Both*, Francesco's narrative opens with this twist, the lines themselves twisting across the page:

>Ho this is a mighty twisting thing fast as a
> fish being pulled by its mouth on a hook
>   if a fish could be fished through a
>   6 foot thick wall made of bricks or an
>   arrow if an arrow could fly in a leisurely
>   curl like the coil of a snail or a
> star with a tail if the star was shot
>   upwards [...][31]

The word 'twist' runs through Francesco's narrative. She admits, for instance, a fondness for 'a twist of yarn' and refers to roads that 'look set to take you in one direction' but 'will sometimes twist back on themselves without ever seeming anything other than straight'.[32] This twist is repeated at the start of George's narrative: George is alone (her mother is dead and her father – barely coping with his own grief – has gone out for the night) and is 'spending the first minutes of the new year looking up the lyrics of an old song Let's Twist Again. Lyrics by Kal Mann. The words are pretty bad. Let's twist again like we did last summer. Let's twist again like we did last year'.[33] Repeating 'Let's twist again, twisting time is here', the word takes on a sexual force; in Francesco's narrative, for instance, the artist recalls encountering an infidel during her travels who utters a word unknown to the narrator: 'It is a benign word as well as a pressing one: something in the sound of it stops me and turns me around on the road.'[34] The infidel tells

Francesco that 'he needs *a twist*', which he explains as a 'need to bind my clothes around me'.³⁵ Providing the infidel with a 'length of rope' from her haversack to function as a belt, Francesco remarks that she had 'never seen such a beautiful man'.³⁶ The couple enter a copse at the side of the road where 'I put my mouth to him and play him like the muse Euterpe plays her wooden flute'.³⁷ *How to Be Both* thus enacts the erotic and linguistic charge of the twist.

Building on this, Smith draws attention to the capacity of the telephone to thwart communication and to twist signification in new ways. Extending Guy Davidson and Monique Rooney's examination of how 'queer objects shape their subjects' and how such objects can 'illuminate, affect and animate queer modes of being', I propose that Smith's queer telephone operates by making the relational strange.³⁸ In the case of *How to Be Both*, the capacity of the telephone to animate queer modes of being is played out between George and her school friend H, who moves with her family to Denmark during the course of the narrative. In the devastation following her mother's death, George receives text messages from H, which arrive 'like information arrows aimed through space at their target, which was George'.³⁹ At first, these texts detail H's research into the historical artist Francesco del Cossa, but when H runs out of things to tell George about Francesco, she instead 'fire[s] mysterious little arrows at George in Latin'.⁴⁰ H's messages are poor Latin translations of popular songs including 'You're The One That I Want'. Listening to H's translated playlist, George reflects: 'It is also like H is trying to find a language that will make personal sense to George's ears. No one has ever done this before for George. She has spent her whole life speaking other people's languages.'⁴¹ These queer texts enable George to begin reorienting herself in the wake of her mother's death and her own desire:

> After she'd downloaded the songs, she'd sent her first reply to H.
> *Let's helix again, like we did last summer.*
> She followed it immediately with a text saying
> (Helix: Greek for twist.)
> Back came a text that pierced whatever was between the outside world and George's chest. In other words, George literally felt something.
> *It's good to hear your voice.*⁴²

Although these 'arrows' make a direct hit, their journey through space is far from straight. Following the twisted path of the helix, the texts between George and H operate according to a queer trajectory – one that opens up to embrace the possibilities of that which is uncertain, athwart or askew. This twist disorients both space and time: in her final messages to H, George tells her about the sculpture of the double helix that marks the start of a cycle trail, and which she has filmed on her phone, wondering if history can be conceived as 'that upward spring, that staircase-ladder thing' – the twist of the double helix.[43] This twisting operates on a structural level too. George repeatedly refers to a 'twist in the plot' or a 'twist in the tale'; Smith's own writing, moreover, appears to take the reader in one direction, only to twist back on itself.[44] Elevating the function of this twist through the two different print versions of the novel, *How to Be Both* thus invites a reading that is not only back to front but also upside down and inside out; the twist in the tale is made manifest on a narrative and a material level.

Getting lost

Playing on the twists in any sending system and enacting the double helix through the novel's structure, *How to Be Both* uses the text message to queer language, space and desire. At the same time, Smith troubles the relationship between technology and orientation by exploring the possibilities for getting lost – a possibility played out in Francesco's remark that 'roads that look set to take you in one direction will sometimes twist back on themselves without ever seeming anything other than straight'.[45] This is extended in Smith's work through her attention to the computational capacities of the smartphone and its potential to both orient and disorient the subject. The possibilities of disorientation are evident when George's mother Carol describes her experience of being in the Italian city as 'very strange', one that she can't quite 'get a grip on':

> She looked at the map on the bed.
> It's as if that map they gave us is nothing to do with the actual experience of being here, she said.[46]

In fact, the experience of strangeness is directly tied to the disconnect between the map and the perception of place:

> They'd been wandering about getting lost the whole day even though they had the map the hotel had given them. Things that looked close by on the map were, when they tried to get to them, actually quite far away; then they'd try to do something that looked like it'd take a very long time to do and they'd find themselves arriving almost immediately.[47]

Their explorations of the town have a disorienting effect – one that, for George, might be sidestepped if her mother had looked up their location online. Access to Googlemaps or Streetview, she informs her mother, would have meant 'they could've got to places with more precision and alacrity'.[48] Here, Smith highlights the ways that cellular technologies have fundamentally transformed the relationship between the telephone and place. Elisabeth Weber, for instance, points out that the mobile phone 'no longer needs an identifiable, permanent location: a building or phone booth. It can be carried anywhere'.[49] For Maurizio Ferraris, moreover, the shift from the landline to the mobile has necessitated an '"inaugurational" transformation' in how we conceptualize the telephone, at the centre of which is the question of location: 'As soon as the other party answers, one feels compelled to ask, "Where are you?"'[50] This question, he points out, would have seemed 'absurd, idiotic' only a few years ago: 'Where do you expect me to be? I am here, I mean there, where you are calling me.'[51] In contrast to the questions asked on the landline, the mobile phone ushers in a situation that he describes as 'completely different': 'The message can reach us anywhere, and, in turn, we could be anywhere ourselves.'[52] As a result of this transformed ontology, he continues, the mobile phone has the capacity to 'dislocat[e] presence'.[53] Perhaps it is for this reason, then, that George's mother Carol resists even turning on her phone: 'Let's follow our noses unbriskly for a change', she says.[54] And even when she forgets the name of the artist Francesco del Cossa, and George suggests, 'I could look it up on your phone', her mother stops herself: 'Let's not look anything up, her mother says. It's so nice. Not to have to know.'[55] Echoing Elsa's 'cloud of unknowing' in Spark's *The Hothouse by the East River*, Carol's own 'cloud of unknowing' in *How to Be Both* thus signifies a productive and creative disorientation that offers new modes of navigating the human condition.[56]

Carol's resistance to the phone in *How to Be Both* celebrates the possibilities of getting lost. Embracing strange connections and queer intimacies, Smith welcomes the uncanny orientations that exist between metaphysical certainties and elsewhere. In many ways, Carol enacts Walter Benjamin's assertion in 'A Berlin Chronicle' that the capacity to lose oneself in a city – what he describes as the 'art of straying' – calls for a certain 'schooling'.[57] Benjamin's conceptualization of getting lost, Rebecca Solnit remarks, is a way 'to be fully present', and to be fully present, she continues, 'is to be capable of being in uncertainty and mystery'.[58] Pointing out that 'the word "lost" comes from the Old Norse *los*, meaning the disbanding of an army', Solnit goes on to express her concern that 'many people never disband their armies, never go beyond what they know'.[59] She appeals instead to 'another art of being at home in the unknown' or of 'being at home with being lost', arguing: 'The question then is how to get lost. Never to get lost is not to live, not to know how to get lost brings you to destruction, and somewhere in the terra incognita in between lies a discovery.'[60] In exploring her characters' capacity to be at home in a 'cloud of unknowing', Smith resists the phone's computational capacities and instead explores the art of finding new ways to travel. Enacting this disorientation through queer forms, she follows the road that takes us in one direction only to twist back on itself – a movement that can be understood in terms of what Daniel Lea describes as her 'but-ness':

> Smith's novels and short stories are always concerned with the pivots that balance alternative perspectives and worldviews, and gain their richness from the divergence from singularity that is implied by 'but-ness'. If what precedes the 'but' is a forceful statement of subjective point of view, that which succeeds it brings depth and polyvocality and, crucially for Smith, opens up the creative possibilities of ambiguity.[61]

Discussing this conjunction, Lea recalls the words of Miles in *There but for The*, who describes the way that the word 'but' 'always takes you off to the side, and where it takes you is always interesting'.[62] But, Lea continues: 'Being taken off to the side, detoured, disoriented, or derailed are adventures to which the reader of Smith must get accustomed.'[63] Here, Lea draws attention to the disorienting effects of her prose and the ways in which her linguistic torsions and narrative twists always take the reader off in queer directions.

The creative ambiguities of getting lost in *How to Be Both* align with Sara Ahmed's assertion in *Queer Phenomenology*:

> In order to become orientated, you might suppose that we must first experience disorientation. When we are orientated, we might not even notice that we are orientated: we might not even think 'to think' about this point. When we experience disorientation, we might notice orientation as something we do not have.[64]

Getting lost, Ahmed argues, 'still takes us somewhere; and being lost is a way of inhabiting space by registering what is not familiar'.[65] Rejecting the perception that the mobile phone can help us navigate – in George's words – with more 'precision and alacrity', Smith explores Ahmed's sense of disorientation as a queer and creative force. In order to develop more fluid ways of thinking and knowing, Smith seems to suggest, we need to reorient ourselves in relation to the world in ways that allow us to go askew. This resonates with Ahmed's argument that 'if orientations are as much about feeling at home as they are about finding our way, then it becomes important to consider how "finding our way" involves what we could call "homing devices"'.[66] But Smith takes this further: her queer mobile operates as an 'unhoming' device, opening up to disorientation, dislocation and the multiple ways in which signification remains unhomed in the text.

Disorientation and displacement

Questions of disorientation are extended in Smith's most recent works. Exploring the relationship between the mobile and practices of unhoming, her seasonal quartet – written at speed in the aftermath of the EU referendum in the UK and published between 2016 and 2020 – oscillates between reorientation and displacement. In *Summer*, for instance, Charlotte resists the computational capacities of contemporary mobile media. This resistance, however, appears as to be as much to do with her desire to explore the art of straying as it is to do with her reluctance to be found. Refusing to own a smartphone, she purchases a Sony C902 from 2008, one that 'came with a special set of decade-old Quantum of Solace tie-ins ready installed' – or, as her former partner Arthur (Art) notes, 'a phone that *won't* do things'.[67] She chooses this device 'so the net would neither own her nor succeed in its mission to become her new phantom limb or brain', and although she '*can* access the web on it', she tells Art that she cannot use it to get online, causing him to refer to her phone as 'Charlotte's non-web'.[68] For Art, the most significant impact of Charlotte's refusal to engage with new technologies is his inability to know where she is:

> If you'd a smartphone, he says now, we'd be able to see each other. I'd be able to see where you are. Where are you?
> Sitting on the stairs, she says.
> It's a lie.
> If you had a smartphone I'd be able to see which stairs you're on right now, he says.
> And why would you want to? she says.[69]

While Art's desire to determine her location via the smartphone suggests the use of videophone technologies to 'see' Charlotte, it also refers to the integrated locative technologies of contemporary mobile media: the contemporary smartphone would enable Art to see Charlotte in more ways than one. In fact, Adriana de Souza e Silva discusses the shift in mobile phone technologies that took place from around 2008 (the year of Charlotte's non-web device), noting that 'although cell phones have always been location aware (because their location could be retrieved by the triangulation of waves), up to that point, GPS-enabled cell phones constituted a very small portion of the market'.[70] Since 2008, the rise of mobile phones with integrated Global Positioning System (GPS) capability has been, in Greg Milner's words, 'meteoric'.[71] The result of this is, for James Bridle, the appearance of a 'monumental network that provides a permanent "You are Here" signing hanging in the sky'.[72] So in choosing her non-web phone, Charlotte resists the phone's capacity to tell her where she is.

But GPS does not only tell us where we are; it tells others too. For Samuel Weber, the development of the phone's locative technologies means that we are 'in a world overseen, in its planetary totality'.[73] As a result, we are even more 'localizable': 'We are, as it were, on call – and from this call it is difficult to imagine any escape.'[74] This is, after all, a world in which, as Smith writes in *Spring*, 'We want to know everything about you. We want to know about all the places you go. We want to know where you are right now.'[75] Charlotte's resistance to the smartphone thus draws attention to the potential for panopticism enabled by locative technologies; her reluctance to being always 'on call' is also a refusal to be seen, tracked and located. This suggests that even as Smith celebrates the joy of following queer trajectories and of losing oneself in the twists of narrative, and in physical and metaphorical space, she also points to the deeply political nature of the phone's locative technologies, and the ways in which disorientation can operate as an oppressive force for those with neither the choice nor the tools to navigate freely.

Such questions of disorientation are repeatedly played out in Smith's quartet, where the connection between telephone technologies and the politics of mapping emerges with increasing urgency. This is evident, for instance, in *Winter* where we first meet Art. In addition to his job to investigate copyright breaches for SA4A – a company that manages detention centres for migrants, and for whom several of the characters across the quartet either work or work against – Art runs the @artinnature blog, where 'art' more often than not signals artifice. Discussing recent posts, he admits that his autobiographical reflections include accounts of places that he has never visited: 'I didn't actually go anywhere. I looked it up on Google Maps and on an RAC route planner, he says.'[76] This is a world in which Google, according to his mother Sophia, is 'the *new* new found land'.[77] But the volatility of social media is exposed when Art's estranged girlfriend Charlotte hacks into his Twitter account and posts the locations of bogus sightings of a Canada warbler in the UK. When Art returns to Sophia's house at Christmas, he discovers it full of people, with a stranger scrutinizing his mother's computer for map coordinates. The stranger, it transpires, is one of the many twitchers who have flocked to the area in the hope of spotting Art's fake warbler. Art is about to confess when the man 'shows him a map of Cornwall with ink crosses marked all over it'.[78] Explaining the attempt to map all the reported sightings using GPS coordinates, the stranger emphasizes the role of telecommunications in tracking the bird, telling him that 'It's all over the net!'[79] Investigating the sightings, the stranger reaches for his mobile:

> He shows Art a photo on his phone, then another, and another.
> It does look like a Canada warbler. And behind the Canada warbler the landscape does look like here.
> It really is, Art says. My God.[80]

The excitement at a warbler that has reportedly migrated from Canada to the UK unfolds against a backdrop of political conflict, where Sophia insists that economic migrants do not simply want better lives: 'They're coming here because they want *our* lives, his mother says.'[81] The 'so-called vote', she continues, 'was a vote to free our country from inheriting the troubles of other countries, as well as from having to have laws that weren't made for people like us by people like us'.[82] Although Sophia's sister Iris and Lux both challenge this perspective, the capacity to trace and map patterns of migration points to the politicization and militarization of the flight path, and the potential for the phone to simultaneously place and displace people who – in Sophia's words – aren't 'like us'.

Thus, while getting lost can invoke a giddy joy for those benefitting from privilege and freedom, it also provokes – as Schmidt di Friedberg notes – 'extreme anxiety' – an anxiety that takes on a new resonance when thinking through the experiences of disenfranchised communities, where lived experience may be one of pervasive physical, cultural or psychological disorientation.[83] In fact, Ahmed stresses the 'significance of "the orient" in "orientation"', pointing out that 'orientations involve the racialization of space'.[84] Discussing what she refers to as 'a migrant orientation', she describes 'the lived experience of facing at least two directions: toward a home that has been lost, and to a place that is not yet home'.[85] Considering this 'double' point of view, Ahmed argues that 'reflecting on migration helps us to explore how bodies arrive and how they get directed in this way or that way as a condition of arrival, which in turn is about how the "in place" gets placed'.[86]

The racialization of space is taken up again in *Spring*, where we encounter Brittany Hall, a 'DCO [Detainee Custody Officer] at one of the IRCs [Immigration Removal Centre] employed by the private security firm SA4A'.[87] At the station on her way to work one day, a schoolgirl approaches Brit and asks for directions to

Kingussie, which is the word written on the back of a postcard, insisting that Brit look it up on her phone. Searching online for routes to Kingussie, Brit ends up following the girl, whose name is reportedly Florence, across the station and on board the next train. Observing the way that Florence seems to have the power to open doors, both literal and metaphorical, she recalls the rumours she has heard at work about a detainee who just '*walked into* the centre' and convinced the management of the centre to deep-clean the toilets.[88] There are also reports that she has persuaded the security at the 'Wood', where her mother is reportedly being held, to 'shut off the system and let her mother out'.[89] Yet despite the obvious connection she feels with Florence, Brit's allegiances ultimately fall with her employer and what she perceives as her country. Shortly after they arrive in Kingussie, and having rescued a filmmaker named Richard (who has also abandoned his phone) from suicide on the tracks, they meet Alda, who appears to be waiting for Florence and who drives them all to Culloden Battlefield. From there, Florence flees with Alda to find her mother, leaving her schoolbag and journal with Brit, who wails: 'She doesn't have a phone.'[90] Despite this – or perhaps because of it – Brit finds herself calling her employers and reporting Florence to SA4A, whose security personnel soon arrive on the scene to forcibly separate Florence from her mother and detain both parent and child.

Smith's challenge to the role of the smartphone in the incarceration of vulnerable people in detainment centres is a reminder of the precarity of place and to whom it is perceived to belong. This is the truth of the situation for Florence, who is unable to escape the planetary surveillance enabled by Brit's smartphone and who is thus simultaneously located and dislocated by a mobile device. Ironically, however, the smartphone not only displaces Florence but also enacts the dislocation of Brit. Thinking through her experience of place on her return, Brit discusses her journey to Kingussie with her fellow SA4A employee Torq. Telling him that she has been to his homeland, he asks – 'Where were you exactly, Britannia?':

> She got up a map on her phone.
> Here. Then here. Then here.[91]

Looking at her location on the phone, he responds in Gaelic – 'that melted sounding language they have there' – a response that makes Brit's 'throat [start] to hurt like it does when you try to stop yourself crying'.[92] Rather than helping her to identify and reaffirm her position in the world, pointing to her location on the smartphone only makes her feel ever more lost. Even as she uses the phone to enable SA4A to locate Florence, the device therefore contributes to her own sense of dislocated presence. In fact, the ability to point to a dot on her phone screen only heightens Brit's uncertain positionality, disconnecting the geographical coordinates from any sense of what it means to be at home.

Unearthly perspectives

Extending Ahmed's interest in the 'orient' in 'orientation', and invoking the locative technologies of the mobile phone, Smith's writing explores the potential for the mobile phone to disorient or unhome. But in order to understand the connection between the telephone and the politics of place, it is important to unpack the phone's relationship to the global imaginary and the wider technological systems that underpin it. In particular, the locative technologies of the smartphone are enabled via global navigational satellite systems (GNSS) of which GPS is the most prominent. For Antony Giddens, the satellite system that facilitates GPS is central to the process of globalization: 'If one wanted to fix its specific point of origin, it would be the first successful broadcast transmission made via satellite.'[93] Tracing the cultural history of the satellite in *Orbital Poetics*, Philip Leonard notes that from '*satelles*', meaning guardian or custodian, satellites can be understood as 'remote devices that guarantee proximity, forging a smooth planetary immediacy and establishing a transparently universal inhabitation.'[94] Appearing to offer a continuous space through the circumnavigation of the earth, satellites hold the promise of instant contact. But rather than abolishing national borders and promoting a sense of global community, locative technologies also have the potential to accentuate cultural, economic and political divisions.[95] This recalls the deeply political history of GPS, which arose in part as a result of Cold War imperatives and the Soviet's launch of Sputnik in 1957. Originally intended for secure use by the military, it is now, Bridle writes, 'a vast structure, a celestial superstructure that we are all living inside.'[96] Bound up with this, as Lisa Parks and James Schwoch explain, are new ways of conceiving of the planet: 'As machines that orbit our planet, satellites are uniquely positioned to visually represent Earth, and their images have been composited to construct Earth as "whole."'[97] But what might be thought of as a celestial superstructure by some is, for others, a symptom of tyrannical rule. Caren Kaplan points out that colonial legacies are inscribed in GPS: when we look up our location on the phone, therefore, we are participating in the 'martial and territorial aspect of mapping throughout the modern period'.[98] In this way, the satellite fixes global divisions and inequalities; it has what Parks and Schwoch describe as a 'dark side'.[99]

This tyrannical rule is evident in Smith's seasonal quartet where, in *Winter*, for instance, '[t]he earth is surrounded with floating space debris, space junk and satellites'.[100] The 'dark side' of the satellite is something of which Sacha, in *Summer*, is more than aware:

> She is a person on a pavement in a city in a country on a planet, seen from above by so many satellites that aren't there so we can see how fine and beautiful our planet is from space but so the people who control the satellites can zoom in on people for all sorts of reasons that are nothing to do with what almost everybody and everything on the planet actually needs.[101]

Here, Sacha draws attention to what Jean Baudrillard has referred to as the 'satellization' of technological control.[102] For Derrida, this can be understood as the sovereignty of the satellite, which is connected to its global power to 'see', to 'have under surveillance', to 'take in' and to 'archive from a superterrestrial height'.[103] Tied to its economic and military strategy, the 'erection toward height', Derrida argues, 'is always the sign of the sovereignty of the sovereign', ensuring that the satellite operates according to a panopticism which plays out the co-implication of technology and the nation state.[104]

But in addition to the tyranny of the panoptic gaze, the satellite also prompts ontological anxiety. Far from disclosing the world, the satellite, for Martin Heidegger, is a symptom of the technoscientific condition that is at once both flawed and dangerous, circumscribing the 'delusion' that the human is the 'lord of the earth'.[105] This disaffection is also evident in the work of Bernard Stiegler, who points to its catastrophic potential. In the first volume of *Technics and Time*, Stiegler stresses the ways that the satellite can reconfigure national and social power, pointing to its role in the West's attempts at 'total territorial extension'.[106] By abolishing the separation of the human from the stars, Stiegler argues that the satellite is 'an astral figure of power, which speaks to a change in epoch, to modern technics' – a change that is disastrous to the human condition: 'Disaster', he writes, 'does not mean catastrophe but disorientation – stars guide'.[107] In *Disorientation*, he goes on to argue that this disaster takes place in the context of capitalism, hyperindustrialization and hyperconnectivity, facets of the contemporary condition that suggest that we live in a disoriented world in which we have lost our 'orientation-markers [*cardinalité*]'.[108] Thus, the extent of our engagement with technology in the contemporary moment brings with it an unprecedented and permanent sense of disorientation. For Stiegler, rather than orienting us in space, the very satellite system that enables the locative capacities of the mobile phone to operate results only in increasing disorientation.

Echoes of Stiegler's critique of the hyperconnectivity of the digital age and the orbital panopticism of GPS can be discerned across Smith's works. Prior to her mother's death in *How to Be Both*, for instance, George gleans entertainment via the screen:

> George is watching a programme about the Flying Scotsman, a train from the past, on TV. But because George came in halfway through this programme and missed the beginning, and because it is an interesting programme, she is simultaneously watching it from the start on catch-up on her laptop.[109]

Moreover, at the same time as watching two screens, George is also 'looking up photobombs on her phone', leading her mother to accuse of being 'a migrant of [her] own existence'.[110] When her mother attempts to persuade the family to venture out to a rural location at night to watch the Perseid shower, George resists: 'It's just pollution. And satellites, George says. There's no point.'[111] Here, George refuses the celestial orientation marker; there is no 'point'. When her mother disappears 'off, or rather into, the face of the earth', however, George searches for new orientation points or cardinal markers.[112] And when attempts to reach her mother by sending messages 'to a phone number that no longer exists' do not provide the reorientation she needs, she explores other ways to connect with the astral.[113] This means shifting the perspective from the satellite's capacity to look down on earth from orbit to the possibility of looking back up into outer space. Rather than tell her father that there is a leak in the roof of her attic bedroom, she conceals the damage, hoping that with 'enough bad weather and the right inattention' her home 'will open to the sky': 'She will lie in bed with all the covers thrown off and the stars will be directly above her, nothing between her and their long-ago burnt-out eyes.'[114] Replacing the panoptic gaze of the satellite with the burnt-out eyes of dead stars, George twists the orbital gaze in order to contemplate new ways of looking beyond the earthly.

George's turn to the stars thus produces new, imaginative cartographies, a reorientation of perspective that can be read in light of Leonard's argument for an 'other cosmographopoeisis'.[115] Leonard does not dispute the satellite's role in global surveillance and regulation, but rather than restricting us only to a 'controlling and globalizing technicity', he explores the ways that it can be 'activated otherwise'.[116] Remapping imperial cartographies, he suggests, the satellite, in its detachment from earth, becomes postcolonial nomad. Moreover, by detaching us from the local, and refiguring our sense of ground, the satellite opens up the possibility of other, 'unearthly' ways of seeing. Thus, the satellite can work both ways: 'It shapes visions of spherical orderliness and of a grounded home, but it also provokes the uncanny sense of a world that is not at home with itself and cannot be subjugated either by circumnavigation or remote observation.'[117] This 'but-ness', as Lea describes it, once again structures Smith's work: the twist in George's perspective suggests that while it represents imperial authority, the satellite also opens out to an orbit that cannot be reduced or contained by a controlling technicity.

A pervasive sense of knowing and unknowing accessed through the celestial emerges again at the end of *Summer*, where Robert, Sacha and Charlotte drive to Roughton Heath in search of the post office where Albert Einstein bought sweets during his time in hiding from the Nazis. They rely on the car's satnav to get there, and by the time they arrive, Sacha is asleep. When Robert and Charlotte get out of the car to contemplate the skies, Robert remarks that Einstein believed that we 'got our best intellectual tools from looking at the stars. But that this doesn't make the stars responsible for what we do with our intellects':

> They stood under a night sky in a car park where Einstein himself perhaps maybe possibly once stood and looked up at the lit pinpoints in the dark that meant the ancient and original and already dead stars, till Robert's sister, waking up and seeing them wave to her, pulled her coat round her shoulders, got out of the car and came over to where they were standing in the cold and they all looked up together to point out which constellations they knew the names for and to guess at the ones they didn't.[118]

Even though Charlotte, Robert and Sacha neither know the names of all the constellations nor their precise position in space, their upward gaze to the 'already dead' intervenes in any sense of their fixed place or time on earth and its perceived epistemological securities. In this way, Smith steers them towards 'the middle of nowhere' in order to find new orientation markers and to reappraise the meaning of home.[119]

It is significant, of course, that neither George in *How to Be Both* nor Charlotte, Sacha or Robert in *Summer* accesses GPS on their phone in order to tell them where or when they are. Here, through its pointed absence, Smith enacts a turning away from the phone's sovereign power. Indeed, time and again in her fiction, characters turn off their phone or opt for an older model with limited functionality: they refuse to allow the phone to tell them where they are or where they should be. But this resistance is not the end of the story: recalling Smith's remark to Beer that she is interested in the potential of the phone to 'hold' narrative, her writing also enacts the capacity for literature to find new ways of reaching orbit and twisting perspective via the telephone. In 'Being Quick', this is framed according to the phone call between the interlocutors – a you-me structure that not only holds the narrative but also enables it to take shape. The story ends with the call, and with its potential to imagine other ways of connecting beyond the earthly, where one tells the other down the line:

> First I was torn off the ground with my legs and arms flailing in the air. Like I was a fish on a hook.
> Eh? You said.
> Like someone in the sky was reeling me in on a huge rod, I said. Or like my middle was tied to a rope and the other end was tied to a plane. And after that, I watched our house collapse in on itself and I spent some time lying in the rubble. Then I vanished completely. I wasn't here at all. Then you phoned.[120]

Here, the narrator offers up her own orbital connection – one in which she is torn from the ground into the sky. Moving beyond the earthly, it is the phone call that brings her back down to the ground. It is the phone call, therefore, that provides the story with its own orientation point. As ever, Smith's treatment of the phone remains nuanced: resisting a straightforward technological determinism and refusing to reduce it to a flawed technicity, she nevertheless calls up its capacity to connect to what Leonard describes as an 'alternative metaphysics' or 'unearthly place'.[121] The story closes:

> Don't go yet, though, you said.
> I looked at the clock.
> Five more minutes? You said.
> Okay, I said.[122]

By highlighting the relation between disorientation and writing, her story is pinned not to a precise location, fixed schema or endpoint. Rather, it points to the phone's uncertain, unknowable and ongoing effects, as well as to its imaginary and unearthly cartographies.

Across a range of her works over the last two decades, Smith's simultaneous celebration and critique of the phone's relation to (dis)location serve not to provide a sense of position but rather to generate an affective disorientation: her question 'WHR R U? XXX' enacts a telephonic textuality cross-wise, the three 'X's' not marking the spot but rather queering questions of orientation. Rather than providing a map or ground for understanding, then, Smith embeds the very possibility of getting lost at the heart of her treatment of the mobile phone, thus inviting us to enter into the text from an uncertain positionality or unearthly place. Politically astute, these dislocations are located in the context of the dangers of technocapitalism and the nation state, but there are also moments of hope to be found in her queer disorientations. In the spirit of her title – *How to Be Both* – and mirroring the structural and ontological twists in her texts – Smith's writing thus opens up the possibilities of a disorientation that works both ways: refusing the rigid orders of mapping, it occupies a space between place and displacement, between orientation and disorientation, between knowing and unknowing, and between earth and orbit.

Notes

1   Ali Smith, 'Being Quick', in *The Whole Story and Other Stories* (London: Penguin, 2004), 27–52 (27).
2   Ibid., 28.
3   Ibid.
4   Ibid., 31.
5   Ibid., 35.
6   Ali Smith, 'The Unthinkable Happens to People Every Day', in *Free Love and Other Stories* (London: Virago, 1998), 129–40 (129).
7   Smith, 'Cold Iron', in *Free Love and Other Stories*, 77–86 (80).
8   Smith, 'Blank Card', in *Other Stories and Other Stories* (London: Penguin, 2004), 37–50 (48).
9   Ben Davies, 'Address, Temporality and Misdelivery: The Postal Effects of Ali Smith's Short Stories', in *British Women Short Story Writers: The New Woman to Now*, ed. Emma Young and James Bailey (Edinburgh: Edinburgh University Press, 2017), 163–78 (173).
10 Ibid., 164.
11 Ibid. See Jacques Derrida, *The Post Card: From Socrates to Freud and Beyond*, trans. Alan Bass (Chicago: The University of Chicago Press, 1987).
12 Davies, 'Address, Temporality and Misdelivery', 167.
13 Smith, 'Being Quick', 48–9.
14 Marcella Schmidt di Friedberg, *Geographies of Disorientation* (London: Routledge, 2019), 15.
15 Ibid., 2.
16 Ali Smith, *How to Be Both* (London: Penguin, 2015). The e-book version is prefaced with a note that asks: 'Who says stories reach everybody in the same order? This novel can be read in two ways and this e-book provides you with both' (n.p.). The

page numbers given in this chapter refer to my own print copy, which presents George's narrative first.

17 Ibid., 229.
18 Ibid., 282.
19 Ibid., 229–30.
20 Jessica Eve Oliver, 'The Raft, the Ladder, the Transitional Space, the Moratorium …': *Digital Interventions in Twenty-First-Century Private and Public Lives* (PhD Thesis, University of Sussex, June 2018), 119.
21 In *Capital*, Marx turns to 'the misty realm of religion' to explain the commodity fetish: 'There the products of the human brain appear as autonomous figures endowed with a life of their own, which enter into relations both with each other and with the human race. So it is in the world of commodities with the products of men's hands. I call this the fetishism which attaches itself to the products of labour as soon as they are produced as commodities, and is therefore inseparable from the production of commodities' (Karl Marx, *Capital: A Critique of Political Economy*, vol. 1, trans. Ben Fowkes (London: Penguin, 1976), 165).
22 Ali Smith, 'Gillian Beer Interviews Ali Smith', in *Ali Smith: Contemporary Critical Perspectives*, ed. Monica Germanà and Emily Horton (London: Bloomsbury, 2013), 137–53 (146, 150).
23 Ibid., 151.
24 Ibid., 146.
25 Ibid.
26 Eve Kosofsky Sedgwick, *Tendencies* (Durham, NC: Duke University Press, 1993), xii.
27 Ibid.
28 See Judith Butler who also uses the language of the 'twist' to argue: 'If the term "queer" is to be a site of collective contestation, the point of departure for a set of historical reflections and futural imaginings, it will have to remain that which is, in the present, never fully owned, but always and only redeployed, twisted, queered from a prior usage and in the direction of urgent and expanding political purposes, and perhaps also yielded in favor of terms that do that political work more effectively' (Judith Butler, 'Critically Queer', in *Playing with Fire: Queer Politics, Queer Theories*, ed. Shane Phelan (London: Routledge, 1997), 11–30 (14)).
29 Sara Ahmed, *Queer Phenomenology: Orientations, Objects, Others* (Durham, NC: Duke University Press, 2006), 162.
30 Ibid., 161.
31 Smith, *How to Be Both*, 189.
32 Ibid., 202, 281.
33 Ibid., 4.

34 Ibid., 5, 283.
35 Ibid., 284.
36 Ibid., 285.
37 Ibid.
38 Guy Davidson and Monique Rooney, 'Introduction: Queer Objects', in *Queer Objects*, ed. Guy Davidson and Monique Rooney (London: Routledge, 2019), 3–5 (3).
39 Smith, *How to Be Both*, 167.
40 Ibid., 168.
41 Ibid., 169–70.
42 Ibid., 170.
43 Ibid., 172.
44 Ibid., 178, 182.
45 Ibid., 281.
46 Ibid., 62.
47 Ibid., 62–3.
48 Ibid., 63.
49 Elisabeth Weber, 'Vectorizing Our Thoughts toward "Current Events": For Avital Ronell', in *Reading Ronell,* ed. Diane Davis (Champaign, IL: University of Illinois Press, 2009), 222–40 (223).
50 Maurizio Ferraris, *Where Are You? An Ontology of the Cell Phone*, trans. Sarah De Sanctis (New York: Fordham University Press, 2014), 11–12.
51 Ibid., 12.
52 Ibid.
53 Ibid., 5.
54 Smith, *How to Be Both*, 63.
55 Ibid., 59, 60.
56 Muriel Spark, *The Hothouse by the East River* (Edinburgh: Polygon, 2018), 136; Smith, *How to Be Both*, 172.
57 Walter Benjamin, 'A Berlin Chronicle', in *Reflections: Essays, Aphorisms, Autobiographical Writings,* trans. Edmund Jephcott, ed. Peter Demetz (New York: Schoken, 1986), 3–60 (9, 8).
58 Rebecca Solnit, *A Field Guide to Getting Lost* (Edinburgh: Canongate, 2009), 6.
59 Ibid., 7.
60 Ibid., 10, 14.
61 Daniel Lea, *Twenty-First-Century Fiction: Contemporary British Voices* (Manchester: Manchester University Press, 2017), 26.
62 Ali Smith, *There but for The* (London: Penguin, 2012), 175; see Lea, *Twenty-First-Century Fiction*, 26.
63 Lea, *Twenty-First-Century Fiction*, 26.
64 Ahmed, *Queer Phenomenology*, 5–6.
65 Ibid., 7.

66 Ibid., 9.
67 Ali Smith, *Summer* (London: Penguin, 2021), 321.
68 Ibid.
69 Ibid.
70 Adriana de Souza e Silva, 'Mobile Narratives: Reading and Writing Urban Space with Location-Based Technologies' in *Comparative Textual Media: Transforming the Humanities in the Postprint Era*, ed. N. Katherine Hayles and Jessica Pressman (Minneapolis, MN: University of Minnesota Press, 2013), 33–52 (46). Although the first commercially available mobile phone with GPS was produced by Benefon Esc! in 1999, it was another decade before this was popularized for the consumer.
71 Greg Milner, *Pinpoint: How GPS Is Changing Our World* (London: Granta, 2016), 119.
72 James Bridle, 'You Are Here', in *Where You Are: A Book of Maps that Will Leave You Completely Lost*, ed. Chloe Aridjis et al. (London: Visual Editions, 2013), n.p.
73 Samuel Weber, *Mass Mediauras* (Stanford, CA: Stanford University Press, 1996), 5.
74 Ibid.
75 Ali Smith, *Spring* (London: Penguin, 2020), 119.
76 Ali Smith, *Winter* (London: Penguin, 2018), 187.
77 Ibid., 192.
78 Ibid., 291.
79 Ibid.
80 Ibid., 291–2.
81 Ibid., 205.
82 Ibid., 206.
83 Schmidt di Friedberg, *Geographies*, 5.
84 Ahmed, *Queer Phenomenology*, 23.
85 Ibid., 10.
86 Ibid.
87 Smith, *Spring*, 151.
88 Ibid., 135.
89 Ibid., 137–8.
90 Ibid., 268.
91 Ibid., 325. It is worth noting that this exchange echoes a conversation between Iona and her taxi driver Wassim in 'The Book Club'. Requesting the precise details of Iona's destination, he insists: 'But where exactly?' (Ali Smith, 'The Book Club', in *The Whole Story*, 123–36 (127)). Pointing to his 'satnav', he explains that the device tells him the fastest and quietest route. When he enters the name of Iona's street 'several maps flash up. That's where you live, isn't it? is that where you live? he is saying. There?' (128). But the emphasis on the question mark that follows the 'there' unsettles the very notion of situatedness and instead disconnects us from our physical position on earth.
92 Smith, *Spring*, 325.

93 Anthony Giddens, *Beyond Left and Right: The Future of Radical Politics* (Cambridge: Polity Press, 1994), 5–6.
94 Philip Leonard, *Orbital Poetics: Literature, Theory, World* (London: Bloomsbury, 2019), 166.
95 See, for example, Peter Dicken and James S. Ormrod, *Cosmic Society: Towards a Sociology of the Universe* (London: Routledge, 2007), 107.
96 Bridle, 'You are Here', n.p.
97 Lisa Parks and James Schwoch, 'Introduction', in *Down to Earth: Satellite Technologies, Industries and Cultures*, ed. Lisa Parks and James Schwoch (New Brunswick, NJ: Rutgers University Press, 2012), 1–16 (3).
98 Caren Kaplan, 'Precision Targets: GPS and the Militarization of U.S. Consumer Identity', *American Quarterly*, 58.3 (2006), 693–713 (698).
99 Parks and Schwoch, 'Introduction', 4.
100 Smith, *Winter*, 239.
101 Smith, *Summer*, 42.
102 Jean Baudrillard, *Simulations*, trans. Paul Foss, Paul Patton and Philip Beitchmann (Cambridge, MA: Semiotext[e], 1983), 62. See also Lisa Parks, *Cultures in Orbit: Satellites and the Televisual* (Durham: Duke University Press, 2005), 5–6.
103 Jacques Derrida, *The Beast and the Sovereign*, vol. 1, trans. Geoffrey Bennington (Chicago: University of Chicago Press, 2008), 289.
104 Ibid. For a detailed analysis of the sovereignty of the satellite in the work of writers and thinkers ranging from Plato to Lisa Parks, see Leonard, *Orbital Poetics*. This chapter owes much to Leonard's critique of the orbital perspective, particularly with regards to its theorization by Derrida, Heidegger and Stiegler.
105 Martin Heidegger, 'The Question Concerning Technology', in *Basic Writings*, ed. D. F. Krell (New York: Harper Collins, 2008), 311–41 (332).
106 Bernard Stiegler, 'Technology and Anthropology', in *Technics and Time 1: The Fault of Epimetheus*, trans. Richard Beardsworth and George Collins (Stanford, CA: Stanford University Press, 1998), 89. See also Leonard, *Orbital Poetics*, 118–20.
107 Stiegler, 'Technology and Anthropology', 89–92.
108 Bernard Stiegler, *Technics and Time 2: Disorientation*, trans. Stephen Barker (Stanford, CA: Stanford University Press, 2009), 2.
109 Smith, *How to Be Both*, 226.
110 Ibid.
111 Ibid., 204.
112 Ibid., 207.
113 Ibid., 133.
114 Ibid., 198.
115 Leonard, *Orbital Poetics*, 30.

116 Ibid., 24, 26.
117 Ibid., 27.
118 Smith, *Summer*, 374–5.
119 Ibid., 368.
120 Smith, 'Being Quick', 45.
121 Leonard, *Orbital Poetics*, 102, 103.
122 Smith, 'Being Quick', 51.

4

Calling without calling

Arriving at the banks of the Jordan River and waiting for permission to cross the bridge into Palestine, Mourid Barghouti writes in *I Saw Ramallah*: 'There is very little water under the bridge. Water without water.'[1] He says that it is 'as though the water apologized for its presence on this boundary between two histories, two faiths, two tragedies'.[2] Recalling Jacques Derrida's use of the Blanchotian syntagma of '*X sans X*', which 'is not a simple negation, nullification, or destruction, but a certain reinscription of X, a certain reversal of the movement of X that still communicates with X', Barghouti's memoir of exile is structured by this impossible logic: for the Palestinian, the river signifies water without water, but this might also be mobility without mobility, place without place, identity without identity, home without home.[3] And to this list, I would like to add: calling without calling. For although Barghouti tells his friend in the memoir, 'Today is the international day of telephones', the lines of communication within and between communities are crossed, corrupted, complicated and very often cut entirely, and the religious, political and geographical boundaries within which Palestinians continue to be entrapped are not only mirrored but are also significantly extended through the telecommunications infrastructure in the Occupied Territories.[4]

Building on my discussion in Chapter 3 of the relationship between telephone technologies, the 'satellization' of experience, and questions of displacement, I wish to turn now to consider the ways in which the telephone connects and disconnects across national and cultural borders. In particular, I focus on the specific situation in Israel-Palestine in order to examine the political implications of telephony and its role in global power structures and oppressive political regimes. Drawing on the work of Mourid Barghouti and Jacques Derrida, alongside research into telecommunications in the region by Helga Tawil-Souri, this chapter examines how Israeli control of infrastructure, cellular networks and airspace contribute to Eyal Weizman's model of the vertical architecture of the state – how, in effect, using the telephone in Palestine often equates to calling without calling. But while the chapter examines the very specific structure of telecommunications in the region, it also hopes to prompt a broader conversation regarding the possibilities for the literary telephone to intervene in debates regarding the relationship between telecommunication technologies, voice and power.

For the Palestinian poet in exile Mourid Barghouti, Israel 'is a nation that sees itself as forever victorious, forever frightened, and forever in the right'.[5] Detailing the support of Israel by the United States and Europe following the Declaration of the Establishment of the State of Israel in 1948 and the 1967 Six-Day War, during which a reported 300,000 Palestinians fled the West Bank, as well as 'the secret collusion of twenty debased Arab regimes', Barghouti notes:

> It is a state that [...] has erected more than six hundred barriers and checkpoints, has built around us a wall 780 kilometers long, detains more than eleven thousand prisoners, controls all borders and crossing points leading to our country by land, sea, and air, and frames its laws with reference to a permanent philosophy that its victories do not change, a philosophy whose core is this mighty state's fear ... of us.[6]

The 'peace process', he remarks, is 'not working'.[7] Echoing Barghouti's view of the failed negotiations, Richard Falk notes that approaches to date, including the Oslo Accords set up between Israel and the Palestinian Liberation Organisation in 1993 and 1995, reinforce the structures of partition:

> The hoped-for end result of achieving 'peace' is generally asserted to be two nominally sovereign states, geographic neighbors coexisting peacefully side by side. (The gross disparities between the two 'neighbors' in their present condition and with regard to any likely negotiated outcome has been treated by mainstream commentators in the West as unmentionable, inevitable, realistic, and intrinsic.)[8]

The imbalance of power here is remarkable, writes Falk: 'One state, Israel, would remain a regional superpower with a formidable arsenal of nuclear weapons; the other, Palestine, would struggle for oxygen.'[9] Without the right of return for Palestinian refugees, and without the shared control of Jerusalem, the situation leads only to a permanent condition of subordination.

Today, the lines of communication around Palestine are more tangled than ever, with the voices of Palestinian authors often excised from public discourse due to anxieties around the charge of anti-Semitism – an anxiety that has sometimes led to the closing down of debate. My engagement with Barghouti in this chapter, however, takes up a different line: rather than aligning itself with either of the opposing 'sides', it expresses a deep commitment to the necessity of speaking across cultural divides and to the essential nature of dialogue within the process of building peace. In order to do so, it focuses on the representation of telephony in the region and the impact of this on cross-cultural conversation between the Palestinians and the Israelis – a conversation, I hope, that might do something towards dispelling both anti-Semitic and anti-Arab stereotypes. Indeed, while scholars such as Anna Bernard, Tahia Abdel Nasser and Salam Mir turn to Barghouti's poetry and prose for a lyrical and provocative account of the Palestinian experience of exile, the relationship between his writing and telecommunications infrastructure – and, in particular, the telephone system – has to date been neglected.[10] In this chapter, I argue for the need to read Barghouti's telephone in both political and aesthetic terms. Certainly, Barghouti's writing exposes the ways that the telephone is not only a lifeline for the Palestinian but – embedded within Israeli infrastructure – is also hooked up with disconnection and death; his memoirs reveal the complex wiring systems that ensure the telephone's contribution to an oppressive political and military regime. Moreover, in considering telephony in Barghouti's work, this chapter also aims to open up broader questions about the possibilities and limitations of the telephone and its capacity to speak across national and political divisions. It does so by interrogating the telephone's role in our understanding of ethical networks and transnational communication, as well as its potential to energize different modes of talking and listening across cultures.

Calling here, calling there

In *I Saw Ramallah*, first published in English in 2000, Barghouti returns to the West Bank after thirty years in exile. In 1966, aged twenty-two and in the face of religious and political conflict, Barghouti left Ramallah and travelled to university in Cairo. Forbidden from returning to Palestine after the Six-Day War in 1967, he has lived in exile ever since, with different members of his family scattered around the globe. In the memoir he recollects the summer following the 1967 conflict when the family met at the Caravan Hotel in Amman in Jordan. Multiple displacements meant that parents and siblings had travelled from many cities: 'I was working in Kuwait. My mother and my youngest brother, 'Alaa, were in Ramallah. My father was in Amman and Majid was at the Jordanian University. Mounif was working in Qatar.'[11] This is symptomatic of the memoir as a whole; his narrative is a transnational one, forged of remote connections with friends and family in exile. But what holds them together, Barghouti says, is the telephone. For the *naziheen*, or displaced ones, Barghouti writes, the telephone is a lifeline: 'The telephone, now that the era of letters is over, is the sacred tie between Palestinians.'[12] The significance and complexity of the telephone call – with its divided geographies and multiplying lines of communication – are evident from Barghouti's ever-expanding catalogue of people and places linked down the wires: 'Mounif is calling me in *America* from *Qatar* about Fahim's martyrdom in *Beirut* and burial in *Kuwait*, and about the necessity of informing *Sitti* Umm 'ata in *Deir Gahssanah* and his maternal grandmother in *Nablus* and my mother in *Jordan*.'[13] The internationalization of this phone is crucial; forced migration means that Barghouti must be able to make long-distance calls in order to ensure the continuation of his family and his community.

Barghouti returns time and again in *I Saw Ramallah* to the role of the telephone in facilitating the closest familial bonds. Following his deportation from Egypt, he lives for some time in Hungary with his wife – the Egyptian writer and translator Radwa Ashour – and his son Tamim. But, Barghouti recalls, he and Radwa decide that Tamim should be educated in an Arab country, and as a result, mother and son return to Cairo while he remains in Budapest. Family life is characterized by separation. Describing the 'dispersal of my family', Barghouti notes: 'From the moment we took that decision our small family was reunited for three weeks in the winter and three months in the summer, from my deportation in 1977 until Tamim was a young man in his final year of high school.'[14] In his experience, the paternal bond can only operate according to the logic of the telephone: 'I had to concede that the telephone would be my permanent means of creating a relationship with a child of a few months.'[15] The family's telephonic connections are extended in Barghouti's second memoir, *I Was Born There, I Was Born Here*. Here, when Barghouti and his son Tamim finally make it to Jerusalem together, it is to the telephone that they turn:

> Tamim dashes into a telephone kiosk in the street and calls Radwa in Cairo. 'Mama, I'm in Jerusalem. I'm at the Damascus Gate. Baba and I are in Jerusalem.' I watch Tamim in the telephone kiosk. I see him in Radwa's arms, right after she left the Dr. Gohar Maternity Hospital. She is standing on the bank of the Nile directly in front of the hospital gate in a light summer dress with a pattern of small roses, holding Tamim in her arms and looking at him.[16]

Here, Barghouti sets up the telephone as an umbilical cord operating along the maternal line; however, this long-distance call also becomes the connecting line between the past and the present, thereby signalling the role of the telephone in maintaining transhistorical and transgenerational networks for communities in exile.

It is this dynamic, then, that leads to Barghouti's statement: 'The Palestinian has become a telephonic person, living by the sound of voices carried to him across huge distances.'[17] Eventually arriving in Ramallah, and wanting to call members of his family in Amman and Cairo, he tells his friend: '"Today is the international day of telephones."'[18] In so doing, Barghouti clearly sets out the value of the telephone as a medium for bridging cultures and locations. But, even as he highlights its role in the global community, he also challenges the telephone's capacity to facilitate communication, returning repeatedly to the difficulties of speaking across the divide. For although the telephone enables long-distance calling, Barghouti's conversations are always haunted by disconnection and death: '"So-and-so, we took her to hospital, but don't worry – it's nothing serious." "So-and-so has passed away, may the rest of his days be added to yours."'[19] As a result, Barghouti admits that the Palestinian 'loves the ringing of the telephone, yet fears it'.[20] Simultaneously a tool for communication and a technology of violence, and always reinforcing his separation from his family, this apparatus is, in Barghouti's words, both 'wonderful' and 'terrifying'.[21] Rather than simply bridging distances in the text, then, the telephone also serves to expose its divisions. Insisting that 'the displaced person can never be protected from the terrorism of the telephone', Barghouti explains:

> The telephone never stops ringing in the night of far-off countries. Someone woken from sleep picks up the receiver and hears a hesitant voice at the other end telling them of the death of a loved one or a relative or a friend or comrade in the homeland or in some other country – in Rome, Athens, Tunis, Cyprus, London, Paris, the United States, and on every bit of land we have been carried to, until death becomes like lettuce in the market, plentiful and cheap.[22]

Barghouti's telephone bell rings as a death knell, playing out Avital Ronell's assertion in *The Telephone Book* that 'the telephone touches the state, terrorism, psychoanalysis, language theory, and a number of death-support systems'.[23] This means that although it facilitates connections between family members, the telephone also participates in and extends the structures of power that keep them apart.

The telephone's participation in the economy of division is seen most explicitly when Barghouti receives a call informing him of his brother's death. In many ways, it is a case of crossed lines:

> One of his friends had called from Geneva and said he had been in an accident in the Gare du Nord in Paris. I called his home and Geneva, trying to find out more. They said that he was alive and they were trying to save him. Then they said he had died. I lived in this confusion before phoning our mother in Amman. I realized they had told her only that he had been hurt in an accident. [...] I called Majid and 'Alaa in Doha. I asked them not to tell our mother about Mounif's death.[24]

And so it continues. Rather than conveying a message, then, news of Mounif's death reaches the family only through a process of distortion and cumulative error, similar to the game that is known as 'Chinese Whispers' in the UK and as the 'Broken Telephone' in the United States. Writing on the politics and poetics of postcolonial telecommunications, Felicia McCarren explains that this game, where the message is always transformed during transmission, is known in French as *téléphone arabe*. She points out, however, that not only does the term '*téléphone arabe*' signify the supposed 'technological naivety of the colonized', but that it also 'resonates now in western ears with the fear of communications technologies such as the cell phone being used not for nationalist, but for internationalist, terrorist ends, linked to Islamic if not "Arabic" extremism'.[25] For this reason, and for many others, the specific relationship between the Palestinian and the telephone, and the connection between the '*téléphone arabe*' and suspected terrorist activities, demands an ever closer ear. Here, we hear the telephone ringing in more ways than one: it signals communication from afar, but it also highlights the distances between people; it puts them in touch, but it also echoes with the impossibility of getting the message through.

This difficulty is taken up once again by Barghouti in *I Was Born There, I Was Born Here*, a title that stresses the operation of distance that structures both communication and community in the Occupied Territories. Reflecting on the ways that the telephone both crosses and extends the distances between places and people, Barghouti notes that 'one of the Occupation's cruelest crimes is the distortion of distance'.[26] Describing his relief at being able to re-enter Jordanian territory – 'where distances always measure the same' – he stresses that distance in Palestine is controlled by the Israeli regime, where it becomes ambiguous and subject to distortion:

> This is a fact: the Occupation changes distances. It destroys them, upsets them, and plays with them as it likes. Whenever the soldiers kill someone, the

customary distance between the moments of birth and death is distorted. The Occupation closes the road between two cities and makes the distance between them many times the number recorded on the maps. [...] The soldier of the Occupation stands on a piece of land he has confiscated and calls it 'here' and I, its owner, exiled to a distant country, have to call it 'there'.[27]

This experience of space in Palestine is reiterated by Juan Goytisolo, who visited the West Bank in 2002 as part of a delegation from the International Parliament of Writers. He describes the topology of power in terms of ripping and appending:

> The landscape of the West Bank and Gaza Strip has been ripped and torn like cloth made from strips of different materials. Barbed wire surrounds Israeli settlements and military posts and the areas theoretically controlled by the Palestinian Authority: it protects and excludes, unites separated zones and separates adjacent territories, weaves in between a labyrinth of islands that are mutually repelled and attracted.[28]

Goytisolo's description of the spatial ambiguities of the region recalls Michel Serres's refiguration of topology, which he presents in conversation with Bruno Latour in terms of a crumpled handkerchief, where 'two distant points suddenly are close, even superimposed'.[29] Serres goes on to explain, however, that if the handkerchief is completely torn, the 'two points that were close can become very distant'.[30] So although, on the surface, the telephone might be said to facilitate this crumpling – a call is made and two distant points are suddenly close, even superimposed – Barghouti shows us that the region's 'topological twists' are only ever manipulated by the Israeli operator, who has the capacity to tear up geography.[31] Thus, even as it has the potential to unite there and here, Barghouti suggests that the present structure of telephony in Israel ensures that people and places always remain at a distance. As the Israeli Minister of Internal Security Uzi Landau remarked in 2002: 'They are there, but we are here and there as well.'[32]

Telephony and infrastructure

The potential for and the limitations of the telephone to cross distance is of course a perspective shared and questioned by many in recent years, with Marie Gillespie's research on the use of telecommunications by refugees pointing to the ways that the smartphone operates according to 'dialectical tensions between threat and resource, invisibility and exposure, and mobility and immobility'.[33] Thus, although we often think of telecommunications as enabling and empowering a host of players in the global community, telephoning practices remain dependent on – and in fact contribute to – imbalances in existing structures of power. McCarren points out, for example, that new developments in global telecommunications indicate 'not equal access to the same level of technology for all, but rather the continuation of a "time-lag" in the former colonies; in spite of the synchronicity and instantaneity of techno-theory, there remain significant differences in techno-practices'.[34] For the Palestinian, this means that calling does not necessarily correspond to getting through.

Barghouti's telephone can be usefully read in the context of Helga Tawil-Souri's extensive research into the relationship between technology, media, territory and politics in the Middle East. Her research confirms that telephony, for the Palestinian, is a political act: 'something as benign as a telephone call – its underlying infrastructure, its political geography, and its political economy', she writes, 'is a dynamic manifestation of the tensions between Israeli practices of control and bordering on the one hand, and Palestinian attempts to mitigate or negate these on the other'.[35] Tawil-Souri states that rather than abolishing distance, the media infrastructure and telephone networks within Israel-Palestine 'are not in and of themselves boundless and open' but function as 'politically defined territorial spaces of control'.[36] Telephone wires and cellular flows are therefore as caught up in the battle for territory as bricks and mortar. Arguing that the telephone is not simply a metaphor for the conflict but is in fact 'the conflict in material form', Tawil-Souri explores the politicization of technology and demonstrates that, for the displaced Palestinian, keeping in touch necessarily demands crossing entrenched geographical, political and cultural lines.[37]

The telecommunication infrastructure in Israel and Palestine has experienced phenomenal growth over the last four decades. This growth, however, is acutely imbalanced, unfairly managed and frequently used to meet political ends. Tawil-Souri points out that mobile phones (and the use of telephone lines to send faxes and emails from the Occupied Territories) were banned under military rule imposed in 1989.[38] Without access to wireless communications, Palestinians had to rely on restricted access to the landline, which was then run by the Israeli Ministry of Communications. Moreover, Bezeq, the government-owned company set up in 1984 to provide all services in the region, was heavily burdened by bureaucracy and inefficient operating systems, and because of this, Palestinian customers often had to wait for years for a line to be installed. These delays meant that, as Tawil-Souri reports, only 2 per cent of Palestinians had a landline installed at home in the early 1990s.[39] Forbidden from developing their own infrastructure, the capacity for Palestinians to make calls was determined entirely by the Israeli regime. 'Circumventing regulations on landlines',

Tawil-Souri points out, was 'impossible': 'if the town was not connected to the network, there was simply nothing to do about it; if the town was connected but Bezeq did not connect the household, or took ten years to do so, nothing could be done about that either.'[40] 'Telephonically', she concludes, 'Palestinians were enclavized, living under a regime that restricted access to the outside world and to each other.'[41]

On the surface, this appeared to shift following the Oslo Accords, with the second 1995 Accord stating: 'Israel recognizes that the Palestinian side has the right to build and operate separate and independent communication systems and infrastructures including telecommunication networks.'[42] This implies that responsibility for telecommunications would be handed over to the Palestinian Authority, enabling it to establish its own infrastructure. However, there are a number of significant caveats: apparently in order to maintain standards, the 1995 agreement also states that while Palestinians are able to develop and import new telephone equipment and services, this can take place 'only when the independent Palestinian network is operational'; moreover, as Hawil-Souri notes, an annex to the Accord insists that 'frequencies will be assigned upon specific requests' or 'as soon as any need arises'.[43] Thus, although Palestinians have the right to establish telecommunications, the Oslo Accords specify that Israel will continue to control the allocation of frequency and bandwidth and will determine when and where new infrastructure can be built. Accordingly, Palestinian networks in the first years of the twenty-first century were quickly saturated. As a result, telephone traffic was rerouted back to Israel's own networks and Palestinians were forced to subscribe to Israeli service providers against their political beliefs.

Indeed, for Barghouti, the telephone's participation in the regime is extended rather than curtailed by the development of cellular technologies. In *I Saw Ramallah*, for instance, he directly addresses the impact of the mobile phone on telecommunications within and beyond Palestine, remarking that 'the latest manifestation of power and status for the Arab parvenu is the mobile phone':

> On the West Bank and Gaza the telephone has developed into the mobile carried in the pockets of the representatives of the newborn Authority in a way that antagonizes ordinary citizens. They are antagonized even though they know that normal landlines are not available on the West Bank and Gaza and that there is a kind of necessity for the mobile.[44]

But the ability to carry a mobile phone in the West Bank and Gaza is, as Barghouti remarks, at odds with the political agency of the Palestinian: 'The marks of personal power do not fit with the absence of their national power or with the power of Palestinians in general according to the strange arrangements of Oslo.'⁴⁵ This is perhaps best exemplified by the fact that, for the Palestinian, sufficient bandwidth to make a call is far from guaranteed. As Tawil-Souri explains: 'While Palestinian mobile phone users can carry their phones around with them (and thus can be considered "mobile"), how far signals reach and where the infrastructure of Palestinian cellular networks reach are territorially defined by the logic of occupation.'⁴⁶ As a result, Barghouti's telephone is caught in a double bind: 'Especially in its dependence on Israeli infrastructure, telecommunications demonstrate Oslo's core paradox: self-determination under continued occupation.'⁴⁷ Another way of putting this: calling without calling.

Although Palestinian networks are now in operation, a number of restrictions on calling remain. This is explored in Yasmin El-Rifae's 2017 essay 'Where Does Palestine Begin?', published in *This Is Not a Border*. Discussing the role of telecommunications in refiguring bordered spaces, and the development of legal Palestinian networks run by Jawwal and Wataniya in the Occupied Territories, El-Rifae writes: 'We drive through Ramallah, capital of politics and finance for the would-be Palestinian state. Here you buy your Jawwal or Wataniya SIM card for use in the West Bank. Palestinian phone operators have not been allowed to provide 3G, although we hear that might change now.'⁴⁸ In fact, according to news reports, spectrum allocation remains a problem to this day, and although 3G service was launched in the West Bank in 2018, service in the Gaza strip at the time of writing is still restricted.⁴⁹ The situation is further compounded by the physical geography of the region. The hilly terrain of the West Bank results in a significantly reduced signal. As a result, El-Rifae points out, Palestinians are forced to circumvent the restrictions: 'Some people manage to buy Israeli SIM cards, either in Israeli cities or from rough neighbourhoods near the separation wall, where they are on sale along with other contraband such as drugs and weapons.'⁵⁰ The Israeli SIM cards – which are strictly forbidden – El-Rifae explains, 'will pick up 3G from settlement communication towers sometimes, especially in the hillier parts of Nablus and Ramallah, near land with the densest settlements'.⁵¹ But for El-Rifae, the construction and location of these cell phone towers are symptomatic of the political climate and imbalance of power: 'If you are looking for a West Bank settlement', she writes, 'look for a tower. They go up first, poking out of the hills like flagpoles, and the settlers follow.'⁵² The erection of Israeli cell phone towers, she continues, is central to the establishment of illegal settlements in Palestinian territory, revealing that rather than reflecting the political dynamic, the construction of telephone infrastructure actively shapes it. And this shaping reveals the three-dimensional nature of border politics in the region: this is not simply the carving up of land but it also involves the battle for air. Describing visiting the old city of Hebron, El-Rifae writes:

> We look up, and Israel lives above the wire mesh which catches its rocks, its garbage, although not its urine. Israel is in the upper floors of houses taken over and occupied by settler families, or turned into watchtowers for the soldiers who protect them. Palestine on the ground floor, on the street level, and Israel between the wire mesh and the sky.[53]

By inviting the reader to 'look up', El-Rifae thus introduces the politics of the sky.

Vertical architecture

The vertical construction of space in Palestine is played out in *I Was Born There, I Was Born Here* when Barghouti recalls his journey by taxi to the border. Attempting to avoid a road block, the car is lifted by a crane over a gaping crater:

> The suspended bubble of air in which we seven are swinging is now our place of exile from this earth. It is our disabled will and our attempt, in a mixture of courage and fear, to impose our will through wit and cunning. This bubble of air is the unyielding Occupation itself. It is the rootless roaming of the Palestinians through the air of others' countries. In the world's air we seek refuge from our earth. We sink into the upper spaces. We sink upward.[54]

The fact that Barghouti seeks freedom in the air is troubled by the military's control of airspace in the Occupied Territories – and this includes, of course, the control of cellular flows, frequencies and bandwidths. By introducing this third dimension, both El-Rifae and Barghouti highlight the ways that the battles for territory extend above ground and into the sky – a dimension of the debate that can be read alongside Eyal Weizman's model of vertical architecture.

Weizman opens *Hollow Land* – his seminal work on the political architecture of Palestine – by recalling that in 1999 a number of Israeli settlers complained of poor cellular reception on a particular bend in the main highway from Jerusalem to the northern West Bank.[55] Although officially owned by local Palestinian farmers, the hilltop overlooking this bend in the road was named after the Biblical town Migron and was occupied by two Israeli settlers. The cell phone provider in the area at that time agreed to erect an antenna on the hill in order to improve communications on the highway. Weizman explains that 'according to the emergency powers invested in the Israeli military [...] the construction of a cellphone antenna could be considered a security issue, and could therefore be undertaken on private lands without obtaining the owners' consent'.[56] Thus, the Israel Electric Corporation connected the hilltop to the grid, although at the time (May 2001), delays meant that only a fake antenna was constructed. A security guard was employed to keep an eye on the fake post; his family moved with him, and then other families joined, and despite being a territory legally owned by Palestinians and overlooked by a fake antenna, Migron eventually established itself as a significant Israeli outpost. In 2011, prior to its dismantlement, it was reported to house fifty families.[57] Migron is not the only outpost established around a cell phone antenna; such cellular hotspots become, Weizman writes, the focus for territorial struggle: 'the energy field of the antenna was not only electromagnetic, but also political, serving as a centre for the mobilizing, channelling, coalescing and organizing of political forces and processes of various kinds'.[58] Built with the aim of influencing state planning and the 'Israeli' frontier, these outposts contribute to what Weizman refers to as the 'political plastic' of the Occupied Territories.

Weizman's *Hollow Land* is interested in reading architecture as 'a conceptual way of understanding political issues as constructed realities'.[59] As such, Weizman points out that the territorial and political boundaries operate across multiple dimensions. Explaining that the division between Israel and Palestine is not simply articulated on the surface of the landscape, but exists 'throughout its depth', Weizman articulates a 'politics of verticality', involving the control by Israel of 'the vast water aquifer in the subterrain beneath them, as well as the militarized airspace above them'.[60] For Weizman, this vertical architecture includes the Israeli control of the electromagnetic spectrum, exposing the ways that territorial conflict operates in political, conceptual, material and immaterial terms, and often in invisible ways.

Connecting impossible lines

In order to think further about this invisible architecture, I'd like to suggest that the core paradox between here and there in Palestine might be read alongside Derrida's writing about the region. Of course, to bring together the work of Barghouti (a Palestinian in exile) and Derrida (a French-Algerian Jew) may appear to cross the wires. However, by arguing that there is a connecting line between these two writers, I hope to demonstrate that their texts have the capacity for cross-cultural conversation. In so doing, I seek to explore the ways that bringing together Barghouti and Derrida might also open up new possibilities of calling the other, perhaps even living together, down the line.

It is necessary to preface this by acknowledging that the relationship between deconstruction and the question of Palestine is a complex and contentious one. Some, such as Christopher Wise, accuse Derrida of a Eurocentric and Jewish-bias, arguing that he ignores the military realities of the Israeli regime.[61] Others, however, argue for a more generous reading: Declan Wiffen, for instance, proposes that the relationship between Derrida and Palestine has been neglected for far too long, and Caroline Rooney suggests that 'the Palestinians are where deconstruction could be in the future'.[62] In fact, for Derrida, 'the war for the "appropriation of Jerusalem" is today the world war. It is happening everywhere, it is the world, it is today the singular figure of its being "out of joint".[63] Jerusalem is, he writes in *The Gift of Death*, 'a holy place but also a place that is in dispute, radically and rabidly, fought over by all the monotheisms, by all the religions of the unique and transcendent God, of the absolute other'.[64] Asking 'Am I in Jerusalem?', Derrida shows that living in Jerusalem is not a straightforward matter:

> This is a question to which one will never respond in the present tense, only in the future or in the past anterior .... Am I in Jerusalem or elsewhere, very far from the Holy City? Under what conditions does one find oneself in Jerusalem? Is it enough to be there physically, as one says, and to live in places that carry this name, as I am now doing? What is it to live in Jerusalem? This is not easy to decide.[65]

Complicating the relations between here and there, near and far, absence and presence, past, present and future, Derrida's question 'Am I in Jerusalem?' mirrors the very same disruptive logic as the telephone. Moreover, it is to the telephone that he once again turns when offering his fullest account of his position on the question of Palestine. This is in conversation with Élisabeth Roudinesco, where he makes it clear that 'I have no particular hostility in principle toward the state of Israel, but I have almost always judged quite harshly the policies of the Israeli governments in relation to the Palestinians'.[66] What is particularly interesting here is that this acknowledgement comes in the form of a telephone call – a passage worth citing in full:

> An anecdote: Some time ago, someone I didn't know called me on the telephone. From the Centre de Documentation Juive: 'My son is writing a thesis on Israel at the Sorbonne. He heard that you were in Tel Aviv two years ago and that you gave a "speech" which the Israeli press reported on. He would like to get a copy.'

I didn't give a lecture a Tel Aviv, I told her; rather I spoke, in front of a large audience and as part of a discussion, about what I thought of the situation and the political stakes, and notably what I disapproved of in Israeli politics. I do so carefully, politely, I believe, but frankly and firmly. Since I had no legible trace of this improvisation, aside from a brief introduction, I told my interlocutor that if her son was interested in what I think of Israel he could find what he's looking for in certain texts of mine. In general, I added, although the conditions of the foundation of the state of Israel remain for me a tangled knot of painful questions that I could not possibly address over the phone (and even if it is considered a given that every state, that every foundation itself is founded in violence, and is by definition unable to justify itself) I have a great many reasons to believe that it is *for the best*, all things considered, and in the interests of the greatest number of people, including the Palestinians, including the other states in the region, to consider this foundation, despite its originary violence, as henceforth irreversible – on the condition that neighbourly relations be established either with a Palestinian state endowed with *all* its rights, in the fullest sense of the term, 'state' (at least insofar as anything remains of this full sense and of sovereignty in general; another very serious question I must leave aside for now while briefly relating, in an interview, a telephone interview), or, at the centre of the same 'sovereign' and binational 'state', with a Palestinian people freed from all oppression or from all intolerable segregation. I have no particular hostility in principle toward the state of Israel, but I have almost always judged quite harshly the policies of the Israeli governments in relation to the Palestinians. I have often said so publicly, in particular in Jerusalem, for example, in a lecture I gave quite a long time ago, which was published in more than one language, during the period when one spoke of 'occupied territories' etc. After a few more sentences along these lines, I heard on the other end of the line: 'I see. Well, that's what I suspected.'[67]

Notwithstanding the significance of Derrida's comments on sovereignty and state in this anecdote, it is thanks to what Martin McQuillan calls 'Derrida's unnamed telephonic interrogator' that we have his much-deferred statement on the Palestinian situation.[68] But while commentators frequently debate Derrida's final position with respect to the conflict, they neglect to interrogate the very self-conscious role of the telephone in this exchange, and the ways in which the telephone itself might contribute to rethinking the relationship between the State of Israel and the Palestinian people.

The year 2012 marked the publication in English of Derrida's own essay on the question of Palestine. In 'Avowing – the Impossible', Derrida argues that living together means 'being-with-oneself', with a oneself that is 'shared or divided, enclosed, multiplied, or torn, open too, in any case anachronistic in its very present, at once increased and dislocated by the mourning or the promise of the other in oneself [...] an other outside of oneself in oneself'.[69] Living together thus means being open to the other, to the other within the self, and to whatever form it may take. He goes on to include the effects of technological others, 'from television to Internet and cell phones, wireless communication, or satellites', all of which 'take into account what occurs [...] to that which is called the proximity of the other in the present'.[70] Multiplying, accelerating and extending the reach of communication, Derrida points to the way that such technologies

> unsettle *at once* all conditions: conditions of being-together (the supposed proximity, in the same instant, in the same place and the same territory, as if the unicity of a place on earth, of a soil, were becoming more and more – as one says of a telephone and in the measure of the said telephone – *portable*) *and* the conditions of the living in its technological relation to the nonliving, to hetero- or homo-grafting, to prosthesis, artificial insemination, cloning, and so on.[71]

All this is in operation throughout Derrida's account of Jerusalem, a Jerusalem where the conditions of being-together – living in proximity, in the same place and in the same territory, at the same time and yet also out of joint – are at once most pressing. We have seen throughout this chapter that the telephone contributes to the distortion of distance in the Occupied Territories, but if the telephone has the capacity to unsettle at once all conditions – the conditions of here and there, distance and proximity, presence and absence, life and death – might it also have the potential to refigure our understanding of territory, of history, and of being (together)? I propose that even as it plays into the topologies of power in Israel-Palestine, the telephone also has the potential to challenge this dynamic, exposing the ways in which notions of self and other are always already ruptured. In so doing, the telephone invites us to rethink what it means to live with the other within oneself, to be together and apart.

Derrida returns to the telephone later in 'Avowing – the Impossible', describing his first visit to Jerusalem in 1982. Michal Govrin, an Israeli friend, takes him to the cemetery at the Mount of Olives in Jerusalem. They enter the Hevra Kadisha, which is, Derrida explains, 'the institution responsible for the difficult administration of the famous cemetery: allocation of plots, decisions as to the "concessions," transport of bodies, often costly operations, from distant countries, and most often the United States, and so on'.[72] Although this is prior to the widespread use of the mobile phone, Derrida is struck by the telecommunication devices that facilitate these negotiations: '[the men]

display a feverish activity around walkie-talkies, telephones, and computers that ostensibly link them to all the places in the world from which one begs them, at any cost, for a place in the cemetery'.[73] It is in the context of this cemetery, and considering the decisions about burial made by the men who work in its office, that Derrida asks: 'What does "living together" mean when the most urgent thing is to choose, while living and in the first place, a last place, an apparently irreplaceable place … ?'[74] Explaining that even before the mobile phone, all these 'little prosthetic machines', as he calls them, make 'all these here-nows infinitely proximate and substitutable', the political situation that keeps Palestinians out of their homeland means that 'New York could appear closer than Gaza (with or without airport), and I could have the feeling of being closer to some other at the other end of the world than to some neighbor, some friend from West Jerusalem or East Jerusalem'.[75] Derrida continues: 'To ask oneself then, on a cell phone, whether Jerusalem is in Jerusalem, is perhaps no longer to trust, like others in older times, the distinction between earthly Jerusalem and heavenly Jerusalem'.[76] Extending the conversation beyond the living, Derrida's spectral telephone not only disrupts the relationship between Palestine and Israel but also ruptures the distinctions between living and dying, then and now, there and here, together and apart.

In a later tribute to Derrida, Govrin turns to the ongoing impact of the telephone on his relationship with Jerusalem. After the initial visit in 1982, she recalls, there were four subsequent visits, and 'following the visits there were books, letters, and phone calls arriving, from Paris to Jerusalem. In our telephone conversations during the short time of peace and many periods of tension and war, always, at a certain point in the conversation, a change in his voice would occur and with it the question: "How is Jerusalem?"'[77] Derrida's contact with Israel is always, in one sense or another, mediated via the telephone. Govrin continues:

> In phone calls to Jerusalem at the time of the first Intifada, at the time of the Gulf War, in the years of the terrorist attacks of the Second Intifada. Always, at a certain point in our conversation the sigh 'Ahh, Jerusalem' was uttered, and in it distance and closeness, criticism and worry, 'the escape from … ' and 'drawing close to' were all interwoven […]. In the coming years, again, as they always did in periods of political violence and terror, anxious phone calls reached Jerusalem from Paris with nearness and distance intertwined.[78]

Referring repeatedly to both the spatial and the temporal ambiguities of the region, Govrin demonstrates the ways that Derrida's proximity to Jerusalem is dissolved through and on the telephone. Moreover, in conversation with Derrida, she shows that this is a call that resonates beyond here and there, then and now; it is a call that always operates in the future to come and beyond the grave.

Notwithstanding their significant differences, both Barghouti and Derrida, therefore, use the telephone to draw attention to the proximity within the distance, to the other within the self, and to the there within the here. And although these two writers are, in many respects, very far apart, their works stage some remarkable connections that play out the paradoxical force of the telephone in order to overturn our commonly held assumptions about who, what and how we call. This is not to diminish the complexity of the situation, nor is it an attempt to reduce the history of the region to a single telephone conversation. But reading the telephone in Barghouti and Derrida does open up new possibilities for talking and listening. For, even as their tele-technological writings repeatedly tap into the syntagmatic logic imposed on Palestine – the fact of calling without calling – the conversation between the texts also suggests the value of a telephonic relation between self and other – the possibility, perhaps, of living with 'the other in oneself [...] an other outside of oneself in oneself'.[79] Thus, I'd like to conclude with the necessary but impossible suggestion that there is a connecting line between these two writers – a line that opens up the possibility that their texts might be calling to each other and, in so doing, renegotiating the limits of the exchange. Moreover, in opening up the lines between Barghouti and Derrida, I propose that a rethinking of the telephone and the structures of power that determine its usage might also ignite new conversations about our capacity to use tele-technologies for talking and listening across different cultures, different places and different times.

Notes

1   Mourid Barghouti, *I Saw Ramallah*, trans. Ahdaf Soueif (London: Bloomsbury, 2005), 11.
2   Ibid.
3   John Caputo, *The Prayers and Tears of Jacques Derrida: Religion without Religion* (Bloomington, IN: Indiana University Press, 1997), 100. See, for example, Derrida's use of 'Suspending without Suspending', in Jacques Derrida, *On Touching – Jean-Luc Nancy*, trans. Christine Irizarry (Stanford, CA: Stanford University Press, 2005), 288.
4   Barghouti, *I Saw Ramallah*, 126.

5 Mourid Barghouti, *I Was Born There, I Was Born Here*, trans. Humphrey Davies (London: Bloomsbury, 2012), 33.
6 Ibid.
7 Ibid., 213.
8 Richard Falk, 'How to Live Together Well: Interrogating the Israel/Palestine Conflict', in *Living Together: Jacques Derrida's Communities of Violence and Peace*, ed. Elisabeth Weber (New York: Fordham University Press, 2012), 275–92 (276–7).
9 Ibid., 277.
10 See, for example, Anna Bernard, *Rhetorics of Belonging: Nation, Narration, and Israel/Palestine* (Liverpool: Liverpool University Press, 2013), 67–88; Tahia Abdel Nasser, 'Between Exile and Elegy, Palestine and Egypt: Mourid Barghouti's Poetry and Memoirs', *Journal of Arabic Literature*, 45.2/3 (2014), 244–64; Salam Mir, 'Mourid Barghouti: The Blessings of Exile', *Arab Studies Quarterly*, 37.4 (2015), 311–33.
11 Barghouti, *I Saw Ramallah*, 24.
12 Ibid., 109–10.
13 Ibid., 108.
14 Ibid., 129, 133.
15 Ibid., 133.
16 Barghouti, *I Was Born There*, 68.
17 Barghouti, *I Saw Ramallah*, 126.
18 Ibid.
19 Ibid., 4.
20 Ibid.
21 Ibid., 126.
22 Ibid., 127, 168.
23 Avital Ronell, *The Telephone Book: Technology, Schizophrenia, Electric Speech* (Lincoln, NE: University of Nebraska Press, 1989), 3.
24 Barghouti, *I Saw Ramallah*, 164. Operating a spectral switchboard, Barghouti's family is haunted by the call of death in the night: 'At one-thirty in the morning Mounif's voice came to me across the phone – my father had died' (Barghouti, *I Saw Ramallah*, 135). In an uncanny scene of repetition, this thanatographical call is repeated seven years later, on 8 November 1993, while he lunches with Radwa and Tamim in Cairo: 'I went to answer. My younger brother 'Alaa's voice, speaking from Doha. His weeping voice said a few words I do not remember. A coldness ran through my shoulders. I do not remember what I said. What I remember clearly is that Radwa jumped out of her seat, her face pale, asking what had happened. I said: "Mounif is dead. Dead"' (164).

25 Felicia McCarren, 'Téléphone Arabe: From Child's Play to Terrorism – The Poetics and Politics of Postcolonial Telecommunication', *Journal of Postcolonial Writing*, 44.3 (2008), 289–305 (290).
26 Barghouti, *I Was Born There*, 79.
27 Ibid., 79–80.
28 Juan Goytisolo, 'Palestinian Notebooks: First Notebook – From Netanya to Ramallah', trans. Peter Bush (n.d.), available at: http://www.mafhoum.com/press3/92Ca11.htm (accessed 6 June 2020), cited in Derek Gregory, 'Palestine and the "War on Terror"', *Comparative Studies of South Asia, Africa and the Middle East*, 24.1 (2004), 183–95 (188).
29 Michel Serres with Bruno Latour, *Conversations on Science, Culture, and Time*, trans. Roxanne Lapidus (Ann Arbor, MI: University of Michigan Press, 1995), 60.
30 Ibid.
31 John Allen, 'Topological Twists: Power's Shifting Geographies', *Dialogues in Human Geography*, 1.3 (2011), 283–98 (284).
32 Foundation for Middle East Peace, 'Sharon's New Map', *Report on Israeli Settlement in the Occupied Territories*, 12.3 (2002), 1–6 (6), cited in Gregory, 'Palestine and the "War on Terror"', 188.
33 Marie Gillespie, Souad Osseiran and Margie Cheesman, 'Syrian Refugees and the Digital Passage to Europe: Smartphone Infrastructure and Affordances', *Social Media and Society*, 4.1 (2018), 1–12 (10).
34 McCarren, 'Téléphone Arabe', 289.
35 Helga Tawil-Souri, 'Cellular Borders: Dis/Connecting Phone Calls in Israel-Palestine', in *Signal Traffic: Critical Studies of Media Infrastructures*, ed. Lisa Parks and Nicole Starosielski (Champaign, IL: University of Illinois Press, 2015), 157–80 (157).
36 Ibid., 158.
37 Ibid., 157.
38 Ibid., 162.
39 Ibid.
40 Ibid., 163.
41 Helga Tawil-Souri, 'Networking Palestine: The Development and Limitations of Television and Telecommunications since 1993', in *The Oslo Accords 1993–2013: A Critical Assessment*, ed. Petter Bauck and Mohammed Omer (Cairo: American University in Cairo Press, 2013), 217–29 (223).
42 Oslo 2, annex III, cited in Tawil-Souri, 'Cellular Borders', 163–4.
43 Ibid., 164.
44 Barghouti, *I Saw Ramallah*, 110, 109–110.
45 Ibid., 110.
46 Tawil-Souri, 'Cellular Borders', 176.

47 Tawil-Souri, 'Networking Palestine', 225.
48 Yasmin El-Rifae, 'Where Does Palestine Begin?', in *This Is Not a Border: Reportage and Reflection from the Palestine Festival of Literature*, ed. Ahdaf Soueif and Omar Robert Hamilton (London: Bloomsbury, 2017), 11–15 (12).
49 Ali Sawafta, 'Palestinians Get 3G Mobile Services in West Bank', *Reuters* (24 January 2018), available at: https://www.reuters.com/article/israel-palestinians-telecom/palestinians-get-3g-mobile-services-in-west-bank-idUSL8N1PJ3FW (accessed 6 June 2020); Mohammad Al-Kasim, 'Palestinians Eagerly Await Arrival of 4G Cellular Service', *Jerusalem Post* (31 August 2021), available at: https://www.jpost.com/middle-east/palestinians-eagerly-await-arrival-of-4g-cellular-service-678301 (accessed 2 February 2022). Digital infrastructure remains significantly underdeveloped in Gaza; on 10 May 2022, the World Bank reported to the Ad Hoc Liaison Committee (AHLC), who coordinate the delivery of international aid to Palestine: 'The GoI [Government of Israel] has not yet released mobile broadband internet frequency spectrum bands for use in Gaza. Internet is available and accessible through Wi-Fi hotspots in Gaza, with one-quarter of households still unable to access the internet' (World Bank, *Economic Monitoring Report to the Ad Hoc Liaison Committee* (Washington, DC: World Bank Group, 2022), 29, available at: https://documents.worldbank.org/en/publication/documents-reports/documentdetail/099407305062233565/idu091fed1da019eb042d6090100a9320aa572de (accessed 7 August 2022)).
50 El-Rifae, 'Where Does Palestine Begin?', 12.
51 Ibid.
52 Ibid.
53 Ibid.
54 Barghouti, *I Was Born There*, 19.
55 Eyal Weizman, *Hollow Land: Israel's Architecture of Occupation* (London: Verso, 2007), 1.
56 Ibid., 2.
57 Chaim Levinson, 'Israel's Supreme Court Orders State to Dismantle Largest West Bank Outpost', *Haaretz* (2 August 2011), available at: https://www.haaretz.com/1.5039235 (accessed 6 June 2020).
58 Weizman, *Hollow Land*, 2.
59 Ibid., 6.
60 Ibid., 4, 12.
61 Christopher Wise, 'Deconstruction and Zionism: Jacques Derrida's "Specters of Marx"', *Diacritics*, 31.1 (2001), 55–72.
62 Declan Wiffen, *Deconstruction and the Question of Palestine: Bearing Witness to the Undeniable* (PhD thesis: University of Kent, July 2014), 7; Caroline Rooney, 'Derrida and Said: Ships That Pass in the Night', in *Edward Said and the Literary,*

Social and Political World, ed. R. Ghosh (London and New York: Routledge, 2009), 36–52 (49).
63 Jacques Derrida, *Specters of Marx: The State of the Debt, the Work of Mourning, and the New International*, trans. Peggy Kamuf (London: Routledge, 1994), 58.
64 Jacques Derrida, *The Gift of Death and Literature in Secret*, trans. David Wills (Chicago: University of Chicago Press, 2008), 70.
65 Jacques Derrida, 'Am I in Jerusalem?', in *Counterpath: Traveling with Jacques Derrida*, ed. Catherine Malabou and Jacques Derrida, trans. David Wills (Stanford, CA: Stanford University Press, 2004), 120–1 (121).
66 Jacques Derrida and Élisabeth Roudinesco, *For What Tomorrow ... A Dialogue*, trans. Jeff Fort (Stanford, CA: Stanford University Press, 2004), 118.
67 Ibid., 118–19.
68 Martin McQuillan, 'Clarity and Doubt: Derrida among the Palestinians', *Paragraph*, 39.2 (2016), 220–37 (225).
69 Jacques Derrida, 'Avowing – the Impossible: "Returns," Repentance, and Reconciliation', trans. Gil Anidjar, in *Living Together: Jacques Derrida's Communities of Violence and Peace*, ed. Elisabeth Weber (New York: Fordham University Press, 2012), 18–41 (20).
70 Ibid., 21.
71 Ibid., 31.
72 Ibid., 40.
73 Ibid.
74 Ibid.
75 Ibid.
76 Ibid.
77 Michal Govrin, 'From Jerusalem to Jerusalem – a Dedication', trans. Atar Hadari, in *Living Together: Jacques Derrida's Communities of Violence and Peace*, ed. Elisabeth Weber (New York: Fordham University Press, 2012), 259–74 (261).
78 Ibid., 267, 272.
79 Derrida, 'Avowing – the Impossible', 20.

5

Distress calls

Shortly after midnight GMT on 27 March 2011, a 10-metre-long rubber boat left the port of Tripoli with seventy-two refugees on board.[1] Also on board was a GPS device and a satellite phone provided by members of the Libyan military, who were fully aware of the boat's 'illegal' passengers and its final destination: the boat was heading for Lampedusa, an island in the Mediterranean Sea off the coast of Southern Italy. Around fifteen hours after its departure from Tripoli, having covered only half the total distance of the journey, with fuel running low and with neither food nor drinking water, the people on board realized they would not be able to reach Lampedusa and used the satellite phone to call for help. The call was answered and requests for assistance were passed to the NATO maritime command in Naples as well as other participating European states. Further, due to the military intervention in Libya launched by the multistate NATO-led coalition just eight days previously, the boat's journey took place during a period of intense maritime surveillance: it is reported that at least thirty-eight naval vessels were in operation in the area at the time of the journey. Despite this, no help was provided and the people on board were left to drift for fourteen days without food, water, fuel or medical assistance – a direct contravention to the 'duty to rescue' set out in the United Nations Convention on the Law of the Sea.[2] On 10 April, the boat was washed up at Zliten, a Libyan coastal city 160 kilometres east of Tripoli from where they had departed. Only eleven of the seventy-two passengers were alive; one of the survivors died on the beach, and another in prison shortly after they were detained by the Libyan military. The nine survivors were eventually released five days later to a situation so desperate that some of them would attempt to make the crossing again: in the words of Christina Sharpe who reads the atrocity in terms of 'wake work', they were 'cast behind, set adrift, once again'.[3]

The incident sparked international outrage and demands for accountability by organizations including Human Rights Watch; the French NGO GISTI; and the Committee on Migration, Refugees and Population of the Parliamentary

Assembly of the Council of Europe, who appointed Dutch Senator Tineke Strik to investigate. Strik's report, 'Lives Lost in the Mediterranean Sea: Who Is Responsible?', was presented in Brussels on 29 March 2012.[4] A year after the atrocity, on 11 April 2012, Charles Heller and Lorenzo Pezzani, researchers working as part of the Forensic Architecture project based at Goldsmiths, University of London, together with SITU Studio, a creative architecture practice based in New York, published 'Forensic Oceanography: Report on the "Left-To-Die Boat"'.[5] Investigating the militarized space of the Mediterranean as a border zone, the researchers describe their technique of using surveillance technologies '"against the grain"' in order to exercise a '"disobedient gaze", one that refuses to disclose clandestine migration but seeks to unveil instead the violence of the border regime'.[6] Building on existing investigations into the incident, the researchers from Forensic Architecture conducted extensive spatial analyses including Synthetic Aperture Radar imagery, geospatial mapping, and drift modelling. Using this data alongside survivor testimonies, their report concludes that the actions and inactions of several international parties including the UK led directly to the 'slow death' of the passengers:

> At least one patrol aircraft, one helicopter, two fishing boats, and a military ship, whose identities still remain unknown, allegedly had direct contact with the boat. Moreover, the Italian and Maltese MRCC as well as participating states/NATO forces present in the area were informed of the distress of the boat and of its location, and had the technical and logistical ability to assist it. Despite all this, none of these actors intervened in a way that could have averted the tragic fate of the people on the boat.[7]

The report by Forensic Architecture provides the source material for two recent poetic responses to the humanitarian crisis: Caroline Bergvall's *Drift* published in 2014 and Asiya Wadud's *Syncope* published in 2019 both draw directly from Forensic Architecture's findings, as well as citing survivor testimonies by Dan Haile Gebre, Abu Kurke Kebato, Elias Mohammed Kadi, Filmon Weldemichail Teklegergis, Bilal Yacoub Idris and Mohammd Ahmed Ibrahim. In so doing, both poets engage with questions regarding refugee voices and the ethics of representation, seeking to move beyond ventriloquism or instrumentalization by staging the failures of speech that demand a listening beyond words.[8] Building on my discussion in Chapter 4 of the capacity for the telephone to connect and disconnect across national and cultural borders in Israel-Palestine, this chapter extends my analysis of the relationship between telecommunications, voice and power by exploring the telephone call in literary representations of refugees lost at sea. In particular, I examine how Bergvall and Wadud enact the 'distress signals' sent and received during the boat's journey as a way to think through the political as well as literary representations of calling.

In order to unpack the complex relationship between telephony, displacement, hospitality and language, however, it is first necessary to outline the geopolitical and military conditions that led to the events in the Mediterranean and to address the interaction of scientific and poetic discourses in the texts that seek to understand the atrocity. I begin this chapter, therefore, with an introduction to Bergvall and Wadud's documentary poetics, and an account of the technical and archival material on which they draw. In the second part of the chapter, I move on to unpack the wider politics of the distress signal in the refugee journey before opening my discussion to a specific reading of the various technological and more-than-human calls that resonate throughout *Syncope* and *Drift*. Following Adelaide Morris's theory of 'forensic aesthetics', the final part of the chapter turns to ways that the patterns of calling and answering in *Drift* and *Syncope* demand a reframing of the ethico-aesthetics of the telephone.[9] In this way, I argue that the distress call issued from the left-to-die boat operates as microcosm for the broader processes of claiming asylum and the nature of host nations' ethical commitment to refugees.

It is important to acknowledge from the outset, however, that – as Heller, Pezzani and Studio SITU take pains to note in the Forensic Oceanography report – the 'left-to-die boat' is just one incident among many.[10] Accordingly, this chapter seeks to simultaneously recognize the specific losses brought about by these crimes and at the same time to observe the incident's place as part of a much wider pattern of human rights violations in the Mediterranean and beyond. The crime of the 'left-to-die boat' took place in 2011, a year described by the United Nations High Commissioner for Refugees in 2012 as the 'deadliest' in the Mediterranean since the organization began recording these statistics in 2006, estimating that over 1,500 people died while fleeing the conflict in Libya.[11] Despite the increased media attention, however, the death toll continues to rise.[12] On 10 December 2021, for instance, the International Organisation for Migration stated that there had been more than 45,000 deaths since 2014.[13] Unable to unpack the scale or complexity of these incidents, this chapter focuses specifically on the role and representation of the distress signal in accounts of the left-to-die boat. It does so in order to think through the possibilities for a poetics of calling and the potential for literature not only to bear witness to the call but also to initiate new conversations about what it means to answer to it.[14] Rather than seeking to homogenize the refugee experience, then, I explore the ways that the telephone call is vocalized in poetic terms as a starting point for thinking through broader questions regarding the ethics and aesthetics of answerability.

Poetic drift

In 2019, Asiya Wadud's published *Syncope*, a eulogy to all those who have attempted to cross the Central Mediterranean. Set out as one long poem in eleven sections and incorporating hymns by Kofi Awoonor, prose extracts by Christian Wiman and prayers cited by Kapka Kaasabova, *Syncope* draws on the first-hand accounts of survivors of the left-to-die boat that are included in the Forensic Oceanography report.[15] Developing a practice of documentary poetics, Wadud explains in an interview that 'I am interested in the fissures and the breaks, what happens just beyond the frame of the official record'.[16] Exploring the gaps in official accounts of the incident, her text is composed in a first-person plural voice interspersed with white space. As such, the poem is 'a reckoning / a recitation / a dirge / an imprint', calling out for international communities to answer to the crime.[17] But how might it be possible to speak of this event while honouring the voices of those lost? And what kind of poem might bear witness to their call?

Wadud opens the text with three definitions of the noun 'syncope': in medicine, it refers to the 'temporary loss of consciousness caused by a fall in blood pressure'; in linguistics, it signals 'the omission of sounds or letters from within a word, e.g., when probably is pronounced "präblē"'; and in music, it indicates 'a change of rhythm and shift of accent when a normally weak beat is stressed'.[18] These senses of syncope work across Wadud's poem; it is a text structured by loss, interruption and omission. This stands to reason given that the collection turns around the lapse in hospitality provided by international agencies to those in need. The history of the left-to-die boat operates according to this interval or abyss: '*No vessel chose to provide any assistance whatsoever to the passengers*' – a lapse that '*appeared to constitute a severe violation of the legal obligation to provide assistance to any person in distress at sea*'.[19] This gap is made manifest on the page from its opening lines:

there were 38 maritime vessels
they were all ocular if they chose to be[20]

Wadud's use of irregular spacing here highlights the failure of international maritime agencies to respond to calls for help from the overcrowded boat. The use of white space is repeatedly deployed by Wadud, with single lines such as 'our bodies became deadweight' presented in isolation on the page.[21] The syncopal break is further heightened, however, through Wadud's particular use of repetition with omission. Towards the end of the collection, for instance, Wadud writes:

> we doubted our own humanity because
> the rescue boats
> each of them
> saw something we couldn't see
> and
> they
> shirked us[22]

These lines are repeated in the subsequent stanza, but in the second iteration, Wadud replaces 'we doubted our own humanity' with 'we doubled down on our humanity' and omits 'each of them / saw something we couldn't see / and / they': what is removed here is not the humanity of the victims but rather the attention of, and hence response by, the would-be rescue boats.[23] The uneven stagger of the statement foretells the last gasps of breath of those on board whose cries for help were denied: 'O here we are just / drifting / O here we are just drifting'.[24]

The notion of drift can in many ways be taken as a model for *Syncope*, where language and form enact interminable drift through disorienting lineation, linguistic omission and interrupted syntax. Overturning chronology and shifting from the present where 'we live with the wreckage' throughout 'these riven two weeks' to the past 'where we drifted', Wadud ruptures time and tense – a breach that also results in an epistemic break, rending means of both thinking and knowing.[25] Without food or clean water, and exposed to all the elements, the poem's voices repeatedly describe the way that 'time ruptured and folded' for the passengers.[26] In his review of *Syncope*, Daniel Moysaenko argues that this use of repetition is not 'purely for aesthetic purposes' but rather functions to 'better parse chronology, decision, and consequence'.[27] Each of the four repetitions of 'time ruptured and folded', he suggests, resituates the break in an altered context and thereby enfolds a continual pattern of omission and loss into the text; the extended use of iteration thus serves to immerse the reader in the ruptures created by the recurring lapses in hospitality. More than this, however, Wadud also uses this pattern of omission and immersion to draw attention to the other gaps in the text, which are suspended as if to hold open space for the reader to acknowledge their complicity in inaction and its consequences. In a sense, then, *Syncope* reminds us of the absurdity of behaving 'as if there were no fault to lay'.[28] Writing that 'if you've decided that / we're / black mules / mules we know / are not / meant / for / rescue', *Syncope* insists that 'bodies became deadweight'.[29] The victims are Eritrean, Ethiopian, Nigerian, Sudanese, Ghanaian, she writes; they are the 'subalterened / we 72 are human / we 72 are oil slick and black / hungry for a spot of water, bread / recognition as human'.[30] Here, the poem not only gives space to the words of the passengers but also refuses to allow the reader to forget that the failure to rescue at sea is a violation of human rights. In this way, it also speaks to Achille Mbembe's discussion of the 'necropolitical' nature of the policing of Europe's borders, in which the predominant expression of sovereignty is 'the right to kill'.[31] As a result, Mbembe argues, 'vast populations are subjected to conditions of life conferring upon them the status of *living dead*'.[32] Recalling Mbembe's '*death worlds*' and enfolding the reader within the poem's repeated violations, Wadud insists: 'don't call this a tragedy'; this is 'calcified violence / this is vile'.[33]

Wadud is not the first poet to reflect on the left-to-die boat and the passengers' attempts to call for help. *Drift* by French-Norwegian multidisciplinary writer and artist Caroline Bergvall is a composition consisting of multimedia performance, installation and book. The multi-form work which, like *Syncope*, draws on the report by Forensic Architecture, was developed by Bergvall alongside collaborations with Norwegian percussionist Ingar Zach, Swiss visual artist Tomas Köppel and Swiss dramaturge Michèle Pralong, and premiered in Geneva in 2012, touring in the UK in 2014. Also in 2014, *Drift* was published in book form by Nightboat Books with accompanying drawings by Bergvall alongside images produced at macro-magnification by photographer Tom Martin.[34] And in early 2015, it was developed into an exhibition for Callicoon Fine Arts Gallery in New York. The text-based version of *Drift*, which forms the focus of this discussion, is arranged into ten main sections consisting of text, maps, photographs and drawings – 'Lines', 'Seafarer', 'Sighting', 'Report', 'Maps', 'Shake', 'Block 16A6', 'Log', 'Noþing' and 'Þ'.[35] Combining poetry, process notes, extracts from the Forensic Oceanography report and verbatim testimonies from survivors, the work resists categorization. Its shifting manifestations – from 'a vast open syntax of textual mass' to live vocal performance, drawings and prints – are integral to its methods.[36] Reflecting on the composition of the work in an essay entitled 'Infra-materiality and Opaque Drifting', Bergvall notes: 'Back and forth between writing, vocal strategies and performance and historic research, this project would keep on asking questions about the handling and processing of the artistic and poetic material in relation to the human dimensions being presented.'[37]

Looking for lost voices, and using hybrid forms to cross media, languages and times, *Drift* draws on two main intertexts: Anglo-Saxon literature and forensic analysis of contemporary human rights violations. Describing the colliding trajectories of the work, Bergvall situates the anonymous tenth-century Anglo-Saxon poem 'The Seafarer' as one of the 'central pieces of the performance and as a template to [her] own writing'.[38] In a review of the work, David Kaufmann points out that 'The Seafarer' is in Anglo-Saxon, a lost or suppressed language.[39] Part of Bergvall's practice here, then, is in excavating this lost dialect – which includes her recovery of the 'Þ' sign as part of the search for her 'Nordic roots in the English language'.[40] But in thinking about lost language, Bergvall is also thinking about other losses; she explains that *Drift* not only provides 'support for my linguistic excavations and translative elegiac meditations on solitary sailing/flailing/failing' but also enables her to 'delve into the unmoored dimensions of contemporary identity'.[41] Exploring the ways in which the ancient literary journey is echoed in contemporary crossings, she states in her 'Log' that the work's development was in part catalysed by an article she encountered in *The Guardian* on 11 April 2012 regarding the report by Forensic Architecture on the left-to-die boat.[42] Using the report as the second main intertext, the poem thus resonates with contemporary atrocities, where nameless refugees 'drifted far and wide on the high sea', leaving 'earthless orphans / hurdled in containers noodled on plastic beach / in the corner coldest of the storm'.[43] Working transhistorically and transculturally to combine modern and archaic languages and forms, Bergvall finds energy in the friction between the ancient seafarer and the contemporary refugee, between a lost language and contemporary witnessing.

Notwithstanding the experiments with language, form and visual image, *Drift* offers a bare and unadorned account of the left-to-die boat in Section 4 of the text, drawing directly on the research undertaken by Heller, Pozzani and Studio Situ. Entitled 'Report' and occupying eleven pages, this section is presented as white text on a black background – a technique that Áine McMurtry suggests enacts the role of visual surveillance techniques in searching for migrants at sea.[44] The clipped syntax and deliberate repetitions, McMurtry continues, call attention to the facts detailed in the report.[45] Refusing embellishment and allowing only the insertion of black space through paragraph breaks and fragments of survivor testimonies presented in italics, the 'Report' works in stark contrast to the experimental forms throughout the remainder of the text; the friction between the different discourses and styles used by Bergvall enacts the affective clash between different political, humanitarian, historical and cultural accounts of the atrocity. Discussing this methodology in her 'Log', Bergvall notes: 'How can I find an archaeological or forensic method that will help me generate a way of writing that can both speak to today and safely point to tagged and numbered teeth items in the ground. How can I find the tools necessary to dig at whatever is driving me.'[46] Adapting and developing the tools of her source text – the Forensic Oceanography report – Bergvall takes a forensic approach to language:

> I decide to use the narrative of the journey and its harrowing drift, the story told by the survivors and corroborated by the forensic findings. My role will be to shorten the narrative and relay the report's complex piece of memorialisation, interpretation and investigation through live recitation. To register the event by recitation.[47]

Picking up on Bergvall's claim that in forensics 'every action or contact leaves a trace', Adelaide Morris draws attention to the different meanings of the word 'forensics'.[48] Discussing Bergvall's *Drift* alongside M. Nourbse Philip's *Zong!*, she explains that the term 'forensic' not only refers to materials prepared for use in a court of law but also 'implies an active, open-ended process of investigation'; accordingly, her approach to forensic imagination prioritizes creative and affective practices that – in the words of Forensic Architecture – enable 'the expansion of the object's or artifact's expressive potential' rather than empirical truth.[49] Bringing this to bear on Bergvall's poem, Morris asks: 'If the sonic profusion of *Zong!* and *Drift* requires the active, rather than passive, reception of forensic or investigative listening, what might it entail, to return to Bergvall's poem, to start to "pay attention"?'[50] Extending Morris's discussion of forensic listening, this chapter now turns to explore ways of attending to the distress call, but rather than asking only what it might mean to start to 'pay attention', it also considers what it might take to respond or answer to that call.

Priority code distress

In 2011, the United Nations Special Rapporteur Frank La Rue declared the 'freedom to connect' and 'internet access' basic human rights.[51] And a year later, in 2012, the World Bank stated: 'Mobile Communication has arguably had a bigger impact on humankind in a shorter period of time than any other invention in human history.'[52] These reports raise urgent questions about the role of communication technologies for the refugee and migrant. Bridging different locations and cultures, the mobile phone has the capacity to connect people separated by conflict, poverty, disease and natural disaster. As a modern computational device incorporating a camera, videophone, GPS, translation tools and social media apps, it also contributes to contemporary political debates regarding the nation state, migration, politics and power. The role of the mobile phone for the refugee or migrant is, of course, a concept frequently covered in international news and social media with headlines ranging from 'Smartphones are the secret weapon fuelling the great migrant invasion' to 'Syrian woman explains why refugees need smartphones'.[53] These narratives convey what Marie Gillespie describes as 'a deep ambivalence in the coverage of "smartphones and refugees" – a vital tool for refugees and also a potential threat for European citizens due to its power to mobilise refugees'.[54] Thus, although it is often conceptualized as both a tool for civic witnessing and a 'lifeline' for the refugee, it is vital to think beyond the reductive model of 'mobility' seemingly promised by the mobile phone. Sara Ahmed points out in *Queer Phenomenology*, for instance, that 'thinking about the politics of "lifelines" helps us to rethink the relationship between inheritance (the lines that we are given as our point of arrival into familial and social space) and reproduction (the demand that we return the gift of the line by extending that line)'.[55] Although Ahmed is referring to a different context here, her words remain resonant for the way that they prompt questions about the lines that are inherited, the lines that are extended, as well as the lines that are held open and answered to.

The role of the telephone as a thwarted lifeline forms a significant strand of the Forensic Oceanography report into the left-to-die boat, which specifically addresses the relationship between telecommunications and the 'Distress Call'.[56] Drawing on survivor testimonies alongside drift models and Synthetic Aperture Radar data from across Europe, as well as official communications from NATO, the authors of the report explain that the passengers on board the zodiac vessel were given a Thuraya satellite phone with failing batteries.[57] Approximately fifteen hours after the boat's departure from Tripoli, having covered only half the total distance of the journey and with fuel running low, the people on board realized they would not be able to reach Lampedusa and used the satellite phone that they had been given to call for help. They called Father Mussie Zerai – also known as Father Moses or Father Mussie – an Eritrean priest based in the Vatican who has received numerous phone calls from refugees needing help at sea.[58] Both Wadud and Bergvall stress the importance of this call to Father Zerai in their work, with Bergvall giving voice to a survivor: '*At the time we called*

*Father Mussie we had not even covered half the distance.*⁵⁹ She also remarks that although 'several calls' were exchanged, the driver was 'not able to read the boat's GPS' and, moreover, 'the connection between Father Mussie and the migrants was made difficult due to failing batteries on the GPS'.⁶⁰ The evidence presented in the Forensic Oceanography report makes it clear that Father Zerai answered the call and immediately passed the information that he had on to the Italian coastguard. The coastguard duly obtained the location of the boat from the satellite phone provider, but because the vessel was outside the Italian search and rescue zone it chose not to intervene. The Italian coastguard did, however, inform the Maltese coastguard as well as NATO's Maritime Headquarters, and also sent distress signals to all nearby vessels – a signal sent at regular intervals, as repeated twice in Wadud's poem:

> The Maritime Rescue Coordination Centre in Rome
> sent calls
>   every 4 hours
>   for 10 days
> the math a facsimile
> of our need⁶¹

Bergvall conveys the specifics of these calls with forensic detail in *Drift*, citing directly from the Forensic Oceanography report and explaining that 'Rome MRCC sent several distress signals, the first an Enhanced Group Call (EGC) broadcast to all ships transiting in the Sicily Channel at 18:54 GMT via the Immarsat C system'.⁶² Despite the fact that the boat was within NATO's maritime surveillance area when the first distress call was made, no help arrived: NATO's practice at the time was to offer minimal assistance in the hope that any migrant or refugee vessels could reach either Italian or Maltese search and rescue zones. Two hours later, however, a military helicopter passed overhead, swooping low to observe the boat. Wadud writes:

> an unidentified helicopter
> lowers
> biscuits and water by rope
> they photograph us on mobiles
> and view us through binoculars⁶³

The mobile phones in Wadud's account are used to take snapshots of the people on the boat, rather than to offer help. Thus, it is, for Wadud, a spectacle without really seeing: 'let us establish a fact: / eyes are for seeing / naming is for subjugating'.⁶⁴ Believing that the arrival of the helicopter meant that help would be on its way, Bergvall cites the report: 'The captain then threw the GPS, satellite phone and compass into the water because he was afraid that if the SAR team found these on board he would be identified as a smuggler and be deported'.⁶⁵ But the helicopter circled and then departed again.

The report by Forensic Architecture makes it clear that not only were their investigators able to identify the 'last signal' from the phone from data provided by Thuraya, but also that Father Zerai confirmed the exact text and dispatch time of an SMS message that he had sent back to the refugees.⁶⁶ Therefore, the vessel's location can be established with reasonable accuracy at three separate points during the journey. From this, the authors of the report insist that they can 'say with certainty':

> NATO maritime command in Naples and participating states/NATO naval assets were informed of the presence of a vessel in distress, respectively by telephone, fax, and via maritime distress signals. The information received clearly indicated the situation of distress and the necessity to assist the migrants.⁶⁷

The word 'distress' is repeated in both collections, with Bergvall emphasizing 'Priority code DISTRESS'.⁶⁸ Indeed, it has been established that the message sent out by the Italian Coastguard as part of the Enhanced Group Call 'had a priority code marked as "distress", the highest possible in a scale that includes, in decreasing order of urgency, "distress, urgency, safety, and routine"'.⁶⁹ The Forensic Oceanography report confirms: 'The 1979 SAR Convention defines distress as "a situation wherein there is a reasonable certainty that a person, a vessel or other craft is threatened by grave and imminent danger and requires immediate assistance"'; moreover, according to this definition, the boat certainly would have 'required "immediate assistance"'.⁷⁰ In addition, the authors of the report explain that on 8 April 2011, just a few days after the distress call and while the boat was still drifting at sea, the UNHCR's Assistant High Commissioner for Protection Erika Feller had stated that 'any overcrowded boat leaving Libya these days should be considered to be in distress'.⁷¹ Despite this – and notwithstanding the fact that the 1982 United Nations Convention on the Law of the Sea (UNCLOS convention) and the 1974 International Convention for the Safety of Life at Sea (SOLAS convention) both state that all maritime vessels, whether civilian or military, are required to be equipped to receive distress signals and are obliged to respond to such calls – the term 'distress' remains contested.⁷² In the context of assisting migrants in the Mediterranean and specifically in the Sicily Channel, a senior officer of the Armed Forces in Malta (who are responsible for search and rescue operations in the region), claimed: 'Distress is the imminent danger of loss of lives, so if they are sinking it is distress. If they are not sinking it is not distress'.[73]

Thus, with their distress signal unanswered and with no further means of calling for help, the passengers resumed their journey towards Lampedusa, knowing that they did not have enough fuel to reach land. During the next few hours, the boat approached a number of other fishing vessels in the area, pleading for assistance – they were desperately low on fuel and they had neither food nor water – but the other boats all turned away. As it grew dark, a second helicopter flew overhead and then departed. The boat continued to drift for a further eight days, encountering a military vessel some time between 3 and 5 April. By this time, half the passengers had died. The military ship circled the migrant boat several times, witnessing the evident distress of the passengers. Then it too turned away. As each day passed and the boat continued to drift, those on board were forced to evacuate all non-essential objects, including the bodies of their loved ones.

More-than-human calls

The left-to-die boat is thus a story of signals – telephonic and otherwise. From the original call made to Father Zerai by satellite phone to the Maritime Rescue Coordination Centre's repeated signals, Bergvall and Wadud expose not only the potential of the telephone to support the safe passage to Europe but also the dynamics of power that structure the ways that we receive and respond to such calls. Bearing witness to the unanswered telephone in *Syncope*, the distress call is translated as incantations, prayers, echoes, shrieks, songs and more-than-human cries. 'Black mules are not worth the rescue', Wadud writes.[74] Reminding us of the old French *'braire'* for 'to cry', she insists: 'no one hears their urgent braying'.[75] In translating the suppressed distress calls of the passengers to the cries of mules, Wadud frames this as a violation of human rights, in which the vulnerable are reduced to bare life.[76] Later, she transmutes the distress signal into the calls of birds:

> these riven two weeks
> the two weeks where we drifted
> our distress calls like urgent plovers[77]

Known for their 'grating alarm call', plovers are typically waders or shore birds, but many are long-distance migrants; Andrew Darby notes that 'they routinely cross hemispheres'.⁷⁸ Wadud returns to the image of the seabird on several occasions throughout the poem, describing the passengers as watching cormorants in order to 'see how they survived'.⁷⁹ The bird call sounds in Bergvall's poem, too, where the seafarers navigate by stars, by the sun, by the currents, by the movements of fish and sea mammals, and by 'types of birds':

> Show me the wave! Powerful arctic birds inout
> of the rollers cranes goldeneagles shearwaters
> pole to pole longhaul navigators Show me the
> wave! Whaup gulls yap yap yap yap firebirds
> griffins dingbats newly released transgenic flying
> organisms prescient caladrius what warns of ills
> terns searns oncwæd what storm the fishing
> beats Show me! Fly me!⁸⁰

By giving voice to the 'yap yap yap' of the gulls, Bergvall experiments with more-than-human ecologies of sound and language. But while the dying passengers long to take flight – in *Syncope*, for instance, 'let us / try our hand at / flight' – the ambivalence of this image in the refugee context must be remembered: 'Associated with freedom, [flight] is also synonymous with fear.'⁸¹

The bird call resounds again, however, when placed in a wider context of human rights violations in the Mediterranean, suggesting that the birds do not merely call across texts but that they also call up other histories. On 3 October 2013, less than three years after the 'left-to-die boat', the media reported that another boat carrying migrants from Libya had sunk off Lampedusa, this time resulting in over 360 deaths.⁸² The incident is discussed by P. Khalil Saucier and Tryon Woods, who explain that 'as the vessel conveying its African cargo caught fire, capsized and sank, people in the vicinity could hear the distress calls coming across the waters; but no one responded (until residents of Lampedusa itself finally organized a rescue party).'⁸³ Some people claimed, Saucier and Woods go on to note, that 'they thought they were hearing a gaggle of seagulls, rather than human beings on the precipice of death'.⁸⁴ According to Sarah Stillman, the mayor of Lampedusa Giusi Nicolini wept at the scene and insisted: 'These bodies are all speaking.'⁸⁵ 'If that's true', continues Stillman, 'it's a troubling sort of ventriloquism. What if next time, such voices weren't invited to the table only as corpses – if their complexities were heard, say, before their callings-out could be taken for the cries of seagulls?'⁸⁶ This act of mishearing demands that we ask questions regarding the politics of listening, and the possibilities for responding to the calls of others. By turning to the bird call, Bergvall and Wadud not only demand that the reader listens to the bodies speaking but they also ask if there are other ways of answering to such a call.

The ethics of answerability

The distress call thus not only plays out, in the words of Emma Wilson, the 'search for emergency help, connection' but also 'comes to speak more widely, and ethically, of response, responsibility, the urgency of hearing and responding to the calls of the living and the dying. Listening, hearing, answering, all take on a live charge'.[87] The question of answerability is one taken up by Avital Ronell in *The Telephone Book*, where she writes:

> And yet, you're saying yes, almost automatically, suddenly, sometimes irreversibly. Your picking it up means the call has come through. It means more: you're its beneficiary, rising to meet its demand, to pay a debt. You don't know who's calling or what you are going to be called upon to do, and still, you are lending your ear, giving something up, receiving an order. It is a question of answerability.[88]

This comes in the context of her analysis of Martin Heidegger's acceptance of a call from the Nazi party during his appointment as Rector of the University of Freiburg between 1933 and 1934, an incident described by Heidegger in an interview in *Der Spiegel* (not published until after his death) in which he admits that 'a telephone call came from Dr. Baumann, S. A. Group Leader in the office of Higher Education of the Supreme S. A. Command'.[89] Ronell explains that while Edmund Husserl – who was Heidegger's mentor and the previous occupant of the office – had insisted on the removal of the telephone from his premises, Heidegger not only had the apparatus reinstalled but also accepted the Storm Trooper's call – something, Ronell points out, for which he refused to apologize. By installing the telephone and accepting the call with neither apology nor accountability, she continues, 'Heidegger answered a call but never answered to it'.[90] Linking telephony to notions of answerability, Heidegger's call thus opens up a number of questions regarding the behaviour of the coastguards, international military vessels, fishing boats, and NATO, all of whom answered the call of the left-to-die-boat but refused to answer to it.

Questions of answerability invariably connect us with moral philosophy, ethics, responsibility and duty – all significantly loaded terms. In *Frames of War*, Judith Butler notes:

> It is not easy to turn to the question of responsibility, not least since the term itself has been used for ends that are contrary to my purpose here. In France, for instance, where social benefits to the poor and new immigrants have been denied, the government has called for a new sense of 'responsibility', by which it means that individuals ought not to rely on the state but on themselves. A word has even been coined to describe the process of producing self-reliant individuals: 'responsibilization'.[91]

Butler goes on to highlight some critical concerns regarding this theory of 'responsibilization': 'am I responsible only to myself? Are there others for whom I am responsible? And how do I, in general, determine the scope of my responsibility? Am I responsible for all others, or only to some, and on what basis would I draw that line?'[92] There are other problems, she notes, not least the pronoun in question. Stressing that 'precariousness implies living socially, that is, the fact that one's life is always, in a sense, in the hands of the other', Butler argues for the need to 'rethink and reformulate a conception of global responsibility that would counter [an] imperialist appropriation and its politics of imposition'.[93] These questions are also addressed by Butler and Athena Athanasiou in *Dispossession: The Performative in the Political*, where they are framed in terms of a 'call' and 'response': 'We might consider what kinds of enabling spaces of politics open up on occasions where we find ourselves affected, undone, and bound by others' calls to respond and assume responsibility.'[94] They continue: 'The question might be whether there can be a way to answer the call of the dispossessed without further dispossessing them.'[95]

Although a full account of ethics and responsibility is beyond the scope of this book, it is important to acknowledge that the politics of answerability to which I refer takes place within unbalanced global structures of power that perpetuate the legacies of colonialism. If this can be understood in terms of a telephone call, then it is essential to recognize that this call is not one that takes place between two equal parties; rather, it is one that evokes questions about the responsibilities of the Global North towards the Global South. Similarly, this chapter resists a humanitarianism that reduces an ethics of answerability to a single call between 'victim' and 'saviour'.[96] Questions of responsibility entail not only responding to the calls of refugees but also answering to the structures and state systems responsible for perpetuating the conditions of colonialism. Reflecting on the attention to the plurality and fluidity of voice in both *Drift* and *Syncope*, and considering the poets' refusal to oversimplify the subject as the voiceless victim, I am thus interested in the role of poetics in thinking through these multiple and complex questions of response.[97] How, in the words of Butler and Athanasiou, might a poem 'answer the call without interpellating the caller and without being interpellated by her?'[98] This is a question with which Wadud and Bergvall are both engaged as they seek to enact what Butler describes in *Frames of War* as 'a different kind of moral responsiveness' – one that employs 'the kinds of utterance possible at the limits of grief, humiliation, longing, and rage'.[99] In so doing, they explore the potential for radical forms of language to simultaneously bear witness to the distress call and expand possibilities for responding well. In the face of the often unspeakable trauma resulting from the unanswered call, this poetics of calling thus inhabits the limits of language and the spaces between and beyond words.

Probing the limits of language and form, the distress call in *Syncope* is structured by omission and suspension – a characteristic of the syncope that can be read in light of work by Catherine Clément and Fred Moten. Noting that 'syncope' is a 'strange' word, Clément stresses the 'miraculous suspension', 'extraordinary short circuit' or even 'absence of self' taking place in medical, musical and linguistic contexts.[100] At its root, the term refers to an interruption or hesitation that results in a suspension of rhythm or 'harmonious and productive discord'.[101] Poetry, Clément goes on to point out, is built on this balance of stress and syncope, and Wadud's habit of emphasizing her own unusual line breaks through iterative techniques creates this syncopated rhythm:

> the extremity of the
> natural world
> how unrelenting the
> light
> can be
> how fissured the dark
> how gaping
> its own ecstatic force[102]

This stanza is repeated several pages later with largely uniform line breaks – 'the extremity of the natural world / how unrelenting the light can be / how fissured the dark / how gaping / its own ecstatic force' – but the isolation and separation of the line 'how gaping' is retained, causing the reader to stumble and catch their breath on the gap left by this 'gaping'.[103] Adhering to Clément's theorization, this syncopation has both aesthetic and political force; inviting us to read that which has been excluded, the gap engendered by the syncope challenges ego psychology and overturns the Western metaphysical focus on the single, unified subject.[104] This reading of the syncopal break can be further extended within the politics of exile. In the collection's notes, Wadud briefly cites Masha Gessen's work on Vladimir Nabokov's *Speak, Memory*, when he writes: 'The break in my own destiny affords me in retrospect a syncopal kick that I would not have missed for worlds.'[105] Picking up on the use of the term 'syncope' to represent the separation from one's homeland, Wadud thereby engages with the ways in which the rupture might determine the rhythm and shape of the text:

> the left-to-die boat
> the demarcated
> boomerang
> this sliver
> the rhapsody
> syncopated
> arrhythmic
> anachronistic
> and exact
>
> time is a heavenly host[106]

Syncopated, arrhythmic, anachronistic, the poem performs rupture and transmutes the unanswered distress signal into a different kind of calling. For Moten – whom Wadud also credits in her notes – the syncope has a 'transportative force'.[107] Thinking through its role in delineating a space where black radicalism is set to work in his text *In the Break*, Moten is interested in those moments 'wherein the primary activity is to catch one's breath, to have one's breath caught'; at such times, he writes (with reference to Billie Holiday), 'one comes back from somewhere and it seems to rupture or arrest all previous itineraries'.[108] Following Moten, Wadud plays on the force of the syncope to rupture the reading experience and, with it, the relationship between call and response. Her use of syncopation pushes the line to the extremity of the breath, causing the gap in the heart's rhythm and, with it, a shudder in the reader: 'this signals the finish / the diminished waning breaths'.[109] As Butler remarks in *Frames of War*, where she reads breath in the poems of detainees at Guantánamo: 'The body breathes, breathes itself into words, and finds some provisional survival there. […] Its breathing is impeded, and yet it continues to breathe.'[110] As 'proof of stubborn life', Wadud's *Syncope* thus enacts the syncopated breath as both 'evidence and appeal' – as a way to bear witness to the call and at the same time to call for new ways of listening, reading and responding.[111]

If Wadud performs the omission of a humanitarian response through silence and syncopation, Bergvall's approach to the call is through a resonant sounding. Reflecting on the process of the poem's composition, she stresses her desire 'to be sounding language, to be calling it up to an audience. Calling up the messengers, root-words, stem-sounds, flowering lines that have nurtured and kept the voices that now have me and egg me on into the story'.[112] Here, she reframes poetry as a way not only of calling out to the reader but also of calling up different language traces, engaging with her source texts 'in a loose homophonic call and response'.[113] Through its rich intertextuality, her poetry operates according to this call and response: '[languages] intermingle and act as obscure relays of one another. They call up all the languages of the world'.[114] Playing out the ways in which these 'obscure relays' operate, Bergvall 'veers off into sound sense', employing interrupted syntax and overlapping poetic time to enact the drift of an interminable passage.[115] Drawing attention to its own materiality, the work consists of foggy lineation, oblique syntax and disorientating multilingualism. The effect is to place the reader at sea in the text. Indeed, as McMurtry notes, this isn't an easy work to navigate: 'the reading process is a disorienting one with few obvious signs to guide the reader'.[116] This is made explicit in the first text-based section of *Drift*, which is entitled 'Seafarer' and which consists of thirty-two poems, sixteen of which are 'songs', eight entitled 'North' and eight entitled 'Hafville' – an Old Norse word which Bergvall translates in the 'Log' as 'sea wilderness, sea wildering'.[117] The blurring of languages and forms is symbolized by the fog in the 'Hafville' poems where, in the first, Bergvall writes: 'The fair wind failed and they / wholly lost their reckoning. They did not know from what direction. / Driven here and there. The fog was so dense that they lost all sense / of direction and lost their course at sea'.[118] In 'Hafville 2', this is iterated as 'Thef air wind f ailed and they wholly l ost their reck their / reckoning did not not know from what direction D riven here and / there The f og was sodense that they l ost all ss ense of dirrrtion and / l ost thr course at sea'.[119] In 'Hafville 3', the orienting vowels are stripped out: 'Th f r w nd f l d nd th y wh ll l st th r r ck th r / r ck n ng Th y d d n t kn w fr m wh t d r ct n D r v n h r nd / th r', and in 'Hafville 4' the text loses entire words and lines until it is left only with the final 't' of 'boat' – a 't t t t t t' that is repeated across three pages in 'Hafville 5' and 'Hafville 6'.[120] Through this sequence, Bergvall enacts the fog of thinking and knowing.[121] This fogginess is vital not only to the drift of the boat but also to the operation of the text: 'Total fumbling. The fog in my mind, my life, my heart.'[122] Thinking through the role of fog in the composition of the poem, Bergvall notes: 'The OED mentions the origin of "fog" as uncertain. Points to the long grass and does not mention the weather system. Fog memory loss identity loss. SIGNAL LOSS. Damaged documents. Fog out the voice the words.'[123] For McMurtry, the amalgamation of forms 'stand[s] for the disorientation of disrupted and indecipherable sign systems – forming a quite literal barrier to comprehension'.[124] By employing these disrupted and indecipherable sign systems, Bergvall enacts what I term the distressed poetics of calling, where 'distress' comes from the Latin *distringere* for 'distrain', meaning 'to draw asunder, stretch out, detain'.[125] *Drift* is thus centrally concerned with the poetic enactment of an epistemic fissure, where the sense of disorientation – or being 'at sea' – is at the heart of a distressed textual process. Accordingly, the material nature of the 'SIGNAL LOSS' runs central to *Drift*, where the failure to respond to 'Priority code DISTRESS' speaks not only to the loss of an ethical compass but also to a loss in the reader's own sense of direction.

The nature of this 'SIGNAL LOSS' is further developed across Bergvall's live and digital vocal performances of *Drift*. In the 'Log', she notes that her multi-form poetry enables her 'to explore the archaic, tribal traffic between voice and drum, between text and beat, between air and skin, voice and breathing'.[126] Her process, she writes, involves 'remind[ing] myself that this text was made for speaking. It will again be spoken, it will again, resonate, exhale, be sung'.[127] From breath to song, the sonic dimensions of the poem are an attempt to reach Butler's 'provisional survival':

> Letting the recitation become a resonating chamber, a ripple effect. Insistent methods in art are intimately connected to processes of receiving and of following. One loads one's vessel for dream-travel and one follows it into hell. A reciting voice remains simultaneously input and output. Resonance is contact ripple. Everything is connected in the vast chamber of the world, beyond the callous, brutal politics. Everything ripples at contact.[128]

In this way, Bergvall's performance becomes the call: the recitation as resonating chamber is a way of making space to receive the lost signal, and the reciting voice is a way of registering the trace of the call. The acoustic echoes of the poem thus ensure that the distress call continues to resound. Returning to Morris's argument that the poem requires an 'active, focused aural attentiveness' rather than a passive reception, the text not only asks its readers to 'pay attention' but, through a productive form of signal loss and distressed language, also instigates new possibilities of answering to the call.[129]

Circling around a telephone call that was not answered to, this chapter is motivated by a need to move beyond the apparatus to a consideration of the relationship between technology and the politics and poetics of calling. In the face of the humanitarian crisis evidenced by the 'left-to-die boat', Bergvall and Wadud use distressed – or stretched apart – forms in order to enact and demand answers to the call. In so doing, they open up an affective space in which readers find themselves – in the words of Butler and Athanasiou – 'affected, undone, and bound by others' calls to respond and assume responsibility'.[130] Thus the literary telephone 'calls out' otherwise unspoken injustices and necropolitics of the global landscape. But in focusing on the nexus between technology, politics, human rights and language, my interest here has been not only to explore a poetics that might operate as both evidence and appeal but also to consider how thinking with the telephone might offer new ways of conceiving of this relationship. Through aporia, distressed language and signal loss, Bergvall and Wadud resist the wordlessness of the refugee imposed by the legacies of colonialism; instead, by staging the failures of speech through the unanswered telephone call, they stress the need to listen for voices that cannot always be heard. Using the motif of the call, then, Bergvall and Wadud oscillate between material text and vocal recitation, between cry and song, between breath and beat, and between space and sound as they explore the possibilities for a poetics of calling to bear witness to an unanswered distress signal and at the same time to appeal for new ways to answer to it.

Notes

1. Although some of the research cited in this chapter (including the *Report on the 'Left-to-Die Boat'* by Forensic Architecture (see n.5)) uses the term 'migrant' to describe the passengers on the left-to-die boat, I have chosen to use the term 'refugee' to denote anyone who migrates out of necessity rather than choice. For a discussion of the controversies surrounding this term, see Peter Gatrell, 'Refugees in Modern World History', in *Refugee Imaginaries: Research across the Humanities*, ed. Emma Cox, Sam Durrant, David Farrier, Lyndsey Stonebridge and Agnes Woolley (Edinburgh: Edinburgh University Press, 2020), 18–35 (26–32).
2. See Irini Papanicolopulu, 'The Duty to Rescue at Sea, in Peacetime and in War: A General Overview', *International Review of the Red Cross*, 92.2 (2016), 491–514.
3. Christina Sharpe, *In the Wake: On Blackness and Being* (Durham, NC: Duke University Press, 2016), 18, 107.
4. See further: Parliamentary Assembly of the Council of Europe, '"The left-to-die boat": there should be no gaps in the division of responsibility for search and rescue' (16 December 2011), available at: https://pace.coe.int/en/news/3759?__cf_chl_jschl_tk__=7uVel6GXYly6BgKFV9ekJgS6zV1yonhcoNP

dm1Xpfos-1643104672-0-gaNycGzNCJE (accessed 18 January 2022); Human Rights Watch, 'NATO: Investigate Fatal Boat Episode' (10 May 2011), available at: https://www.hrw.org/news/2011/05/10/nato-investigate-fatal-boat-episode (accessed 18 January 2022); GISTI, 'Le Gisti va déposer plainte contre l'OTAN, l'Union européenne et les pays de la coalition en opération en Libye' (9 June 2011), available at: http://www.gisti.org/spip.php?article2304 (accessed 18 January 2022).

5   Charles Heller, Lorenzo Pezzani and Situ Studio, *Report on the 'Left-to-Die Boat'* (Goldsmiths, University of London: Forensic Oceanography, 2012), available at: https://content.forensic-architecture.org/wp-content/uploads/2019/06/FO-report.pdf (accessed 18 January 2022). This research also led to a short film entitled 'Liquid Traces' produced for the *Forensis* exhibition at Haus del Kulturen der Welt in Berlin in 2014 (Charles Heller and Lorenzo Pezzani, 'Liquid Traces', 17 min, 2014. Animation produced for the exhibition *Forensis*, available at: https://forensic-architecture.org/investigation/the-left-to-die-boat (accessed 18 January 2022)).

6   See 'Methodology' at Forensic Architecture, *The Left-to-Die Boat* (11 April 2012), available at: https://forensic-architecture.org/investigation/the-left-to-die-boat (accessed 18 January 2022).

7   Heller, Pezzani and Studio Situ, *Report on the 'Left-to-Die Boat'*, 10, 9.

8   For Liisa Malkki, the refugee suffers from 'a particular kind of speechlessness in the face of the national and international organizations whose object of care and control they are'; the refugee is thus 'commonly constituted as a figure who is thought to "speak" to us in a particular way: wordlessly' (Liisa H. Malkki, 'Speechless Emissaries: Refugees, Humanitarianism and Dehistoricization', *Cultural Anthropology*, 11.3 (1996), 377–404 (386, 390)).

9   Adelaide Morris, 'Forensic Listening: NourbeSe Philip's *Zong!*, Caroline Bergvall's *Drift*, and the Contemporary Long Poem', *Dibur Literary Journal*, 4 (2017), 77–87 (82 n. 17).

10 The report states that 'it should be recalled once again that this is only one amongst the many incidents that have caused the deaths of more than 13,417 deaths [*sic*] at the maritime borders of the EU over the last 20 years' (Heller, Pezzani and Studio Situ, *Report on the 'Left-to-Die Boat'*, 10).

11 UNHCR, 'Mediterranean takes record as most deadly stretch of water for refugees and migrants in 2011', Briefing Notes (31 January 2012), available at: https://www.unhcr.org/4f27e01f9.html (accessed 18 January 2022). See Heller, Pezzani and Studio Situ, *Report on the 'Left-to-Die Boat'*, 9.

12 Writing for *Fortress Europe* on 2 February 2016, for instance, Gabriele Del Grande notes that 'since 1988 at least 27,382 migrants have died trying to conquer Fortress Europe' (Gabriele Del Grande, *Fortress Europe*, available at: http://fortresseurope.blogspot.com/ (accessed 18 January 2022)).

13   International Organisation for Migration, 'Rising Migrant Deaths Top 4,400 This Year: IOM Records More Than 45,000 since 2014' (10 December 2021), available at: https://www.iom.int/news/rising-migrant-deaths-top-4400-year-iom-records-more-45000-2014 (accessed 18 January 2022).
14   While recognizing the broader pattern of human rights violations of which the incident is a part, it is important to resist the temptation to provide an ahistorical account of the losses of life at sea by acknowledging the specificity of this crime and policy differences in the treatment of asylum seekers by different nation states.
15   Asiya Wadud, *Syncope* (New York: Ugly Duckling Presse, 2019). Wadud notes, for instance, that she cites a prayer from Kapka Kassabova's *Borders: A Journey to the Edge of Europe* (Minneapolis, MN: Graywolf Press, 2017) and a stanza from Kofi Awoonor's 'Hymn to My Dumb Earth', in *The Promise of Hope: New and Selected Poems 1964–2013* (Lincoln, NE: University of Nebraska Press, 2014). She includes an extract from the *Report on the 'Left-to-Die Boat'* in the opening pages of the collection (9) and acknowledges the importance of the report in her notes (68).
16   Asiya Wadud, 'Burnished, Etched, Emblazoned: Asiya Wadud Interviewed by Emily Skillings', *BOMB Magazine* (27 March 2020), available at: https://bombmagazine.org/articles/asiya-wadud/ (accessed 11 December 2020).
17   Wadud, *Syncope*, 13.
18   Ibid., n.p.
19   Heller, Pozzani and Situ Studio, *Report on the 'Left-to-Die* Boat', cited in Wadud, n.p.
20   Wadud, *Syncope*, 17.
21   Ibid., 23.
22   Ibid., 51.
23   Ibid.
24   Ibid., 49.
25   Ibid., 56, 57.
26   Ibid., 28, 29, 34, 38.
27   Daniel Moysaenko, '*Syncope*: A Review', *Harvard Review Online* (3 March 2020), available at: https://harvardreview.org/book-review/syncope/ (accessed 18 January 2022).
28   Wadud, *Syncope*, 21.
29   Ibid., 23.
30   Ibid., 18.
31   Achille Mbembe, 'Necropolitics', trans. Libby Meintjes, *Public Culture*, 15.1 (2003), 11–40 (16).
32   Mbembe, 'Necropolitics', 40.
33   Mbembe, 'Necropolitics', 40; Wadud, *Syncope*, 46.

34 Discussing the photographic work that appears in *Drift*, Bergvall explains that she invited Martin – who had experience of working in war zones and documenting conflict – to 'reflect on the image that has been widely circulated online: the image of the zodiac of migrants at the start of their journey, photographed by a French military helicopter'. Alongside this, she was keen for Martin to draw on his interest in printing processes: 'The question I ask of him here is how one might unpack the cruel scandal that this image reveals and that is "about to" take place.' The macro magnification operating in the images produced in 'respon[se] to this call' is, she says, 'unreadable, yet potentially decipherable' (Caroline Bergvall, 'Infra-materiality and Opaque Drifting', in *Minding Borders: Resilient Divisions in Literature, the Body and the Academy*, ed. Nicola Gardini, Adriana X. Jacobs, Ben Morgan, Mohamed-Salah Omri and Matthew Reynolds (Cambridge: Modern Humanities Research Association/Legenda, 2017), 67–75 (71–2)).

35 Unless otherwise stated, this chapter refers to the book version of *Drift* (New York: Nightboat Books, 2014).

36 Ibid., 140.

37 Bergvall, 'Infra-materiality and Opaque Drifting', 67.

38 Bergvall, *Drift*, 130. I. L. Gordon (ed.), *The Seafarer* (London: Methuen, 1960), 1–2. A 125-line poem, 'The Seafarer' falls into two parts, the first devoted to recounting the hardships of life at sea, and the second, a religious paean to God. See David Kaufmann, '*Drift*: Book Review', *Asymptote* (October 2014), available at: https://www.asymptotejournal.com/criticism/caroline-bergvall-drift/ (accessed 18 January 2022); Áine McMurtry, 'Sea Journeys to Fortress Europe: Lyric Deterritorializations in Texts by Caroline Bergvall and José F. A. Oliver', *The Modern Language Review*, 113.4 (October 2018), 811–45 (814).

39 Kaufmann, '*Drift*: Book Review'.

40 Bergvall, *Drift*, 177. For further discussion of Bergvall's use of the 'thorn' sign, see, for instance, Kate Lewis Hood, 'Clouding Knowledge in the Anthropocene: Lisa Robertson's *The Weather* and Caroline Bergvall's *Drift*', *Green Letters*, 22.2 (2018), 181–96, and Kaufmann, '*Drift*: Book Review'.

41 Bergvall, 'Infra-Materiality and Opaque Drifting', 69.

42 Bergvall, *Drift*, 132.

43 Ibid., 36, 48.

44 McMurtry, 'Sea Journeys to Fortress Europe', 831.

45 Ibid.

46 Bergvall, *Drift*, 143.

47 Ibid., 134.

48 Ibid. Morris notes that Bergvall echoes the definition of 'forensic imagination' that appears in the 'Lexicon' published by Forensic Architecture in *Forensis*, which states that 'in forensic science, every contact is perceived as leaving a trace' (Forensic

Architecture, *Forensis: The Architecture of Public Truth* (London: Sternberg Press, 2014), 746, cited in Morris, 'Forensic Listening', 80).
49 Morris, 'Forensic Listening', 80; Forensic Architecture, *Forensis*, 746.
50 Morris, 'Forensic Listening', 85.
51 Frank LaRue, 'Report of the Special Rapporteur on the Promotion and Protection of the Right to Freedom of Opinion and Expression', in *UN General Assembly, Human Rights Council* (Geneva: UN Printing Office, 2011), available at: https://digitallibrary.un.org/record/706200?ln=en (accessed 18 January 2022).
52 Michael Minges, 'Overview', in *Information and Communications for Development 2012: Maximizing Mobile*, ed. World Bank (Washington: World Bank Publication, 2012), 11–30 (11).
53 Dominic Lawson, 'Smartphones Are the Secret Weapon Fuelling the Great Migrant Invasion', *Daily Mail* (28 September 2015), available at: https://www.dailymail.co.uk/debate/article-3251475/DOMINIC-LAWSON-Smartphones-secret-weapon-fuelling-great-migrant-invasion.html (accessed 18 January 2022); Will Worley, 'Syrian Woman Explains Why Refugees Need Smartphones', *The Independent* (12 May 2016), available at: https://www.independent.co.uk/news/world/europe/why-do-refugees-have-smartphones-syrian-woman-explains-perfectly-refugee-crisis-a7025356.html (accessed 18 January 2022).
54 Marie Gillespie, Lawrence Ampofo, Margaret Cheesman, Becky Faith, Evgenia Iliadou, Ali Issa, Souad Osseiran and Dimitris Skleparis, *Mapping Refugee Media Journeys: Smartphones and Social Media Networks* (Milton Keynes: The Open University / France Médias Monde, 2016), 9.
55 Sara Ahmed, *Queer Phenomenology: Orientations, Objects, Others* (Durham, NC: Duke University Press, 2006), 17.
56 See Heller, Pezzani and Situ Studio, *Report on the 'Left-to-Die Boat'*, 19, 34–6.
57 Ibid., 13, 38, 10. The report notes that 'Thuraya Telecommunications Company is a world-leading mobile satellite service provider of voice, data, maritime, rural telephony, fleet management and other telecommunication solutions in remote areas. Providing mobile satellite communications to over 140 countries around the world, Thuraya offers a congestion-free network that now covers most of the planet, encompassing Asia, Africa, Australia, the Middle East and Europe' (Heller, Pezzani and Situ Studio, *Report on the 'Left-to-Die Boat'*, 18).
58 According to the Italian Coast Guard, Zerai's calls have helped save five thousand lives. See Mattathias Schwartz, 'The Anchor', *The New Yorker* (21 April 2014), available at: https://www.newyorker.com/magazine/2014/04/21/the-anchor (accessed 18 January 2022).
59 Bergvall, *Drift*, 73.
60 Ibid.
61 Wadud, *Syncope*, 21, 58.
62 Bergvall, *Drift*, 74.

63 Wadud, *Syncope*, 21.
64 Ibid., 20.
65 Bergvall, *Drift*, 76.
66 See Heller, Pezzani and Situ Studio, *Report on the 'Left-to-Die Boat'*, 20, 13.
67 Ibid., 46.
68 Bergvall, *Drift*, 74.
69 Heller, Pezzani and Situ Studio, *Report on the 'Left-to-Die Boat'*, 36.
70 International Maritime Organisation, *International Convention on Maritime Search and Rescue (SAR Convention)*, adopted 27 April 1979, entered into force 22 June 1985, available at: https://www.imo.org/en/About/Conventions/Pages/International-Convention-on-Maritime-Search-and-Rescue-(SAR).aspx (accessed 18 January 2022), cited in Heller, Pezzani and Situ Studio, *Report on the 'Left-to-Die Boat'*, 36.
71 UNHCR, 'UNHCR Calls on States to Uphold Principles of Rescue-at-Sea and Burden Sharing', Press Release (8 April 2011), available at: https://www.unhcr.org/uk/news/press/2011/4/4d9f1f7e6/unhcr-calls-states-uphold-principles-rescue-at-sea-burden-sharing.html (accessed 18 January 2022), cited in Heller, Pezzani and Situ Studio, *Report on the 'Left-to-Die Boat'*, 36.
72 Article 98 (1) of the United Nations Convention of the Law of the Sea states: 'Every State shall require the master of a ship flying its flag, in so far as he can do so without serious danger to the ship, the crew or the passengers: (a) to render assistance to any person found at sea in danger of being lost; (b) to proceed with all possible speed to the rescue of persons in distress, if informed of their need of assistance, in so far as such action may reasonably be expected of him' ('The United Nations Convention on the Law of the Sea' (10 December 1982), 1833 U.N.T.S. 397 (UNCLOS), 60, available at: https://www.un.org/depts/los/convention_agreements/convention_overview_convention.htm (accessed 18 January 2022), cited in Forensic Architecture, *Forensis*, 655 n. 2). Further, Article 98 (2) states: 'Every coastal State shall promote the establishment, operation and maintenance of an adequate and effective search and rescue service regarding safety on and over the sea and, where circumstances so require, by way of mutual regional arrangements cooperate with neighbouring States for this purpose' ('The United Nations Convention on the Law of the Sea', 60). Alongside this, Regulation 10 of Chapter V of the 1974 International Convention for the Safety of Life at Sea (SOLAS Convention) states: 'The master of a ship at sea, on receiving a signal from any source that a ship or air craft or survival craft thereof is in distress, is bound to proceed with all speed to the assistance of the persons in distress informing them if possible that he is doing so' (International Maritime Organisation (IMO), *International Convention for the Safety of Life at Sea (SOLAS convention)* (1 November 1974), 1184 UNTS 3, 414, available at: https://www.imo.org/en/KnowledgeCentre/ConferencesMeetings/Pages/SOLAS.aspx) (accessed 18 January

2022)). It is worth noting that the Spanish Ministry of Defence denied that their vessels received this signal. See Jack Shenker and Giles Tremlett, 'Migrant Boat Disaster: Spain Challenges NATO over Distress Call Claim', *The Guardian* (29 March 2012), available at: http://www.guardian.co.uk/world/2012/mar/29/migrant-boat-disaster-spain-nato (accessed 18 January 2022), cited in Heller, Pezzani and Situ Studio, *Report on the 'Left-to-Die Boat'*, 36 n. 121.

73 See Silja Klepp, 'A Double Bind: Malta and the Rescue of Unwanted Migrants at Sea, a Legal Anthropological Perspective on the Humanitarian Law of the Sea', *International Journal of Refugee Law*, 23.3 (2011), 538–57 (553–4). See also Heller, Pezzani and Situ Studio, *Report on the 'Left-to-Die Boat'*, 36 n. 123.

74 Wadud, *Syncope*, 38.

75 Ibid.

76 Giorgio Agamben, *Homo Sacer: Sovereign Power and Bare Life*, trans. Daniel Heller-Roazen (Stanford, CA: Stanford University Press, 1998). McMurtry reads border control practices in terms of Giorgio Agamben's 'states of exception', noting that 'Agamben's state of exception is not an uncontroversial concept and has come under particular critique for its ahistoricity and quasi-ontological foundation, which have been found to neglect socio-political specifics in understanding the *homo sacer* as a transhistorical figure of exclusion'. However, she goes on, her aim is neither to 'follow Agamben in conceiving present-day refugees in terms of the *homo sacer*' nor to 'pass judgement on the overarching coherence of the state of exception throughout Agamben's thought'; rather, she 'employs the arresting thought-image of the camp to conceptualize the political situation of displaced people and mass drowning in the Mediterranean today' (McMurtry, 'Sea Journeys to Fortress Europe', 813).

77 Wadud, *Syncope*, 57.

78 Andrew Darby, *Flight Lines* (Crows Nest, NSW: Allen & Unwin, 2020), 4, 3.

79 Wadud, *Syncope*, 54.

80 Bergvall, *Drift*, 128, 46.

81 Wadud, Syncope, 55; Michael Jackson, *The Politics of Storytelling: Variations on a Theme by Hannah Arendt* (Copenhagen: Museum Tusculanum Press, 2013), 99.

82 BBC, 'Lampedusa Boat Tragedy: Migrants Raped and Tortured' (8 November 2013), available at: https://www.bbc.co.uk/news/world-europe-24866338 (accessed 18 January 2022).

83 P. Khalil Saucier and Tryon P. Woods, 'Ex Aqua: The Mediterranean Basin, Africans on the Move, and the Politics of Policing', *Theoria: A Journal of Social and Political Theory*, 61.141 (2014), 55–75 (66).

84 Ibid.

85 Sarah Stillman, 'Lampedusa's Migrant Tragedy, and Ours', *The New Yorker* (10 October 2013), available at: https://www.newyorker.com/news/daily-comment/lampedusas-migrant-tragedy-and-ours (accessed 18 January 2022).

86 Ibid.
87 Wilson is referring here to the distress calls featured in the film *Fuocoammare* (Gianfranco Rosi (dir.), *Fuocoammare* (Stemal Entertainment, 2016); Emma Wilson, 'Telephone Calls in Gianfranco Rosi's Fire at Sea (Fuocoammare, 2016)', *Alphaville: Journal of Film and Screen Media*, 17 (2019), 12–23 (13)).
88 Avital Ronell, *The Telephone Book: Technology, Schizophrenia, Electric Speech* (Lincoln, NE: University of Nebraska Press, 1989), 2.
89 Martin Heidegger, '"Only a God Can Save Us": The Spiegel Interview (1966)', in *Heidegger: The Man and the Thinker*, ed. Thomas Sheehan (London: Routledge, 2017), 45–68 (47). See Ronell, *The Telephone Book*, 29.
90 Ronell, *The Telephone Book*, 5.
91 Judith Butler, *Frames of War: When Is Life Grievable?* (London: Verso, 2016), 35.
92 Ibid.
93 Ibid., 14, 35.
94 Judith Butler and Athena Athanasiou, *Dispossession: The Performative in the Political* (Cambridge: Polity, 2013), 106.
95 Ibid., 112.
96 See, for instance, Mariangela Palladino and Agnes Woolley, 'Migration, Humanitarianism, and the Politics of Salvation', *LIT: Literature Interpretation Theory*, 29.2 (2018), 129–44.
97 This builds on Anna Bernard's discussion of 'literature's capacity to generate a shared sense of responsibility among non-refugees'. Bernard points to the ways in which literature foregrounds a sense of shared responsibility while also acknowledging that 'writing and reading about refugees is not a sufficient form of action in itself' (Anna Bernard, 'Genres of Refugee Writing', in *Refugee Imaginaries: Research across the Humanities*, ed. Emma Cox, Sam Durrant, David Farrier, Lyndsey Stonebridge and Agnes Woolley (Edinburgh: Edinburgh University Press, 2020), 65–80 (77)).
98 Butler and Athanasiou, *Dispossession*, 112.
99 Butler, *Frames of War*, 58.
100 Catherine Clément, *Syncope: The Philosophy of Rapture*, trans. Sally O'Driscoll and Deirdre M. Mahoney (Minneapolis, MN: University of Minnesota Press, 1994), 5, 10.
101 Ibid., 4–5.
102 Wadud, *Syncope*, 39.
103 Ibid., 50.
104 Clément's work on the syncope addresses this sense of disappearance – something that she argues has been neglected by Western philosophy – across a range of contexts but with a particular appeal to the Indian *renonçant* who, by renouncing the village and embracing vagrancy, serves to open up space (Clément, *Syncope*, 6).

105 Vladimir Nabokov, *Speak, Memory: An Autobiography Revisited* (New York: Vintage, 1989), 250, cited in Masha Gessen, 'To Be, or Not to Be', *New York Review of Books* (8 February 2018), available at: https://www.nybooks.com/articles/2018/02/08/to-be-or-not-to-be/ (accessed 18 January 2022). See Wadud, *Syncope*, 67.
106 Wadud, *Syncope*, 24.
107 Fred Moten, *In the Break: The Aesthetics of the Black Radical Tradition* (Minneapolis, MN: University of Minnesota Press, 2003), 236. See Wadud, *Syncope*, 67.
108 Moten, *In the Break*, 163, 165. Extending Clément's work, Moten is interested in the racialization and sexualization of the syncope. See especially Moten, *In the Break*, 163–6.
109 Wadud, *Syncope*, 55.
110 Butler, *Frames of War*, 61–2.
111 Ibid., 62.
112 Bergvall, *Drift*, 128–9.
113 Ibid., 144.
114 Ibid., 161.
115 Ibid., 131.
116 McMurtry, 'Sea Journeys to Fortress Europe', 818.
117 Bergvall, *Drift*, 153.
118 Ibid., 36.
119 Ibid., 37.
120 Ibid., 38.
121 Discussing this passage, Kate Lewis Hood notes: '"The fair wind failed" is a direct translation of the phrase "tók af byri", which […] usually precedes references to hafvilla in the sagas […]. Repeated and retranslated to form a linguistically dense passage, the text is caught up in its own fog of sources' (Lewis Hood, 'Clouding Knowledge in the Anthropocene', 190).
122 Bergvall, *Drift*, 138.
123 Ibid., 157.
124 McMurtry, 'Sea Journeys to Fortress Europe', 818–19.
125 'distrain, v.', *OED Online* (Oxford: Oxford University Press, 2022), available at: www.oed.com/view/Entry/55738 (accessed 18 March 2022).
126 Bergvall, *Drift*, 128.
127 Ibid., 152.
128 Ibid., 134–5.
129 Morris, 'Forensic Listening', 84–5.
130 Butler and Athanasiou, *Dispossession*, 106.

6

Missiles and missives

Discussing the technoaesthetics of nuclear culture in *The Nuclear Borderlands*, Joseph Masco draws attention to an interactive exhibit on display at the Bradbury Science Museum at Los Alamos National Laboratory.[1] At the centre of the display is an old telephone and a prompt: 'What does this phone have to do with nuclear weapons?'[2] The accompanying text explains that, like many weapons in the nuclear arsenal, the telephone was manufactured in the late 1960s. Set up as an analogy to the Science-Based Stockpile Stewardship (SBSS) – the United States' management programme to ensure both the safety and viability of nuclear weapons as they age – the exhibit is designed to prompt visitors to reflect on how, following the Partial Test Ban Treaty of 1963 and Comprehensive Nuclear Test Ban Treaty of 1996, they might test a nuclear weapon without actually using it.[3] The text reads:

> Suppose this telephone is reserved only for emergency calls – no exceptions! Suppose, too, that there's a strict rule that says you are not allowed to test the equipment by placing or receiving an actual phone call. Are you confident the phone will work if you need it?[4]

For Masco, the exhibit suggests that 'a nuclear weapon is like a 911 emergency call'.[5] But the initial question – 'what does this phone have to do with nuclear weapons?' – resonates in other ways too: by what means are telephone systems and communication networks bound up in nuclear culture? What kinds of telephones are imagined in the event of nuclear catastrophe? And how might a telephone call also operate as a nuclear missile? This chapter seeks to explore ways of addressing these questions, unpicking the relationship between the telephone and nuclear weapons in Cold War fiction, as well as its entanglement in textuality, aesthetics, politics and power.

My attempt to think with and through nuclear culture draws on seminal debates in a 1984 special issue of *Diacritics*, in which the editors define two forms of nuclear criticism: 'the sort that reads other critical or canonical texts for the purpose of uncovering the unknown shapes of our unconscious nuclear fears' and the kind that 'aims to show how the terms of the current nuclear discussion are being shaped by literary or critical assumptions whose implications are often, perhaps systematically ignored'.[6] There is an explicit ethical imperative here that 'critical theory ought to be making a more important contribution to the public discussion of nuclear issues'.[7] Although attention to nuclear criticism waned following the fall of the Berlin Wall and the emergence of the War on Terror, nuclear weapons – and the ethical, political and environmental concerns regarding their development, storage and disposal – persist long beyond the end of the Cold War. Masco remarks:

> At the beginning of the twenty-first century these technological systems remain firmly in place: the United States and Russia each maintain over ten thousand nuclear weapons in their arsenals and continue to have nuclear submarines on constant alert, positioned to launch immediate and overwhelming nuclear (counter)strikes. Thus, the technological infrastructure of the Cold War lives on, as do the cultural and environmental effects of our first half century in the nuclear age.[8]

I write at a time when nuclear rhetoric is being actively employed by aggressors during the invasion of Ukraine by Russia; it is also a time when the impact of human-induced climate change has reached unprecedented levels.[9] These discussions, therefore, feel as pressing as ever. Necessarily limited, however, this chapter does not attempt to provide a comprehensive analysis of literary telecommunications in the atomic age; rather, by focusing on a cluster of texts published during the build up to the Cuban Missile Crisis, it hopes to initiate new conversations regarding the relationship between the Cold War telephone and the question of literature, and the ways in which both are bound up with what Martin Amis has called the 'unthinkability' of nuclear war.[10] In so doing, it takes my discussion of distressed language and signal loss in Chapter 5 in new directions by exploring the ways in which the ethics of the telephone are bound up with other failures of speech. Although limited in focus, my discussion speaks to wider concerns with regard to the telephone's relationship with global networks, questions of responsibility and the limits of language.

The connection between the nuclear missile and communication systems is, of course, not a new one. The same special issue of *Diacritics* also includes a neglected but provocative essay entitled 'On Nuclear Communication' in which Derrick de Kerckhove argues that the presence of the nuclear bomb operates as a force for change: 'beside threatening global destruction', he suggests, 'it can also serve the purpose of educating us to a new global maturity'.[11] Acknowledging its devastating potential, he nevertheless proposes that the bomb functions as both a unifying force and an incentive for action. At the heart of his claim is the statement that 'as a ground for the policies of deterrence, the nuclear bomb has become, quite unexpectedly, the greatest communication medium mankind has ever invented, not for information but for transformation'.[12] Notwithstanding the significant and controversial implications of his wider statements, the relationship between the nuclear bomb and communication demands further thought. Writing in the same issue, Michael McCanles remarks: 'If deterrence necessarily involves some sort of threat and a threat is in turn a communication, then deterrence depends not so much on possessing military capability and the willingness to use it, as on the communication of messages about that capability and that willingness.'[13] The premise of mutually assured destruction (MAD) thus depends not simply on the presence of nuclear weapons but on the devices that facilitate the communication of this fact: as Edward Kaplan puts it, nuclear operations are 'an abstract form of direct communication between national leaders'.[14] But for de Kerckhove, it goes further than this: the bomb prompts a rethinking not simply of how we communicate with each other in a crisis but also how and what nuclear technologies might communicate to us. With this in mind, the present chapter hopes to return to the question introduced by the Bradbury Science Museum in order to open up new ways of thinking about the relationship between the telephone and the nuclear missile, and the implications of this for reframing communications warfare.

The hotline

In 1958, four years prior to the Cuban Missile Crisis, Peter George, a former RAF major, published the novel *Red Alert* under the name Peter Bryant. In this novel, Major Howard learns that Brigadier General Quinten, Commanding Officer of Sonora Air Force Base, has taken it upon himself to independently launch a preventive nuclear strike on the Soviet Union. Committing suicide rather than facing capture, Quinten takes the recall codes with him to his death. His reasoning, Howard later explains, "'boiled down to the fact if we didn't destroy the Russians now, they would certainly destroy us in the next year or so'".[15] When the US President learns of the situation, he calls for a direct link to Moscow involving 'two microphones and two speakers' which 'were linked to a radio net flung across an ocean and a continent to the Kremlin'.[16] The ability to speak directly to the Soviet Union appears to be critical, with the transmission of the voice facilitating the urgency of the message and enabling the expression of both spoken and unspoken emotion. '"How long will it take?"' the President asks a general down the line. Calculations related to 'bomb time' occupy the strategists, with Zorubin – the Russian Ambassador to Washington – deducing 'Not just two hours to bomb time. But two hours to doom'.[17] Translating for the President, Zorubin listens 'keenly' for any expression of emotion in the Russian Marshall's voice, telling the President: 'It is the end' and 'I can tell it from his voice'.[18] The presumed immediacy and authenticity of the spoken word enable the President to convince the Kremlin that this is an accident, thereby making it possible for them to assist the Soviets in intercepting the American planes. In fact, all but one of the American bombers are successfully shot down; only a single plane, the Alabama Angel, continues on her route to Kotlass, the US target, with a damaged radio preventing further contact. Under duress, and as payment for their error, the President grants the Soviets the right to destroy Atlantic City in the place of Kotlass. Speed of communication and the affective register of the voice are vital to this agreement:

> The reply took only a few seconds to come. 'The President's offer is unacceptable. The American bomber has chosen its target. We wish to choose ours.'
> 'No.' The President's tone was unequivocal. 'I will not accept that. My offer is final and I will not argue about it. I am ready to go so far to preserve peace. I will not be pushed further.'[19]

Despite the initial refusal, the President's 'unequivocal' tone convinces the Kremlin to accept the offer. Ultimately, however, the proposed retaliatory strike on Atlantic City is not necessary and catastrophe is averted when the Alabama Angel fails to destroy its target: the explosion that takes place is small, the bomb falling on an uninhabited area 15 miles south-east of Kotlass. Nuclear war is thereby avoided and the novel concludes when the President asserts: 'We must take steps immediately to see this does not happen again'.[20]

Notwithstanding the problematic representation of masculine strength and a conservative worldview typical of the Cold War thriller, Bryant's fictional scenario – and the role of telecommunications in averting catastrophe – is an influential one; it became the basis for Stanley Kubrick's 1964 farce *Dr. Strangelove, Or How I Learned to Stop Worrying and Love the Bomb* in which the US President Merkin Muffley telephones the Premier of the Soviet Union Dmitri Kissov, bringing to even greater public attention the role of communication in a crisis, as well as its comedic potential.[21] The similarity between *Red Alert* and a later novel by Eugene Burdick and Harvey Wheeler entitled *Fail-Safe* is so marked that Bryant, together with Kubrick, launched what David E. Scherman described in *Life Magazine* as 'a megaton lawsuit over who got airborne with the idea first'.[22] The influence of *Red Alert* extends beyond popular culture and literary legal battles, however; reading it as a warning, nuclear strategist Thomas Schelling was so impressed by Bryant's fictional account of how nuclear war might start that he purchased a number of copies of the novel to give to colleagues and friends.[23] His review of *Red Alert* was published in the *Bulletin of Atomic Scientists* as 'Meteors, Mischief, and War', where he argues that 'the sheer ingenuity of the scheme, beautifully analyzed in "realistic" detail, with emphasis on the system rather than on personalities, exceeds in thoughtfulness any nonfiction available on how war might start'.[24] For Schelling, as he explains in his later *Arms and Influence*, the installation and maintenance of effective communication channels are imperative: 'There is probably no single measure more critical to the process of arms control than assuring that if war should break out the adversaries are not precluded from communication with each other'.[25] Schelling's 'emphasis on the system' thus places the telecommunications infrastructure at the heart of nuclear deterrence. This was a strategy worked out in fiction first; as David Seed notes: 'The description of the hot line in *Red Alert* led Thomas Schelling to suggest to the Eisenhower government that they set one up'.[26]

In Bryant's phonocentric novel, the hotline consists of a pair of microphones and speakers, linked via radio. Accordingly, tone and intimacy of expression are central to the action, speaking to the ways in which power and authority are bound up with logocentric notions of voice, immediacy and (tele)presence. However, Bryant was not the only writer exploring the role of telecommunications in the atomic age; nor was he alone in situating the spoken word as central to the drama. In fact, a number of writers proposed a Direct Communications Link (DCL) between Washington and Moscow, and more often than not this took the form of a telephone exchange, connecting the resolution of conflict with dialogue at a distance. For instance, Leo Szilard – an exiled Hungarian physicist and leading figure in the Manhattan Project – published his own version of the telephonic hotline in the *Bulletin of Atomic Scientists* in 1961, just one year after Schelling's review of *Red Alert*. Accompanying the text is Szilard's note: 'In spite of its fictional form, the article is technically correct. The form permits the author to be more enlightening by being more entertaining'.[27] Based on game theory, 'The Mined Cities' develops Szilard's theory of 'metastability', in which the recognition of the potential for destruction on both sides is guaranteed through the carefully managed sacrifice of cities in an agreed 'tit-for-tat'.[28] Set in a futuristic 1980, the story features Dr Jones who has awoken from an eighteen-year sleep to learn that all but a handful of nuclear missiles have been destroyed; those remaining have been 'mined' beneath an equal number of cities in the United States and in the Soviet Union as a mutually assured deterrent – apparently the idea of a character named Szilard who presented his theory in the form of fiction in the *Bulletin of the Atomic Scientists* in 1961. However, Jones learns that a year previously the Soviets had suddenly evacuated their mined cities without warning, prompting the US government to issue an ultimatum, which is quickly resolved when the 'President got through to the Chairman in Moscow on the telephone and the two of them talked for hours on end'.[29] Jones is advised that, as a result of a student prank, 'the telephone line directly connecting the White House with the Kremlin had been installed just a few months before this incident'.[30] For Szilard's characters, the telephone facilitates the direct and intimate dialogue necessary for successful negotiation. Horn explains that, by establishing 'communication in a situation that was frozen in hyper-rational, yet abstract speculations between enemies', Szilard's telephone becomes part of the 'control and communication' strategy whose aim it is to prevent unintended war.[31]

The motif of the hotline is central to 'Abraham '59', a story by 'F. B. Aiken' that appeared in the anti-McCarthyism *Dissent* magazine in 1959.[32] Like *Red Alert*, the story follows the actions of the President when one 'berserk squadron' fails to return from a routine flight only in order to radio its intention to attack Moscow once it is far enough away to avoid interception. Under pressure, the President searches for a possible way to convince his Soviet counterpart that the attack is accidental. To do this, he enlists a translator who is required to 'provide the President with a concurrent translation in a transatlantic telephone communication with Khrushchev'.[33] The President's plan is to launch a second Strategic Air Command (SAC) squadron over New York City, the destruction of which he feels would represent a '"comparable loss"' to the destruction of Moscow and thus '"prove to him our sincerity"'.[34] But the President's exchange with the Kremlin cannot take place via a standard telephone line; challenging the easy talk of Szilard's story, 'Abraham '59' depicts a more formal 'four-way telephone connection' between the President, Khrushchev, the American Embassy in Moscow and the Soviet Consulate in New York.[35] For Tobias Nanz, this four-way hotline 'constitutes the basis of the trust that needs to be restored, since the destruction of New York can be transmitted in real time thanks to the transatlantic telephone connection'.[36] It is worth pointing out, however, that although this transatlantic telephone might appear to promise direct communication in real time, the conversation is always mediated by other interlocutors, who are crucial to reading the situation and managing the transmission of any response. Moreover, as Nanz also observes, the operation of the hotline depends on not only the transmission of the voice but also its cessation: 'If the plan goes according to this schedule, two stations in our telephonic network will drop off dead before we are through'.[37] In other words, if the connection between Washington and Moscow is severed, the President will know to order the release of bombs on New York City, the reality of which will also be conveyed to Khrushchev through a second disrupted connection. In 'Abraham '59', however, the telephone conversation and its effects remain deferred; interrupting the narrative, the story ends when the President reaches for the handset. Operating as the vehicle for the story's action and yet hovering at the limits of the fiction, the telephone is thus both a critical object and one that remains at the margins of the text.

Challenging perceptions of the telephone call as a conversation between two parties, the representation of the hotline in 'Abraham '59' suggests that Cold War negotiations are bound up within a more complex communication system involving not only the immediate interlocutors but also their translators and interpreters, as well as the effects of both sound and silence. This system is extended in *Fail-Safe*, a novel co-authored by Eugene Burdick and Harvey Wheeler and published in the United States on 22 October 1962 in the midst of the Cuban Missile Crisis. When an unknown aircraft in US air space is detected, SAC follows protocol and alerts its bombers, who proceed to their 'fail-safe' point – a strategy designed to prevent US bombers from accidentally crossing into Soviet air space and thus inadvertently initiating nuclear war – where they await further command. The Positive Control Fail-Safe system, as advisor to the White House Professor Groteschele explains, 'is the ultimate protection against mechanical failure'.[38] But Groteschele's explanation is accompanied by a 'nervous chuckle': 'The whole system had one big flaw in it. Nobody could ever be certain that the black boxes would actually work properly in a showdown.'[39] Therefore, like the telephone on display at the Bradbury Science Museum, Burdick and Wheeler's 'Fail-Safe machines could be truly tested only once: the single time they were used'.[40] When the unknown aircraft in the novel is identified, the threat level is reduced and the bombers recalled. But a malfunction in 'Machine No. 6' means that rather than receiving the signal to return to base, Group Six receive the attack codes instead. In the absence of further radio contact (which has been blocked by the Soviets noting the presence of bombers and fearing attack), Group Six conclude that nuclear war is underway and that they must follow the order to launch a retaliatory strike on Moscow.[41] In an attempt to avoid total nuclear war, the President uses the 'hot wire' to connect to the Kremlin. As in 'Abraham '59', a four-way telephone line is established between the Pentagon, Khrushchev, the US ambassador in Moscow and the Soviet ambassador in Washington, and negotiations commence with the President offering New York as his sacrifice. But whereas the telephone call in 'Abraham '59' hovers at the limits of the fiction, in *Fail-Safe* the call itself is launched. Dispatching expressions of masculine strength as well as strained and strategic silences down the line, a translator named Buck takes on a mediating role: 'There was a long moment of tension after Buck had translated. Buck felt squeezed buglike between the wills of two men. Although they were separated by thousands of miles it was almost as if their strength poured through the line.'[42] Once again highlighting the role of the mediating party inserted between interlocutors, Buck is attuned to the resonance of each word, as well as all that remains unspoken:

> The moment he heard the voice something in Buck's mind went alert. He heard perfectly and literally what Khrushchev said, but he also sensed something else. It was the same person speaking but in a different voice. The voice ended each sentence with an odd lifting sound.
> As Buck translated the literal words he searched back over his experience. Something was there, elusive and subtle, but heavy with meaning.[43]

Enacting the importance of pitch and pause, and questions of their translation and interpretation, this telephone call operates beyond a single mouthpiece; instead, it contributes to a heterogeneous and complex system involving both spoken and unspoken language. Moreover, this system is part of a vast assemblage of machines that is dependent on both human and nonhuman actors. The system that enables 'Condition Red' to operate is an 'immense man-machine [that] activated itself, checked itself, coordinated itself, restrained itself, passed information to itself, carefully filtered incoming information, automatically tripped other systems that were serving it'.[44] In this way, Burdick and Wheeler move beyond Szilard's representation of the Cold War telephone as a self-contained and fully functioning material object and instead demonstrate its multiple and fallible textual codes. A vehicle of dramatic action, the hotline in *Fail-Safe* is thus bound up with phonocentric notions of voice and sovereignty, even as it exposes the spoken and unspoken traces that operate as part of a wider system of relations. Both deferring and resolving the crisis, the hotline simultaneously holds the novel's conclusion and the nuclear missile in suspension, while at the same time always moves the narrative forward.

From missive to missile

On 12 December 1962, less than two months after the publication of *Fail-Safe* and the resolution of the Cuban Missile Crisis, the United States submitted a working paper entitled 'Reduction of the Risk of War through Accident, Miscalculation, or Failure of Communication' to the Eighteen Nation Disarmament Conference. This paper proposed the creation of a DCL between Washington and Moscow – a proposal that was accepted by the Soviet Union on 5 April 1963.[45] On 20 June 1963, the US and Soviet governments both signed the memorandum to establish a DCL designed to prevent misunderstanding that might put pressure on the fragile balance over the deliberate or mistaken use of nuclear arms – an agreement that came into effect on 30 August 1963. When it was finally installed, however, the hotline – designed to operate as a rapid communication link between international heads of state to reduce the danger of accident or misadventure – consisted not of a telephone connection but rather a teletype system between two terminal points in Washington and Moscow. American teleprinters and encoding devices were set up in the Kremlin to receive messages written in English, with the equivalent Soviet machines installed in the Pentagon for Russian-language communications. This hotline, as Miller notes, 'represent[s] an emergency mechanism that sits astride the paths to nuclear war – an insurance policy worth having'.[46] But although this system enabled the parties to send, receive, decode and translate messages in minutes, it avoided the direct and immediate transmission of the voice which was so central to the popular conception of the telephone hotline in the literary imagination. In fact, as Nanz explains, strategists decided on the use of a teletyper 'precisely in order to avoid the emotions that in discussions via telephone could lead to an escalation of the situation'.[47] As such, he argues, it operates as a 'temporizing device that allows one to buy time in a crisis'.[48] Nanz thus makes a clear distinction between the DCL actually established between Washington and Moscow – a link that consisted of 'terminals, telexes, cables, operators and translators' through which standardized test messages were transmitted at designated times – and the popular representation of the telephone hotline which operates as a dramaturgical device in literary culture.[49]

While the recurring representation of the hotline as telephone call can of course be attributed to the dramatic effects of dialogue at a distance in literature and film, Nanz argues that it also draws attention to the telephone as an 'object in which a number of epistemological questions come together: how is the political imaginary generated in times of crisis and what role is assigned to human and non-human actors in this process?'[50] Nanz proposes that the Cold War telephone operates as *dispositif* – in other words as both material object and system of relations.[51] In this way, the nuclear telephone is not only a technological and military device, but it is also bound up with a complex and heterogenous ensemble involving a range of human and nonhuman components. Moreover, as a military and political strategy that was realized in fiction first, the hotline occupies an important place in our understanding of nuclear culture. This means, Nanz argues, that the telephone is not simply a material object but is a 'hybrid object' through which 'materiality and factuality are intermingled with stories and fictions'.[52] Here, Nanz emphasizes the role of the telephone in complicating the relation between both human and non-human actors while also demonstrating the entanglement of fiction and politics in nuclear culture. In so doing, Nanz is of course referring to Jacques Derrida's influential essay 'No Apocalypse, Not Now (Full Speed Ahead, Seven Missiles, Seven Missives)', which was published in the 1984 special issue of *Diacritics*. Here, Derrida describes nuclear warfare as 'a phenomenon whose essential feature is that of being fabulously textual, through and through'.[53] By this, Derrida means that the reality of nuclear war is 'constructed by a fable, on the basis of an event that has never happened'; as a result, the phenomenon is textual 'to the extent that, for the moment, a nuclear war has not taken place: one can only talk and write about it'.[54] Notwithstanding the 'massive "reality" of nuclear weaponry', Derrida argues that total nuclear war 'has never occurred, itself; it is a non-event'.[55] As such, fiction is not only the medium through which we seek to understand the reality of nuclear catastrophe, but it is also critical to the ways that the reality of nuclear war and its outcomes are shaped and contested.[56] Certainly, as works such as *Fail-Safe* attest, its manifestation in the literary imagination means that – like a nuclear weapon – the Cold War telephone is fabulously textual through and through.

Nanz's argument is a persuasive one, but although he outlines the ways in which the hotline participates in Derrida's fabulous textuality, he does not pursue Derrida's account of the relationship between nuclear weapons and telecommunications. In fact, Derrida goes on to point out: 'Nuclear weaponry depends, more than any weaponry in the past, it seems, upon structures of information and communication, structures of language, including non-vocalizable language, structures of codes and graphic decoding'.[57] Here, Derrida draws attention to the ways in which nuclear culture is also bound up with communication networks and the operation of language, including literary language. He states:

> [A]ll language, all writing, every poetico-performative or theoretico-informative text dispatches, sends itself, allows itself to be sent, so today's missiles, whatever their underpinnings may be, allow themselves to be described more readily than ever as dispatches in writing (code, inscription, trace, and so on).[58]

For Derrida, both the missile and the missive are subject to dispatch. Thus, reflecting on the ways in which a telephone call is also dispatched, it is perhaps helpful to reframe the question posed at the Bradbury Science Museum: to what extent is the telephone call missive and to what extent is it missile? As Daniel Cordle remarks, Derrida's conceptualization of the textuality of nuclear weapons suggests that they – much like literary texts – are 'not only missiles but missiles that are held in suspension, ready to be launched from, and by, vast interconnected informational networks'.[59] Held in suspension, their power, in other words, is bound up in the kinds of informational and intertextual networks through which nuclear war can actually exist. What is proposed here is that the nuclear telephone is not simply a device through which we communicate, nor is it merely part of a cybernetic system consisting of human and nonhuman speaking machines; rather it is itself a missile/missive held in suspension.

The red telephone

The possibility for the hotline to operate as missile opens up the ways that the Cold War telephone functions as 'nuclear dispositive' on multiple levels.[60] For not only does it contribute to arms regulation and political negotiation in the attempt to prevent an unintended war, but it also has the capacity to do precisely the opposite – in other words, the telephone has the potential to serve as 'doomsday device', triggering a nuclear strike.[61] The terrifying ease with which the Cold War telephone call slips from missive to missile is made clear in both fictional representations of atomic culture and their theoretical analyses. At the centre of this slippage is the allegorical 'red telephone', an object that for Sean Maloney is 'the quintessential symbol of the nuclear age'.[62] But this is also an object that appears to oscillate in the cultural imagination between serving as the hotline between Washington and Moscow and symbolizing the communications link between the US President and his own military command – two distinct and separate systems.[63] My discussion here owes much to Nanz's reading of the red telephone as hybrid object, in which he draws attention to the representation in popular culture of the hotline as attached to a red handset. Nanz is correct: according to the editors of *Electrospaces*, for instance, the Jimmy Carter Library and Museum once displayed a red telephone with the exhibition text: 'During Jimmy Carter's presidency, the "red phone" was a hotline to the Kremlin in Moscow. A U.S. president could pick up the phone and speak directly to Soviet leaders in times of crisis.' However, the museum label was later altered to clarify that 'the "red phone" was in fact used to communicate with U.S. military command centers in a crisis' and was 'not the hotline to Soviet leaders'.[64] Although Nanz acknowledges that the red telephone in *Fail-Safe* actually had a quite different function to the hotline (rather than connecting Washington and Moscow, it enabled the President to talk directly and urgently to his own military command), at critical points in his analysis he actually appears to perpetuate the conflation of the two systems. In his reading of 'Abraham '59', for instance, he remarks: 'The American ambassador in Moscow and the Soviet ambassador to the UN in New York have now been brought into a conference call on the red telephone.'[65] Notwithstanding the ways that the hotline might be symbolically perceived as 'red', it is worth noting that there are in fact no references to the red telephone in this story, suggesting that the two separate communication networks – which have quite different functions – have become inextricably crossed in Nanz's own analysis.[66] In fact, Nanz frequently turns to the 'red telephone' as the device that 'offers the last chance for a solution to be found', pointing out that 'if the negotiations via the "red telephone" should fail, then war appears inevitable'.[67] By framing his discussion in this way and conflating the two communication systems, the red telephone – by which I mean the telephone connections between the President and his Strategic Command rather than the link between Washington and Moscow – is rendered all but invisible. In fact, the communications link between the President and his staff is an important one in *Fail-Safe*:

> [Buck] had never heard the sound before, but instantly he knew where it came from. In the second drawer of his desk there was a red telephone. When he had been given the office and his instructions, he had been told that this telephone would ring only in case of emergency and was never to be used for ordinary communications. The black telephone on top of the desk was to be used for normal business. He had also been told that when the red phone did ring it would not give the short intermittent rings made by an ordinary telephone, but would give off a steady sharp sound until it was answered.[68]

The red phone's ring punctuates the narrative at key moments in the novel, where it not only operates as dramatic device but also functions as a sanitized symbol for the network of technological, military and state power: 'A phone had rung. It did not ring loud, but it did ring distinctively. A steady persistent unbroken ring. It was the red phone.'[69] Although the negotiations via the hotline hold the missile in suspension, the order to launch the nuclear strike on New York City comes through the President's internal telecommunications system: '"Gentleman, I have had to make a terrible decision," the President said.'[70] When he issues the final order to General Black who is circling above New York City, the message is not conveyed as part of a standardized and carefully managed protocol but takes the form of a more personal and direct connection between friends: 'Blackie, this is it. The bombs have just fallen on Moscow. Release four bombs according to our predetermined pattern.'[71] Black's co-pilot is the next to speak, reaching for the 'bright red key which controlled communications with the White House', he says: '"Mr. President, this is Major Callahan. The mission has been accomplished. The four bombs have exploded 5,000 feet over New York. General Black has killed himself with his suicide kit."'[72] Apparently unthinkable, the bombs and their effect are not featured in the novel: instead, the actions are reduced to a call, and the final words of the President – an order to award Black a posthumous 'Medal of Honor' – heard only as an audible aside down the line. In this way, the internal communications system offers a sanitized outcome: war is tragic but limited. Not only is this the result of a successful negotiation via the hotline, but it is also expertly and heroically managed and implemented via the internal line. Thus, on one level at least, nuclear communication in *Fail-Safe* appears to preserve the masculine authority of the President of the United States and as well as the efficiency and obedience of his men.

The role of the red telephone in nuclear communications, and its association with authority and power, is also evident in Pat Frank's 1959 novel *Alas, Babylon!* where it contributes to a large ensemble of heterogeneous information systems from the domestic phone call to emergency broadcasting through the CONELRAD (Control of Electromagnetic Radiation) service. In this novel, which is described by Cordle as both 'a polemic in favour of civil defense' and a 'stage on which a survivalist fantasy can be played out', Randy Bragg, an Army Reserve Officer living in Fort Repose in Central Florida, receives an urgent message from his brother Mark, relayed to him via Florence Wechek, the manager at Western Union: 'Urgent you meet me at Base Ops McCoy noon today. Helen and children flying to Orlando tonight. Alas, Babylon.'[73] Randy recognizes the 'family signal' from his brother Mark, who works for SAC intelligence.[74] With his concerns regarding a nuclear strike growing, Mark has promised to give Randy warning so that he can be prepared: "'I won't call you up and say, 'Hey, Randy, the Russians are about to attack us.' Phones aren't secure, and I don't think my C-in-C, or the Air Staff, would approve. But if you hear "'Alas, Babylon'", you'll know that's it'.[75] While Randy makes preparations for the attack, Mark is recalled to the War Room. With him is Ace Atkins, the Senior Controller, who sits with 'the red phone a few inches from his fingers. One code word into Ace's red phone would cock SAC's two thousand bombers and start the countdown at the missile sites'.[76] Here, the representation of the red telephone in the text comes close to its parallel function as a missile with the capacity to dispatch not words but atomic bombs. Particular attention in the text is drawn to the red phone in light of the recent silence from Moscow; clearly, on this occasion, the hotline is not working as it should. Mark explains to Ace that it is the silence that is most disconcerting: 'Not a word. Not a whisper. Usually Radio Moscow would be screaming bloody murder. That's what worries me. As long as people keep talking they're not fighting. When Moscow quits talking, I'm afraid they're acting'.[77] In contrast to *Red Alert* and *Fail-Safe*, then, it is not the negotiation with the enemy via the hotline that provides the dramatic action. In fact, as Seed points out, the novel is marked by 'the complete absence of any visible enemy'.[78] Thus, rather than concentrating on the communication link between the United States and Moscow, Frank's focus is on the red telephone and its symbolic status as the mechanism for launching a missile strike. Demonstrating America's military might and its relation to both technological and state power, the red telephone is transformed into a cultural fetish. Indeed, the narrator's gaze lingers over the way in which Ace's 'fingers stroked the red phone'.[79] The gendered and sexualized language used in Frank's description of the phone – from its potential to 'cock SAC's two thousand bombers' to Ace's erotic handling – speaks to the biological determinism of Helen Caldicott's *Missile Envy*, in which she examines the psychosexual overtones with which the language of the military is laden, evident in phrases such as 'missile erector, thrust-to-weight ratio, soft laydown, deep penetration, hard line, and soft line'.[80] Here the violent sexual dynamics of nuclear war extend to those technologies that hold it in suspension.

In many ways, the red phone in both *Fail-Safe* and *Alas, Babylon!* can be said to function as synecdoche for the authority and power of nuclear communications in the United States, marking the move from call as missive to call as missile. In *Alas, Babylon!*, furthermore, it is raised to the level of cultural fetish – a condition to which William Prochnau also draws attention in *Trinity's*

Child where the red telephone appears 'encased in glass like a prized butterfly on a pedestal just inside the door' of Strategic Air Command, where its mythic function is exposed:

> A small bronze plaque notes that this is the original red phone, donated by the Bell Telephone System in appreciation of its historical significance. The real phone, the line to the President, is downstairs. It is yellow. It also is dirty, as if the janitorial service dusts everywhere but there.[81]

But in Frank's novel, the red phone's metafictional status as mythic object is part of a larger move towards exposing the fictionality and fallibility of US communication networks. Indeed, despite the initial association of nuclear communications with state power and military authority in texts such as *Alas, Babylon!* and *Fail-Safe*, these works remain haunted by communication anxiety and the vulnerability of both technological and linguistic systems. The Cold War telephone, in other words, not only exemplifies our concerns regarding the fallibility of telecommunications but also prompts new questions about the limits of human language, and what might happen to the word in the event of the atomic bomb.

The atomization of language

On the one hand, the literary representation of the nuclear telephone in the countdown texts of the late 1950s and early 1960s points to a device that has the capacity to either prevent nuclear catastrophe or to launch a carefully controlled yet heroic sacrificial strike: either way, it operates as cultural fetish in the service of Western capitalism. On the other hand, however, the telephone remains an anxious object, forever threatened by human error, technological disruption, mistranslation or other failures of language. In Bryant's *Red Alert*, for instance, the red telephone takes on a life of its own not simply by becoming the vehicle for communication but by seeming to sound on its own terms. At the start of the novel, Howard delivers a letter from Strategic Air Command to Quinten, remarking: 'My red line's still out, General. [...] They haven't located the fault yet.'[82] Immediately, then, the authority of the red line is disrupted. Only a minute later, Howard is summoned back to the room where he finds the General clutching the telephone: 'his voice was quite firm as he said, "I understand," and replaced on its rest the red instrument, the telephone which linked directly with SAC operations room.'[83] Quinten has apparently received a call with the order to issue 'Warning Red', meaning that an air attack by Soviet forces is imminent.

Picking up the phone again, he puts into motion a preventative nuclear attack, ordering a complete ban on telecommunications: 'No calls from inside go out. No calls from outside are even answered, let alone put through. No calls. You understand?'[84] Although at first Howard believes that an attack is underway, he soon starts to have doubts: his suspicion rests on the ringing of the red telephone, which continues to clamour 'loudly and imperatively' at key moments.[85] When the ring prompts Howard's realization that he had not heard the telephone bell at all when the fatal call came, he deduces that Quinten has taken it upon himself to launch a preventive nuclear strike on the Soviet Union: the call is entirely phoney. This suggests that the red telephone is not simply the medium through which words are exchanged in the crisis; instead, it speaks on its own unruly terms. Rather than operating solely as a symbol for logocentric order and authority, the materiality of the call communicates its own disruptive potential.

Although the red telephone operates without fail in *Fail-Safe*, the failure of almost all other communication devices (including the eponymous fail-safe system) is striking, enacting Derrida's connection between 'the destinerrance of the envois, (sendings, missives, so to speak)' and the operation of 'incalculability'.[86] For Buck, it is the material basis of the hotline and its potential for disruption that is most pressing. While he is on the extension line translating for the President and Khrushchev, he notes: 'The silence on the line went past the point of tension. The tiny, and usually inaudible, screech of static now seemed to be a scream in their ears', and when Khrushchev finally spoke, 'it was to Buck like a bell fractured, a flash that ripped darkness, a pinprick through the eardrum'.[87] Later, when Khrushchev learns of the President's proposition to demonstrate the authenticity of his promise by bombing his own city, the Soviet Premier is reduced to silence, which Buck struggles to translate: 'Suddenly, like a mechanical mockery, there was a flare-up of static on the line. It sounded like some macabre laugh, something torn from the soul of the mechanical system.'[88] Reflecting on this, Nanz rightly points out that the telephone in *Fail-Safe* 'opens up an arena in which the technical aspects such as telephone lines, extensions, microphones, or static interference and other forms of signal noise come together with human actors'.[89] Moreover, as he goes on to note, the noise of these operations and their disruptions are always 'actively disclosed' in the text.[90] In this way, he argues, the hotline 'reverses' McLuhan's argument that media disguise their own operations, suggesting that 'disruption seems to be the standard case'.[91] Supporting his argument, Nanz makes reference to Claude Shannon and Warren Weaver's theory of noise, in which they posit that during the process of transmission, distortions of sound or other errors are added to the signal which must be removed in order to get 'the useful information'.[92] But in *Fail-Safe*, as Nanz points out, the noise is integral to the signal; rather than requiring 'subtraction', it is part of the 'useful information': 'disruption in the communication channel is to be viewed as a message source on par with a message transmitter'.[93] The President explains that when the first bombs are dropped, the telephone 'will give off a distinctive shrill sound as it melts from the heat of the fireball. We know; we have tested. When we hear that sound we will know that the American Ambassador to Moscow is dead'.[94] When the scene is played out in the novel's climax, Buck is unable to subtract the noise from the ambassador's message, which is 'drowned in a screech that had an animal-like quality to it. The screech rose sharply, lasted perhaps five seconds, and then was followed by an abrupt silence'.[95] Communicating the noise of its own destruction, the telephone's screech shatters language, its 'animal-like quality' speaking beyond human communication before falling into total silence.

This screech contributes to what Masco has called 'a new sensorium tuned to the nuclear age'.[96] Examining the relationship between the nuclear bomb and sensory experience, Masco is concerned with what he terms the 'technoaesthetics' of the Cold War. More often than not, the visual effects of nuclear war occupy the cultural imaginary where, as Masco notes, descriptions of the atomic bomb focus on the 'visual intensity of a nuclear explosion' which, he explains, 'reaches the brilliance of [a] thousand midday suns' and 'readily blinds'.[97] But Masco is also interested in the 'auditory dimension' of nuclear culture – a dimension that intersects in curious ways with the noise of the telephone.[98] Nevertheless, it is worth noting that both the bomb's effects and its after-effects are transmitted as silence down the line in Frank's *Alas, Babylon!* when Florence, who is compelled to return to work on the day war breaks out, attempts to communicate with the outside world and discovers that only official government messages can be transmitted. The phone line is out at the bank, too, and its president Edgar Quisenberry rushes to Western Union where he insists that Florence send a message on his behalf:

> 'I HAVE MESSAGE FOR JX SUB-BRANCH OF FEDERAL RESERVE. SENDER IS EDGAR QUISENBERRY, PRESIDENT OF FIRST NATIONAL BANK. WILL YOU TAKE IT?' JX replied: 'IS IT AN OFFICIAL DEF …' Florence blinked. For an instant it seemed that someone had flashed mirrored sunlight into her eyes. At the same instant, the message from JX stopped.[99]

Although Edgar notices 'nothing but a little flash of light', this pause signifies the complete annihilation of Palatka, Jacksonville.[100] Florence's remark to Edgar hovers between bathos and despair: "'I'm very sorry, Mr. Quisenberry,' she said, "but I can't send this. Jacksonville doesn't seem to be there any more.'"[101] Providing a marked counterpoint to the screech of the melting phone in *Fail-Safe*, the dead line in *Alas, Babylon!* is conspicuously understated: both, in the end, are reduced to silence.

The silence of the dead telephone is something that recurs time and again in fiction of the Cold War, not only signalling the ways that a nuclear apocalypse is represented down the line but also suggesting that our fears of extinction are conceptualized in terms of total disconnection and the erasure of human language. For instance, in Helen Clarkson's often neglected 1959 novel *The Last Day* – a novel rich in auditory detail – making contact in a post-nuclear society is critical for Lois's husband Bill:

> Listening to all this, I feel strongly that everything depends on our getting in touch with the outside world as soon as we can. [...] Civilization is communication. Without modern communications, we'll be reduced to barbarism, just as without language, we'd be reduced to animals.[102]

For Bill, the maintenance of modern communication networks is essential to the logocentric order; his reference to 'animals', moreover, recalls the 'animal-like screech' of the melting telephone in *Fail-Safe* and thus speaks to the perceived connections between language, technology and the human. But those surviving on Selsea Island soon come to realize that there are '[n]o telephones working – no electricity'.[103] In fact the drugstore telephone – usually the first to be repaired following a hurricane – becomes the site of tension when the islanders rush to make contact with the outside world, despite the local doctor Joel Franklin's insistence that 'no telephone in the village is working'.[104] The radios are all out too, but when Eric volunteers to travel to the next town to try to source spare parts, he returns with the news: 'I didn't talk to anyone. They were all dead. There were no radio parts. There was no telephone. There was no town. Just rubble.'[105] And even when they do eventually locate undamaged spare parts for the radio-telephone on a cabin cruiser from further down the coast, they are unable to make contact: 'There isn't a voice or a signal anywhere.'[106] By the end of the novel, the sole survivor Lois eventually comes to understand that the silence down the line not only signifies the annihilation of all humanity beyond Selsea Island but also means a life 'without language'. She is alone except for the 'last bird of all', which has sheltered from the radioactive fallout in a hollow: 'Why sing if there is no one to hear you? I sat and listened while he poured forth the most joyous song I have ever heard.'[107] The bird's song is neither the barbarism that Bill fears nor the animal-like screech of *Fail-Safe*; it does, however, speak beyond the human to the devastation of the planet, resonating with Lois's final recognition that 'I shared the guilt of all my species'.[108] Discussing the death of birds in nuclear texts, Cordle describes their absence as 'an unsettling of the natural order that is disturbing for its ubiquity':

> By roaming across and beyond the geographical and political borders that define the human imagination of space, they illuminate the interconnection of complex ecosystems around the planet and their presence also challenges our sense of the human view as the authoritative one; they imply a different understanding of space.[109]

Disrupting the anthropocentric world view, the final bird's song thus serves as a reminder of the interconnection of the planet's ecosystems. But this bird's song is haunted by its own impending cessation: without another bird to answer it, the song hangs suspended, like an unanswered call. From the silence of the telephone line to the last notes of the bird's call, the auditory dimensions of atomic culture connect us not merely to a world without humans but to a world devoid of human ways of making sense: 'Soon', Clarkson writes, 'there would be no form, no color, no light – only a vast, monstrous pulsation of electric and magnetic forces without purpose or future'.[110]

From Bryant's *Red Alert* to Clarkson's *The Last Day*, the telephone veers between missive and missile, thereby communicating its own resistance to (human) language. Reduced to a dead line, it inevitably exposes the capacity for nuclear communication to destroy itself and, in so doing, it speaks to the ways in which the termination of the phone call is bound up with the termination of all life forms on the planet. Certainly, as Seed points out, 'narratives of nuclear war constantly problematize their endings'; in many ways, he continues, 'it is impossible to conceive of an ultimate ending because the very existence of the physical text presumes a kind of survival'.[111] The problematics of the ending, and its relation to language, form and technology, is central to the structure of Mordecai Roshwald's *Level 7*.[112] In this novel, the narrative's survival beyond its own ending is guaranteed only by the arrival of 'The Martian Institute for Archaeological Excavations in the Solar System' some '1550 years after the Great Fire on Earth'.[113] What is more, the 'Great Fire' has been brought about through a device known as the 'atomphone' – an apparatus that speaks to the potential for nuclear communication to destroy itself. The novel features the diary of Officer

X-127 who, because of his 'personal qualities', is sent to Level 7 of the underground military-industrial complex that has been constructed during escalating tensions with an unnamed enemy.[114] X-127 has been assigned as a 'PBX' or 'push button officer' where it is his task to respond to the order to activate atomic destruction. The 'elaborate communications system' operating underground is key to life on Level 7 and Roshwald makes much of the various systems and devices that operate not only within the complex but also between the different levels and the outside world.[115] However, the question of communication becomes increasingly absurd after the bombs have been dropped and the remaining survivors, who are restricted to life underground, make radio contact with the unnamed enemy to discuss the situation. Although the enemy initiated the conflict when twelve rockets were launched by accident – 'the result of a technical failure' – they maintain that 'to retaliate with two thousand bombs was a war crime of the worst sort'.[116] The response is that the enemy should never have reacted to this bombing with an even more violent attack and 'the argument went on in this fashion for some time' until X-127's commander reveals: 'Our leaders did not give the order! It was given automatically when your twelve H-bombs exploded in our country!':

> He went on to explain that for safety's sake we had not relied entirely on our leaders, who, being human, were subject to human weakness and fallibility and could be sick, meet with accidents and what not. Certainly they *could* have given an order to attack, but in fact they did *not* issue such an order. It was done by a mysterious gadget called an 'atomphone'.[117]

It transpires that the atomphone is 'an intricate and ingenious device which was said to be sensitive to atomic explosions occurring within a limited range'; once it had 'registered an atomic explosion, it would automatically issue the order for retaliation of the appropriate strength'.[118] What is more, it appears that the enemy has a similar device: 'The retaliation was automatic. So was the retaliation to the retaliation, and so on. […] Thus the progress of the war resembled the chain reaction going on inside the atomic bomb itself.'[119] By this account, Roshwald's atomphone operates according to the same logic as nuclear fission: the successful operation of the device splits signification and at the same time releases new energy, setting off a chain reaction that not only brings about the destruction of the subject but also leads to the atomization of meaning.

Combining the Greek *atomos* for 'indivisible' and *phōnē* for 'voice, sound, language', the chain reaction initiated by the atomphone operates through the fission of language.[120] In *Level 7*, communication with the enemy is conducted via radio link, but it is only when this conversation falls silent that X-127 understands the extent of the devastation: 'They are silent. They must have died. [...] There is no longer even an ex-enemy to communicate with.'[121] Realizing that '[w]e *are* alone now, literally and absolutely alone', an accident during repairs to their own nuclear energy supply means that all on Level 7 are wiped out. X-127's final words enact the failure of language:

    I   cannot   see   Oh   friends   people   mother   sun   I   I[122]

Here, the atomphone launches the devastation of the planet and the destruction of writing; the fragmentation of thought that accompanies the disintegration of life is enacted in the complete atomization of language. In the end, then, the atomphone speaks only to and with silence: as Derrida warns us, the nuclear apocalypse is an event without remainder, marking the potential end of thought itself.

Roshwald's atomphone operates in a logocentric society that combines nuclear technologies with the speaking machine, thus enacting the complex system of human and nonhuman voices. This focus on the technological voice – and its ultimate disintegration – is a recurring motif in the fiction of the Cuban Missile Crisis. Initially seeming to offer a sanitized view of limited nuclear war that serves to maintain the gendered language of weaponry, the fetishization of the nuclear telephone in the texts that I have considered repeatedly points to a belief in the importance of telecommunications in the resolution of conflict, the restoration of Western power, and the possibility of the resurrection of human civilization. At the same time, however, nuclear communication in these texts remains both anxious and vulnerable and is always haunted by human, technological and linguistic error. In this way, it becomes a critical fault line along which to read the intersections of global power, the relationship between technology and language, and the link between human communication and the destruction of the planet. Indeed, by working towards both resolution and deferral, nuclear communication holds the terminal point always in suspension by suggesting that the speech act can only ever be incomplete. Thus, thinking through the question posed by the Bradbury Science Museum – 'What does this phone have to do with nuclear weapons?' – the atomic telephone slips all too easily from missive to missile, not merely connecting interlocutors but demonstrating the potential collapse of human meaning. With its accompanying screeches and silences, its animal-like sounds and its dead connections, the telephone is always on the verge of atomizing the text.

Notes

1 Joseph Masco, *The Nuclear Borderlands: The Manhattan Project in Post-Cold War New Mexico* (Princeton, NJ: Princeton University Press, 2006), 89.
2 Exhibition photograph, sent to the author by Wendy Strohmeyer, Artifact Collection Specialist at Bradbury Science Museum (personal email correspondence 27 April 2022).
3 Bureau of Arms Control, Verification, and Compliance, 'Treaty Banning Nuclear Weapon Tests in the Atmosphere, in Outer Space and under Water' (signed Moscow 5 August 1963; entered into force 10 October 1963), https://2009-2017.state.gov/t/isn/4797.htm (accessed 2 March 2022); Bureau of Arms Control, Verification, and Compliance, 'Comprehensive Nuclear Test Bay Treaty' (opened for signature 24 September 1996; not yet entered into force), available at: https://2009-2017.state.gov/t/avc/c42328.htm (accessed 2 March 2022).
4 Exhibition photograph, sent to the author by Strohmeyer (27 April 2022). According to personal correspondence with Strohmeyer, the exhibit was on display from circa 2002 until 2018.
5 Masco, *The Nuclear Borderlands*, 89.
6 'Proposal for a Diacritics Colloquium on Nuclear Criticism', *Diacritics*, 14.2 (1984), 2–3 (2).
7 Ibid.
8 Masco, *The Nuclear Borderlands*, 8–9.
9 See, for instance, Daniel Boffey, 'Russia Reasserts Right to Use Nuclear Weapons in Ukraine', *The Guardian* (26 March 2022), available at: https://www.theguardian.com/world/2022/mar/26/russia-reasserts-right-to-use-nuclear-weapons-in-ukraine-putin (accessed 29 April 2022); Robinson Meyer, 'On Top of Everything Else, Nuclear War Would Be a Climate Problem', *The Atlantic* (9 March 2022), available at: https://www.theguardian.com/world/2022/mar/26/russia-reasserts-right-to-use-nuclear-weapons-in-ukraine-putin (accessed 29 April 2022).
10 Martin Amis, *Einstein's Monsters* (New York: Harmony Books, 1987), 10. See also Herman Kahn, *Thinking the Unthinkable* (New York: Horizon Press, 1962).
11 Derrick de Kerckhove, 'On Nuclear Communication', *Diacritics*, 14.2 (1984), 71–81 (71).
12 Ibid.
13 Michael McCanles, 'Machiavelli and the Paradoxes of Deterrence', *Diacritics*, 14.2 (1984), 11–19 (11).
14 Edward Kaplan, *To Kill Nations: American Strategy in the Air-Atomic Age and the Rise of Mutually Assured Destruction* (Ithaca, NY: Cornell University Press, 2015), 181.
15 Peter Bryant, *Red Alert* (Las Vegas: Wolfpack, 2020), 150.
16 Ibid., 102.

17 Ibid., 131.
18 Ibid., 102, 130.
19 Ibid., 166.
20 Ibid., 182.
21 For a discussion of the 'hypermasculinity of national policy' in the fiction of the Cold War, see Susanne Clarke, *Cold Warriors: Manliness on Trial in the Rhetoric of the West* (Carbondale and Edwardsville, IL: Southern Illinois University Press, 2000), 3, et passim. Kubrick's black comedy frequently draws attention to the failures of telecommunication technologies (Stanley Kubrick (dir.), *Dr. Strangelove or: How I Learned to Stop Worrying and Love the Bomb* (Hawk Films/Columbia Pictures, 1964)). David Seed, for instance, points out: 'One of the many ironies of *Dr. Strangelove* is that the military machines function only too well while the means of communication constantly break down'. He cites as an example the scene where British Exchange Program liaison officer Lionel Mandrake runs out of coins when trying to telephone in the recall code to the president: 'one machine has to be "shot" (a Coca-Cola dispenser) in order to give access to another, the telephone' (David Seed, *Under the Shadow: The Atomic Bomb and Cold War Narratives* (Kent, OH: Kent State University Press, 2013), 188). Although it is beyond the scope of this chapter, the telephone – and its failures – is a recurring motif in films of nuclear war. See further Sean M. Maloney, *Deconstructing Dr. Strangelove: The Secret History of Nuclear War Films* (Lincoln, NE: Potomac Books, 2020), 110, 115, 148, 155, 164–5.
22 David E. Scherman, 'The Doomsday Lawsuit', *Life Magazine* (8 March 1963), 49–50 (49).
23 Dan Lindley, 'What I Learned since I Stopped Worrying and Studied the Movie: A Teaching Guide to Stanley Kubrick's "Dr. Strangelove"', *PS: Political Science and Politics*, 34.3 (2001), 663–7 (666).
24 Thomas C. Schelling, 'Meteors, Mischief, and War', *Bulletin of the Atomic Scientists*, 16.7 (September 1960), 293–300 (293).
25 Thomas C. Schelling, *Arms and Influence* (New Haven, CT: Yale University Press, 1966), 263–4.
26 Seed, *Under the Shadow*, 266 n. 28. Tobias Nanz argues that the model for the hotline 'is doubtless the radio-telephone link between Washington and London that was set up under the strictest secrecy during the Second World War and first used in 1943' (Tobias Nanz, 'The Red Telephone: A Hybrid Object of the Cold War', trans. Gregory Simms, in *Disruption in the Arts: Textual, Visual, and Performative Strategies for Analyzing Societal Self-Descriptions*, ed. Lars Koch, Tobias Nanz and Johannes Pause (Berlin: De Gruyter, 2018), 275–89 (279)).
27 Leo Szilard, 'The Mined Cities', *Bulletin of the Atomic Scientists*, 17.10 (1961), 407–12 (408). Despite his significant contribution to the development of the atomic bomb, Szilard had grave concerns about its use, explaining in an interview that in March 1945 he had prepared a memorandum to be presented to Roosevelt which

warned that the use of the atomic bomb in Japan would initiate an arms race with Russia. Shortly after, Szilard turned away from research and began campaigning for arms control, often making use of fiction to develop and disseminate his ideas. See Seed, *Under the Shadow*, 19.
28 For an account of Szilard's understanding of metastability, see Eva Horn, 'The Apocalyptic Fiction: Shaping the Future in the Cold War', in *Understanding the Imaginary War: Culture, Thought and Nuclear Conflict, 1945–90*, ed. Matthew Grant and Benjamin Ziemann (Manchester: Manchester University Press, 2016), 30–50 (41).
29 Szilard, 'The Mined Cities', 408.
30 Ibid., 409.
31 Horn, 'The Apocalyptic Fiction', 43.
32 Attributed to 'F. B. Aiken', the story was actually written by Harvey Wheeler in 1956 (Nicholas Ruddick, 'Adapting the Absurd Apocalypse: Eugene Burdick's and Harvey Wheeler's *Fail-Safe* and Its Cinematic Progeny', in *Future Wars: The Anticipations and the Fears*, ed. David Seed (Liverpool: Liverpool University Press, 2012), 161–79 (164)).
33 F. B. Aiken, 'Abraham '59 – a Nuclear Fantasy', *Dissent*, 6 (1959), 18–24 (21).
34 Ibid., 23, 24.
35 Ibid., 23.
36 Nanz, 'The Red Telephone', 276.
37 Aiken, 'Abraham '59', 24.
38 Eugene Burdick and Harvey Wheeler, *Fail-Safe* (New York: RosettaBooks, 2013), 159.
39 Ibid.
40 Ibid.
41 Nanz points out that whereas in *Red Alert* and 'Abraham '59', the crisis was the result of human action, here the crisis is technical – a possibility that provoked outrage in some quarters. In his book *The Fail-Safe Fallacy*, for instance, Sidney Hook not only objects to what he perceives as a sympathetic portrayal of Khrushchev but also insists that the multiple levels of security ensure that nuclear war will never be triggered by a technical defect. Afraid of the influence it might have on readers, the novel, as Nanz explains, represented 'a danger to national security' (Nanz, 'The Red Telephone', 285). See also Sidney Hook, *The Fail-Safe Fallacy* (New York: Stein and Day, 1963).
42 Burdick and Wheeler, *Fail-Safe*, 190.
43 Ibid., 213.
44 Ibid., 68.
45 Steven E. Miller, 'Nuclear Hotlines: Origins, Evolution, Applications', *Journal for Peace and Nuclear Disarmament*, 4.1 (2021), 176–91 (177).
46 Ibid., 176.
47 Nanz, 'The Red Telephone', 286.
48 Ibid., 286–7. The Stanford Arms Control Group confirms that 'it was decided that if the leaders spoke over a telephone they would have to rely too heavily on rapid

translation. Printed messages would provide greater clarity and give either party time to reflect before replying' (Stanford Arms Control Group, *International Arms Control: Issues and Agreements*, 2nd edition, ed. Coit D. Blacker and Gloria Duffy (Stanford, CA: Stanford University Press, 1984), 118).
49 Tobias Nanz, 'Communication in Crisis: The "Red Phone" and the "Hotline"', *Behemoth: A Journal on Civilization*, 2 (2010), 71–83 (80). It is worth noting that Nanz's discussion here – and in his essay 'The Red Telephone' – revolves around the distinction between the historical hotline and representations of a more informal telephonic communication frequently symbolized in popular culture by a red telephone. This distinction will be addressed later in the chapter.
50 Nanz, 'The Red Telephone', 278.
51 Ibid., 279. For Michel Foucault, the *dispositif* is 'a thoroughly heterogeneous ensemble consisting of discourses, institutions, architectural forms, regulatory decisions, laws, administrative measures, scientific statements, philosophical, moral and philanthropic propositions' (Michel Foucault, 'The Confession of the Flesh,' in *Power/Knowledge: Selected Interviews and Other Writings*, trans. Colin Gordon, Leo Marshall, John Mepham and Kate Soper, ed. Colin Gordon (New York: Pantheon, 1981), 194–228 (194)).
52 Nanz, 'The Red Telephone', 279. This builds on Bruno Latour's interest in 'hybrids of nature and culture'. Discussing the tendency of the modern critical stance that relies on the 'separation between scientific power charged with representing things and the political power charged with representing subjects', Latour challenges the notion that 'subjects are far removed from things' and argues that the 'modern constitution allows the expanded proliferation of the hybrids whose existence, whose very possibility, it denies' (Bruno Latour, *We Have Never Been Modern*, trans. Catherine Porter (Cambridge, MA: Harvard University Press, 1993), 10, 29, 35).
53 Jacques Derrida, 'No Apocalypse, Not Now (Full Speed Ahead, Seven Missiles, Seven Missives)', trans. Catherine Porter and Philip Lewis, *Diacritics*, 14.2 (1984), 20–31 (23).
54 Ibid.
55 Ibid.
56 See also Horn, 'The Apocalyptic Fiction', 31.
57 Derrida, 'No Apocalypse, Not Now', 23.
58 Ibid., 29.
59 Daniel Cordle, 'Cultures of Terror: Nuclear Criticism during and since the Cold War', *Literature Compass*, 3.6 (2006), 1186–99 (1188).
60 This draws on Horn's discussion of 'the Bomb' as a 'nuclear dispositive' that operates on three levels 'which cannot be seen separately and which constitute the intricate correlation of "fiction" and "political reality" at the heart of Cold War politics'. According to Horn, '[t]he Bomb is (1) a weapons technology that is characterised by its unprecedented destructive potential; it designates (2) a political

and military strategy of different options to use this weapon (deploying or not deploying); and it calls (3) for instruments to regulate and control the weapons technology, but also for communication structures within these political strategies' (Horn, 'The Apocalyptic Fiction', 33).

61 'The Red Phone that Was Not on the Hotline', *Electrospaces* (30 August 2013; updated 5 March 2016), available at: https://www.electrospaces.net/2013/08/the-red-phone-that-was-not-on-hotline.html (accessed 8 May 2022).

62 Maloney, *Deconstructing Dr. Strangelove*, 155. Maloney notes that the symbolic red telephone can be found on the cover of Herman Kahn's *Thinking the Unthinkable* as well as on the stained-glass window in the Strategic Air Command chapel at Offutt AFB. He also goes on to note: 'There were actually several Red Phones, as well as other important colored phones in the SAC Control Center. […] The Red Phone was really a voice alternative or backup to the Primary Alerting System panel. For example, when General Power contacted his forces during the various crises, he did that using the Red Phone' (155).

63 This points to the need for a broader discussion regarding the tensions between military and civilian administration of, and control over, nuclear weapons.

64 'The Red Phone that Was Not on the Hotline'; the curator at the Jimmy Carter Library confirms that the museum label was changed following consultation with Vice President Mondale's office (personal correspondence with Museum Curator, Jimmy Carter Library, 8 May 2022). The editors of *Electrospaces* go on to suggest that although the red phone sets were never used for the hotline between Washington and Moscow, they were in fact regularly used as part of the secure voice network used by the US military.

65 Nanz, 'The Red Telephone', 275.

66 In her reading of 'The Mined Cities', Horn also suggests that Szilard 'invents a device that was supposed to prevent war much more effectively than the highly dangerous Doomsday Device, the famous "red telephone"' (Horn, 'The Apocalyptic Fiction', 43).

67 Nanz recognizes that in contrast to the red handset used to link the President's bunker with his own Strategic Command in *Fail-Safe*, the direct line to Moscow 'is not yet assigned any specific color' (280). Despite this acknowledgement, however, there are occasions in his analysis when he appears to conflate the red telephone and the hotline.

68 Burdick and Wheeler, *Fail-Safe*, 22–3.

69 Ibid., 164.

70 Ibid., 265.

71 Ibid., 283.

72 Ibid., 284.

73 Daniel Cordle, *States of Suspense: The Nuclear Age, Postmodernism and United States Fiction and Prose* (Manchester: Manchester University Press, 2008), 5; Pat Frank, *Alas, Babylon!* (New York: Bantam Spectra, 1976), 1.

74   Frank, *Alas, Babylon!*, 14.
75   Ibid., 17.
76   Ibid., 81.
77   Ibid., 82.
78   Seed, *Under the Shadow*, 64.
79   Frank, *Alas, Babylon!*, 82.
80   Helen Caldicott, *Missile Envy: The Arms Race and Nuclear War* (New York: Bantam Books, 1986), 238.
81   William Prochnau, *Trinity's Child* (New York: G. P. Putnam's Sons, 1983), 30.
82   Bryant, *Red Alert*, 9.
83   Ibid., 10.
84   Ibid., 12.
85   Ibid., 11.
86   Derrida, 'No Apocalypse, Not Now', 29.
87   Burdick and Wheeler, *Fail-Safe*, 214.
88   Ibid., 262.
89   Nanz, 'The Red Telephone', 281–2.
90   Ibid., 282.
91   Ibid.
92   Claude E. Shannon and Warren Weaver, *The Mathematical Theory of Communication* (Urbana, IL: University of Illinois Press, 1964), 19.
93   Ibid., 283.
94   Burdick and Wheeler, *Fail-Safe*, 261.
95   Ibid., 279.
96   Masco, *The Nuclear Borderlands*, 10.
97   Ibid., 9–10. Horn also attests to the residing image of the nuclear sublime as '[t]he radiant flash of light, the mushroom cloud and a destroyed landscape reaching up to the horizon' (Horn, 'The Apocalyptic Fiction', 30); see also Frances Ferguson, 'The Nuclear Sublime', *Diacritics*, 14.2 (1984), 4–10.
98   Masco, *The Nuclear Borderlands*, 141. The visual intensity of the blast is well documented, whereas its auditory dimensions – experienced after a lapse of time – are typically neglected. However, for Otto Frisch, Masco notes, '[I]t was not the light or heat, but the sound of the explosion that terrified, and decades later he claimed he could still hear it' (Ferenc Morton Szasz, *The Day the Sun Rose Twice: The Story of the Trinity Site Nuclear Explosion, July 16, 1945* (Albuquerque, NM: University of New Mexico Press, 1984), 88, cited in Masco, *The Nuclear Borderlands*, 58). The literary representation of the sound of the bomb and its resistance to recording and transmission merits a separate discussion.
99   Frank, *Alas, Babylon!*, 111.
100 Ibid.

101 Ibid., 112.
102 Helen Clarkson, *The Last Day* (New York: Torquil, 1959), 76.
103 Ibid., 54. It appears that this is the effect of an electromagnetic pulse (EMP), an effect that became more widely understood in the 1980s; see, for instance, Caldicott, *Missile Envy*, 288–90. EMP is a common feature of later Cold War novels such as Prochnau's *Trinity's Child* and Whitley Strieber and James Kunetka's *Warday* (New York: Holt, Rinehart and Winston, 1984) as well as more recent works such as Don DeLillo's *The Silence* (New York: Simon & Schuster, 2020).
104 Clarkson, *The Last Day*, 61.
105 Ibid., 115.
106 Ibid., 124.
107 Ibid., 183.
108 Ibid.
109 Daniel Cordle, *Late Cold War Literature and Culture: The Nuclear 1980s* (London: Palgrave, 2017), 127.
110 Clarkson, *The Last Day*, 175.
111 Seed, *Under the Shadow*, 5.
112 Roshwald claims that he began working on *Level 7* in the summer of 1957, during a time of 'mad competition' on the international scene, where the second strike capability meant 'the capacity to annihilate the enemy after having been destroyed by a surprise attack' (Mordecai Roshwald, 'Looking Back in Wonder: The Author's Reminiscences and Reflections' (September 2003) in *Level 7*, xxix–xliii (xxix)).
113 Mordecai Roshwald, *Level 7* (Madison, WI: University of Wisconsin Press, 2004), xlv, xlix.
114 Ibid., 22.
115 Ibid., 48.
116 Ibid., 125.
117 Ibid., 126.
118 Ibid. This is similar to the more famous doomsday device in *Dr. Strangelove*, which consists of pre-positioned hydrogen bombs that will automatically detonate if the system's sensors detect attack (Kubrick (dir.), *Dr. Strangelove*).
119 Roshwald, *Level 7*, 126, 127.
120 'atom, n.' and '-phone, comb. form.', *OED Online*, Oxford University Press, March 2022.
121 Roshwald, *Level 7*, 176.
122 Ibid., 176, 183.

7

Remains

Prior to the emergence of the Georgia Flu in Emily St John Mandel's *Station Eleven*, Clark finds himself frustrated at 'iPhone zombies, people half his age who wandered in a dream with their eyes fixed on their screens'.[1] However, when the virus takes hold, he – like most others – turns to his phone:

> It occurred to Clark that he should call someone, actually everyone, that he should call everyone he'd ever loved and talk to them and tell them all the things that mattered, but it was apparently already too late for this, his phone displaying a message he'd never seen before: SYSTEM OVERLOAD EMERGENCY CALLS ONLY.[2]

Seemingly so crucial to surviving Day One, by Day Eight, with the failure of power grids and loss to network coverage, the mobile is rendered worthless. By Day One Hundred, Clark has accepted that his phone will no longer offer any assistance at all. That does not mean that it is without value in the post-pandemic world, however, and rather than discarding it, he chooses to preserve it: entering the Skymiles Lounge at Severn City Airport where his plane was diverted during the first hours of the pandemic, Clark 'place[s] his useless iPhone on the top shelf'.[3] With it, he puts an Amex Card and a driver's license, and within a few hours others have added a second iPhone, a pair of stilettos and a snow globe.[4] This is the beginning of the 'Museum of Civilization': 'There seemed to be a limitless number of objects in the world that had no practical use but that people wanted to preserve: cell phones with their delicate buttons, iPads, Tyler's Nintendo console, a selection of laptops.'[5] The founding object is the smartphone, which represents life 'before' the Georgia Flu: it was a time when you could 'lift a receiver or press a button on a telephone, and [...] speak to anyone'; significantly, however, it was also a time when you could 'leave your garbage in bags on the curb', where a truck would collect it and transport it 'to some invisible place'.[6]

In many ways, the Museum of Civilisation is Clark's answer to the questions posed by Jennifer Gabrys in *Digital Rubbish*: 'How do electronics die? Where do they go to die? How do they transform and decompose? What (and whom) do they leave behind?'[7] But although *Station Eleven* engages with the relationship between technology, catastrophe and contemporary life, it neither addresses the spatiality of waste nor what Rob Nixon calls the 'slow violence' of its environmental impact.[8] Of course, the problem of rubbish is not simply a contemporary concern; developing an anthropology of waste has been a long-standing project, with seminal twentieth-century works in the field including Robert Hertz's 1907 study of burial rites, Marcel Mauss's 1925 essay on the notion of reciprocity and the gift, Mary Douglas's 1966 examination of pollution and taboo in *Purity and Danger* and Michael Thompson's 1979 *Rubbish Theory*.[9] But while Brian Neville and Johanne Villeneuve note that 'our age is by no means unique in its wastefulness', they also point out that 'it certainly has the dubious honor of creating waste of kinds and quantities as yet unseen'.[10] In fact, the production of electronic waste in particular, as Gabrys remarks, is growing at an unprecedented rate.[11] Challenging privileged Western perceptions of the recycling of electronic goods as an unproblematically ethical practice, Gabrys points out that it frequently involves transporting electronic goods for salvage to the Global South, where environmental laws are lax and labour is unregulated and cheap. It turns out, she argues, that the digital revolution is 'littered with rubbish'.[12] With electronics such as the smartphone now being produced at an explosive rate, discarded goods are transported to Mandel's 'invisible place' where they pile up and damage the ecosystem of the poorest communities – what Zygmunt Bauman calls 'ready-made dumping sites for the human waste of modernization'.[13]

Such sites include Guiyu in Guangdong Province, China – a once-rural rice-growing community transformed into a vast e-waste processing machine. For many years, Guiyu was the recipient of discarded and obsolete electronics from all over the world; this was despite the 1989 Basel Convention, which forbids the trade of hazardous goods across international borders.[14] Often mixed with scrap metal shipments to avoid detection, these goods were processed in unsafe working conditions by the poorest and most vulnerable communities.[15] Following a 2001 investigation, a report by Basel Action Network and the Silicon Valley Toxic Coalition described the export of electronic waste to Asia as the 'dirty little secret of the high-tech revolution'.[16] Numerous studies have since evidenced the high concentrations of heavy metal pollution from electronic waste recycling in the area, and in 2013, a United Nations report labelled Guiyu an 'environmental calamity', explaining that 'informal processing often leads to detrimental effects on the environment and the health and safety of workers and local communities'.[17] Following the efforts of environmental activists and international media interest, the local government in Guangdong approved a plan to construct a major new industrial park in 2013, and in 2017 the Chinese Ministry of Environmental Protection notified the World Trade Organization that it would by the end of that year be banning imports of highly polluted solid waste.[18] In 2021, it extended this move and banned all solid waste imports.[19] But although recycling processes in the region have been formalized, this has had other cultural and economic impacts, leading to an effective monopoly on most forms of recycling, lower wages for workers and increased deprivation.[20] Moreover, environmental activists point out that while Guiyu appears to be free from further toxic waste, the trade has simply shifted to other locations.[21] Thus, rather than changing disposal practices and addressing the increasing traffic in toxins, the sites to which electronic waste from around the world is sent have merely shifted elsewhere; as Mengtian Sun points out: 'The tide of waste keeps adjusting its course in relation to cheap labour.'[22]

Despite its diminutive size and seeming immateriality, the smartphone is a major player in the exportation and trade of digital rubbish. Throughout its lifecycle, the phone contributes to unsafe and abusive labour practices including the mining of metals, the trade in conflict minerals, the production of microchips using toxic solvents, and the handling of hazardous components, as well as the environmental damage caused by its manufacture, transportation, consumption and disposal. In *Made to Break*, Giles Slade notes that in the United States mobile phones have 'achieved the dubious distinction of having the shortest life cycle of any electronic consumer product in the country, and their life span is still declining'.[23] According to a report by the United States Environment Protection Agency, an estimated 151 million phones a year – approximately 416,000 a day – were thrown away in 2014 in the United States alone, a figure that many suggest continues to grow.[24] This, combined with their 'miniaturization', Slade notes, marks the phone as a 'significant toxic hazard': it is both difficult and expensive to disassemble the tiny components of the mobile phone so that the materials can be reused, he remarks, noting that because of their size, most mobile phones are simply dumped in rubbish bins for transportation to landfills or incinerators.[25] This is despite the fact that mobile phones contain high levels of permanent biological toxins (PBTs) including arsenic, antimony, beryllium, cadmium, lead, nickel and zinc. If discarded phones are burned, Slade points out, toxins are released into the air; if they are buried, pollution seeps into the groundwater.[26] The toxins, scientists remark, persist in the environment for protracted periods of time, meaning that ecological devastation is not a short-term local problem but has lasting planetary consequences.[27]

Exploring the afterlife of electronics as well as the invisible sites of their disposal, this chapter reads the toxic remainder of electronic goods and their resistance to both material and conceptual dissolution.[28] Focusing on literary depictions of Guiyu, and drawing on work by Jennifer Gabrys, Kevin Hetherington and Rob Nixon, among others, it considers literary waste in order to rethink the impact of the telephone on multiple and entangled ecologies. Reflecting on the rapid obsolescence of the mobile phone as just one element of a much wider concern, I first seek to examine the effects of electronic waste in work by Chen Qiufan, Sally Wen Mao and Rita Wong, exploring the ways that these texts dissolve human-waste relations through toxic languages and forms. Moving on to focus specifically on the afterlife of the mobile phone and its environmental impact, I consider the relationship between the telephone and ecocide. But whereas my account in Chapter 6 of Cold War calling was interested in what happens to the telephone when it is destroyed, this chapter turns instead to the refusal of the telephone to disappear entirely. Resituating the phone as remains, it examines the stubborn material resistance of digital technology, arguing that works by Qiufan, Mao and Wong enact the interminability of the phone call while simultaneously exploring the ways that its material, conceptual and linguistic errancy persists long into our imagined telefutures.

The spatiality of disposal

The afterlife of electronics is at the heart of Chen Qiufan's science fiction ecothriller *Waste Tide*, which is set in a fictional city named 'Guiyu'.[29] Chen's play on the name of this city is significant: the 'Guiyu' (硅屿) of Waste Tide means 'silicon island'; however, the real city of 'Guiyu' (貴嶼) in Guangdog means 'precious island'. As homophones, only the Chinese characters mark the difference.[30] The first chapter of *Waste Tide* brings together the irony of the fictional Guiyu's dual legacy when Scott Brandle visits the 'overly air-conditioned Museum of Silicon Isle History', where he contemplates 'the fine, handcrafted wooden model of the junk at the center of the glass display case'.[31] In place of a digital display, Scott contemplates a 'hand-drawn map of Silicon Isle' which forms the backdrop to the exhibit, against which the junk 'glisten[s] with the reddish-brown varnish intended to give it an antique air'.[32] This is not a convincing replica: 'the mapmaker strained too hard to show the natural beauty of the local scenery, and the excessive application of colorful paint appeared unnatural'.[33] In this way, the curator avoids the use of twenty-first-century technologies in the exhibition, opting instead for a false antiquity. The simulation is especially ironic given that Silicon Isle is the place to which discarded electronics are sent to be processed from all over the planet and that this is a world in which the rich 'switch body parts as easily as people used to switch phones'.[34] In fact, Scott recognizes this incongruity: 'The museum was too bright, too clean, just like the whitewashed and rewritten history it tried to present, just like the version of Silicon Isle that the natives tried to show outsiders.'[35] Well aware of the harm inflicted on vulnerable communities by global electronic waste, Scott acknowledges the false technological optimism depicted in the museum display. Notably, the exhibit that catches Scott's eye is translated by Ken Liu as 'junk' – a word that signifies not only 'a sailing vessel of a kind used in East and South-East Asia, typically having fully-battened lugsails' but also 'old or discarded items or materials that may be reused or recycled [...]; waste, refuse, rubbish'.[36] In this way, Chen unsettles the relation between electronic matter, its preservation in the archive and its exclusion through disposal practices. In fact, as he departs the museum, Scott reflects: 'The model junk seemed to him the perfect metaphor: a play on words was perhaps the sole remaining thread connecting the museum and this island of junk.'[37] Not only does the metaphor operate on a linguistic level, but it also serves as the remainder that connects the preservation and eradication of matter. The twin sites of museum and dump thus invite us to rethink, in Ioana Jucan's words, the 'matter and temporality of remains'.[38] By placing the museum and the e-waste processing centre side by side, Chen asks us not simply to question our assumptions about global recycling efforts but to rethink the meaning and value of material permanence.[39]

A self-confessed 'economic hit man' who represents TerraGreen Recycling, Scott has visited waste-processing sites around the globe.[40] His mission in Guiyu is to persuade the clan leaders to allow the company to take control of the process in exchange for local economic and environmental benefits – a trade that also, of course, results in huge financial gain for the United States. Scott's occupation thus exposes the corruption of global recycling practices, enacting Gabrys's argument that current recycling initiatives do not remove waste but merely displace it:

> When we recycle, we repeat the process of delaying the inevitable return to rubbish. Electronic waste may be discarded in one location but then surfaces in another to be processed as goods with marginal scrap value. Yet when that scrap is processed into new electronic components, for instance, it re-enters a value system that will mobilize again toward rubbish.[41]

Gabrys's theory of digital rubbish builds on Mary Douglas's conceptualization of dirt as 'the by-product of a systematic ordering and classification of matter, in so far as ordering involves rejecting inappropriate elements'.[42] As 'matter out of place', dirt, Doulas argues, threatens to pollute when it is in the wrong place.[43] Transporting electronic waste overseas is similar to the creation of rituals and taboos examined by Douglas; in other words, it is another way of attempting to contain and control our relation to dirt by placing it out of sight. For Kevin Hetherington, this demonstrates that disposal 'is not primarily about waste but about placing. It is as much a spatial as a temporal category'.[44] Considering the ways that waste is so often placed elsewhere, Hetherington's 'spatiality of disposal' proposes that the lifecycle of electronics is bound up in a recursive process that operates across a global stage – a practice that simultaneously exposes and heightens global divisions.[45]

The spatiality of waste is influenced by both socio-economics and race and makes manifest the ways that vulnerable and disenfranchised communities and places are – in the words of Stacy Alaimo – 'literally dumped upon'.[46] This is made explicit in *Waste Tide* when Scott travels to the villages of Guiyu from Silicon Isle town, the site of the museum and where the leaders of the three local feuding clans who control e-waste processing in the region enjoy reasonable air quality, uncontaminated food and drinkable water. In contrast, the workers live in chaos and squalor in the villages, which are shrouded in 'waves of heat, clouds of toxic miasma, and streets full of filth':

> Metal chassis, broken displays, circuit boards, plastic components, and wires, some dismantled and some awaiting processing, were scattered everywhere like piles of manure, with laborers, all of them migrants from elsewhere in China, flitting between the piles like flies. The workers sifted through the piles and picked out valuable pieces to be placed into the ovens or acid baths for additional decomposition to extract copper and tin, as well as gold, platinum, and other precious metals. What was left over was either incinerated or scattered on the ground, creating even more trash. No one wore any protective gear.[47]

The villagers who have been hired by the clans to process the toxic rubbish are known as 'waste people': 'For the Luo clan, a waste girl wasn't a person, but more akin to a sheep, a farming implement, a bag of seeds.'[48] If waste people are injured during the course of the work, or if they overdose on the digital mushrooms introduced by the clans as a means to maintain control, they too become 'bugs, disposable trash', demonstrating the destabilization of human-waste relations.[49]

Chen's waste people thus mirror Bauman's description of 'human rejects' or 'wasted humans' whose task it is to deal with 'the rejects of consumer feasts; indeed, they seem to have been made for each other'.[50] Describing the real Guiyu as an 'electronic junkyard', Bauman exposes the ways in which vulnerable workers 'have fallen (or been thrown) overboard from the vehicle of economic progress'.[51] The concept of 'waste people' or 'wasted humans' thus not only overturns ontological categories but also exposes the destruction of both human and more-than-human ecologies.

Destabilizing human-waste relations

Contaminants seep through the pages of *Waste Tide*. Throughout the text, the boundaries of the human body are repeatedly permeated by toxic materials:

> Everything was shrouded in a leaden miasma, an amalgamation of the white mist generated by the boiling aqua regia in the acid baths and the black smoke from the unceasing burning of PVC, insulation, and circuit boards in the fields and on the shore of the river. The two contrasting colors were mixed by the sea breeze until they could no longer be distinguished, seeping into the pores of every living being.[52]

If, as Douglas asserts, 'dirt offends against order', Chen's waste people not only illustrate the violation of human rights embedded at the heart of current disposal practices but also expose the interaction between the human body and anthropogenic waste.[53] These human-waste relations are further threatened when Scott's covert mission is revealed: in addition to his job at TerraGreen Recycling, he is also on the lookout for a prosthetic device that carries a biological weapon known as the Suzuki virus. Capable of causing mass hallucination, the virus has been sent to Guiyu, and Scott's bosses are keen to see it returned so that they can maximize its potential as a military weapon. Initially unaware of this context is Scott's translator Kaizong, a first-generation Chinese-American history graduate driven by nostalgia for his homeland. During the visit, Kaizong becomes infatuated with Mimi, a worker who has been infected by the Suzuki variant and who is captured and tortured by the Luo clan. But the virus mutates when it encounters the heavy metals in her body and, when she is beaten, raped and buried by members of the clan, Mimi's consciousness fuses with the body of a discarded mecha and she is transformed from Mimi 0 to Mimi 1, a powerful cyborg capable of connecting directly to wireless networks in order to wreak vengeance on her oppressors and galvanize the workers into uprising. In this way, the human-waste cyborg in *Waste Tide* challenges the divisions between organic life and electronics, and between the destruction of the human body and ecological devastation.[54]

The novel's treatment of human-waste relations enacts Alaimo's argument that the human and the environment are never entirely separate. Proposing a theory of 'trans-corporeality', in which the human and more-than-human are entangled, Alaimo argues that the 'trans-' not only points to the movement across sites but also 'opens up a mobile space that acknowledges the often unpredictable and unwanted actions of human bodies, nonhuman creatures, ecological systems, chemical agents, and other actors'.[55] This trans-corporeality is enacted by Mimi, whose body ruptures conventional divisions between the natural and the artificial, the human and the machine. By presenting the transformation of Mimi 0 to Mimi 1 in terms of contamination across both temporal and spatial dimensions, Chen suggests that electronic waste can neither be contained nor fully broken down. Moreover, by embodying human-waste entanglement, Mimi enacts Alaimo's claim that the movement of toxins across human and more-than-human bodies ruptures knowledge practices and demonstrates that trans-corporeality is 'never an elsewhere but is always already here'.[56] In other words, the toxic body indicates not only the inseparability of the human and the environment but also the here and the elsewhere, and the deep past and the distant future.

Trans-corporeality is simultaneously embodied by Mimi and embedded in *Waste Tide* at the level of form. Bringing together cyberpunk and traditional Chinese literary tropes, and mixing superstition and animism with speculative technologies and ecological realism, the novel's generic hybridity stages the movements between the local and the global, and the human and the more-than human.[57] This correlates with Peter Vermeulen's observations regarding the limitations of literary realism and its ability to capture the 'unruly realities' of the Anthropocene.[58] Noting that 'genres are not only templates for organizing our experiences of the world, they are also affective scenarios through which we orient ourselves in a world whose coordinates we haven't yet fully understood', Vermeulen argues that 'it might be the friction between generic templates that provides the best intimation of a nonhuman reality'.[59] In this way, as Cara Healey affirms, by blending elements of cyberpunk with elements of twentieth-century Chinese realism rather than placing literary traditions in opposition to each other, *Waste Tide* plays out the ways that the human and more-than human worlds are always enmeshed.[60] Speaking both to the specific conditions in China, and to worldwide concerns with ecocide, *Waste Tide*'s hybridity thus opens up questions regarding the ways that the Anthropocene demands a rethinking of literary languages and forms.

Generic hybridity and toxic poetics

The toxic effects of e-waste, the interchange between human-waste relations, and generic hybridity are also at the heart of poetic representations of Guiyu, which include Sally Wen Mao's poem 'Electronic Necropolis' from her 2019 collection *Oculus* and Rita Wong's 'sort by day, burn by night' published in her 2007 collection *forage*.[61] Mao's Guiyu is a 'glowing, dying / circuit', the place of 'black digital water' where fish scales shoot 'jets of bitumen'.[62] Representing Guiyu as the 'sum of foreign / dross', Mao emphasizes the entanglement of the natural and the artificial:

> I douse
> the hardware in pyretic acids
> before it scrapes me, enters me, a lather of data
> against my organs, bless them,
> my warring insides.[63]

In the poem, the hardware doused in acid is a poisoned body, the discarded machine is skinned, and data is blood. Mao thus enacts Alaimo's trans-corporeality through the entangling of bodies and forms, with her machines supplying both 'food' and 'harm'.[64] Mao's emphasis on flesh and hardware reinforces the materiality of electronic waste and its tangible impact on both human and more-than-human bodies; here, even sleep is 'short-circuiting'.[65] The destabilization of epistemological categories is extended through Mao's choice of language. Splicing together images of the human body with vocabulary associated with electronic engineering, digital culture and recycling processes, she forges a poetics of dismemberment: 'We unsolder our duress / with wire splinters, all lodged in our flesh / as if powering us.'[66] In bringing together intimate, informal, biological and scientific registers, Mao translates toxicity into a contamination of the text. This can be framed in terms of what Ocean Vuong has referred to as Mao's use of 'acidic language'. Describing Mao's work as 'reclaim[ing] for itself an acidic possibility, corrosive to monuments of thought', Vuong points to language as matter and its potential to break down ideology.[67] This is evident in 'Electronic Necropolis' where Mao's acidic language destabilizes the boundaries between human and waste, and exposes the inequalities of disposal practices and their relation to place and race. In so doing, Mao corrodes master narratives regarding technology and notions of historical progress. The effects of environmental degradation are ever present in the poem through an entanglement of human-waste relations, where under the 'skein' of the Lianjiang River, the 'foreign dross' is '[r]iven, rising: a bloodless organ'.[68] The present participle 'rising' indicates that the movements between the human and the more-than-human are mobile and ongoing; the material remainder of electronic waste, in other words, continues to spread across both temporal and spatial dimensions.

Referring both to 'these nights' and the Lianjiang River that 'flows onward, toward the purple rusk, the limestone cliffs', Mao's 'Electronic Necropolis' brings together both the present moment and geological deep time.[69] This stages the shift from linear teleology to what David Farrier describes as 'thick time' – or 'the lyric's capacity to put multiple temporalities and scales within a single frame, to "thicken" the present with an awareness of the other times and places'.[70] In fact, toxic pollution remains long after the death of the human; although the poem opens with the suggestion that its speaker 'tend[s] to disappearance', Mao shows us that waste and its by-products refuse to disappear, instead remaining 'incant like ghosts'.[71] Serving as an unsettling reminder of the permanence of toxic matter, then, Mao draws attention not only to the movement between body and waste but also to the ways in which discarded and dismantled electronics never truly vanish, creating instead new geologies that continue to haunt the planet.

Exposing the trade of global waste and its inequalities, Mao's 'Electronic Necropolis' thus demonstrates that despite their perceived immateriality, we are haunted by the stubborn afterlife of electronic goods. This spectrality recalls Hetherington's theory of material remains, in which rubbish refuses to disappear entirely but instead returns in unexpected ways and in different forms.[72] Reframing the conduit of disposal as a 'door' rather than a 'rubbish bin', Hetherington argues that 'disposal is never as final as is implied by the notion of rubbish but involves issues of managing social relations and their representation around themes of movement, transformation, incompleteness, and return'.[73] He suggests that we must challenge the notion of waste as a singular act of disposal or as a 'final state of rubbishing' and thus move from conceptualizing waste as something that we need to get rid of towards an emphasis on 'the recursivity of disposal in a fuller sense'.[74] This means thinking about the ongoing impermanence of non-biodegradable materials and their unexpected return. Mirroring Mao's haunting incantations and drawing on a language of spectrality, Hetherington states that 'in consumption practices there are many ghosts'.[75] But while this language of spectrality points to the perpetual return of waste, the association of ghosts with ephemerality and immateriality doesn't fully acknowledge the material impact of technology's afterlife. Arguing that 'waste always returns', Gabrys goes on to stress that 'digital technologies, so apparently immaterial, also have their substantial remainders'.⁷⁶ Discussing the contemporary emphasis on virtuality and immateriality, Jonathan Sterne also points out that '"new" media technologies as we know them, and all of their components, are defined by their own future decomposition'.⁷⁷ Noting that even compressed digital formats have a material basis, he argues that 'the entire edifice of new communication technology is a giant trash heap waiting to happen'.⁷⁸ Challenging our sense of the ephemerality or immateriality of information culture, then, both Gabrys and Sterne argue that portable electronics such as the smartphone rematerialize with sometimes unexpected remainders and effects.

For Hetherington, this remainder can be understood in terms of the resistant 'tackiness' of things.⁷⁹ Certainly, this material resistance is at work in 'Electronic Necropolis', where the ghosts are not simply immaterial spirits but are imbued with a sticky resistance. Evident in the return of pyretic acids and other toxins, this tackiness is also enacted at the level of language and form where words and images adhere across lines and at the same time show a resistance to being worked through. The 'skinless clouds', for instance, stick to 'skinned machines' with the verb 'to skin' (meaning 'to remove the skin from') attaching itself to its adjectival form (meaning 'endowed with or possessing (a) skin'), where it denotes precisely the opposite.⁸⁰ Sticking together the 'lather of data / against my organs' with the 'foreign dross' that forms a 'bloodless organ', Mao stages the trans-corporeality of waste, binding together organs from the human and more-than-human world and in so doing re-organizing human-waste relations. In this way, her poem not only exhibits an acidity capable of corroding ways of thinking but also performs the resistant tackiness of toxic remains through a stickiness that operates across and between signifiers.

The quick and the slow

This sticky resistance is extended in the work of Rita Wong, a poet who draws on indigenous, feminist and environmental thought. Examining global capitalism, environmental justice and decolonial approaches to intertwined ecologies, the cover of her 2007 collection *forage* features a photograph of Guiyu by Lai Yun for Greenpeace: in the foreground is a mountain of circuit boards; the natural hills of Guiyu rise in the background. Focusing on Guiyu, the poem 'sort by day, burn by night' forms what Samantha Walton describes as the book's centrepiece.⁸¹ Composed after watching the Basel Action Network film *Exporting Harm*,

Wong's depiction of Guiyu draws attention to the circulation of matter in the manufacture and disposal of electronics, asking:

> where do metals come from?
> where do metals return?[82]

Here, Wong speaks to the inevitable return of matter in disposal practices. Focusing on the circuit board, she turns our attention to the 'hundred thousand people' who work in Guiyu. Enacting the global movement of materials from manufacture to consumption to dump, and stressing the irony through quotation marks, Wong addresses those who

> 'liberate recyclable metals'
> into the canals & rivers
> turning them into acid sludge,
> swollen with lead,
> barium leachate, mercury bromide.[83]

Justified right, the placing of these lines emphasizes the spatiality of displacement, suggesting a toxicity that seeps across the page. Like Mao, Wong's poetry blends diasporic and scientific languages in order to enact the trans-corporeality of electronic waste. Indeed, with its 'compilation of lead, aluminium, iron, / plastics, orchestrated mercury, arsenic antimony … ', the poem reads as a catalogue of toxicity, staging the insistent return of waste contaminants.[84]

Riffing on this toxic materiality, Wong's poem explores what Jussi Parikka calls the 'toxic legacies of technological culture'.[85] Investigating the spatiality and temporality of toxic waste, Parikka discusses the ways that discarded goods refuse containment and instead leak across times and places.[86] For Jucan, this leakiness can be understood as a form of 'ongoingness' that operates across 'extended temporal and spatial intervals and scales'.[87] Wong's text is concerned with precisely this 'ongoingness' and the spillage of matter across extended intervals and scales. This effluence is evident in her claim that 'economy of scale / shrinks us all' as well as in the irregular arrangement of lines leaking across the page as matter is transformed from the 'shiny laptop' to the 'acid sludge' of the dump.[88] Furthermore, textual leakage – made manifest through the material arrangement of Wong's poem – spreads beyond the frame of the poem to the reader's own complicity in toxic legacies: 'what if your pentium got dumped in guiyu village? / your garbage, someone else's cancer?'[89] The unfolding effects of waste across temporal and spatial dimensions – 'global whether / here or there' – are reframed in light of Wong's citation of Whitman's 'One's-Self I Sing': 'Yet *utter the word Democratic, the word En-masse*'. By omitting the preceding line of Whitman's poem – 'One's-Self I sing, a simple separate person' – Wong transforms the song of myself to the 'toxic ditty of silica', thereby speaking to the perceived limitations of the lyric I ('a simple separate person') to encompass ecological entanglement in the age of the Anthropocene.[90] Drawing on Farrier's argument that the Anthropocene destabilizes the stable perspective of the lyric subject, Walton proposes that not only is the singular subject position insufficient to capture the 'huge scale of interconnections, bodies, agencies and materials' in Wong's work, but the epic form is likewise rejected for being 'too preoccupied with closed, heroic and anthropocentric narratives'.[91] Wong's alternative is open field poetics, which Walton explains functions through fragmentation and juxtaposition in order to reject master narratives in favour of ecological entanglement and trans-corporeality.[92] In this way, the poem moves beyond a single, stable or closed perspective and instead opens to a leaky poetic form that maps the uneven spatio-temporal dynamics of disposal while emphasizing its planetary devastation across deep time. Enacting the displacement of electronic waste through its ongoingness, 'sort by day, burn by night' thus exposes the toxic materiality of global capitalism, stressing the materiality of digital rubbish and its unequal, insistent and leaky return.

This sense of a material remainder also operates in Wong's recent collection *undercurrent*, where in 'pollution dodged?' contamination is 'relocated, lodged / in moist flesh folds'.[93] In this poem, Wong enacts the traffic of toxins by exposing the trade of one person's waste for another's poison, the movement signified by the displacement of the line:

> tricks of the global trade
>
> my endocrine disruption
>
> for your muted phone
>
> your cancer
>
> for my keyboard[94]

The remainder is once again insistent in Wong's poem, where 'dispersed histories bioaccumulate / returning in media res ICYMI' and 'bloodstream's poisoned gift' keeps 'giving & giving & giving'.[95] Exposing the trade of global waste and its inequalities, Wong's poem pays particular attention to the ways in which our move to smaller, lighter and faster electronics contributes to ecological damage, noting that while we remain on the 'techno treadmill' our 'eyes stay on the screen / that gets smaller & smaller / faster & faster'.[96] For Wong, global capitalism is a 'toxic roller coaster' in which digital culture appears to manifest as immateriality, disposability and instantaneity, culminating in the 'Great Acceleration' of the Anthropocene.[97] But at the same time, Wong undercuts this with the reminder that for all its perceived immediacy and immateriality, the speed of digital media such as the smartphone results in what she describes as 'a slow release traffic jam'.[98] This speaks to Rob Nixon's theory of slow violence, by which he means 'a violence that occurs gradually and out of sight, a violence of delayed destruction that is dispersed across time and space, an attritional violence that is typically not viewed as violence at all'.[99] Opposed to our customary sense of violence as a sudden, visible and often spectacular event in time, Nixon argues that we need to engage with 'a different kind of violence' – one that is 'incremental and accretive, its calamitous repercussions playing out across a range of temporal scales'.[100] Explaining that we must address the 'long dyings' that are the result of 'slow-motion toxicity', Nixon calls for new ways of addressing and exposing acts of slow violence that may be incremental, intergenerational and dispersed but that have a long-lasting and catastrophic impact on the planet.[101] Responding to this, Wong's shifting forms bring together the ongoing acceleration of global capitalism with the slow release of toxins and their interminable effects, thus forging alternative ways of thinking about trans-corporeality, slow violence and the digital afterlife.

These changing scales and speeds, moreover, speak to the planned obsolescence of digital media in which, as Gabrys writes, 'materials are caught in a tension between the quick and the slow': 'Ephemerality can only hold at one level; it instead reveals new spaces of permanence. Throw away plastic to discover it lasts for an ice age. The balance of time shifts.'[102] This shifting temporality is central to Wong's poetics, which moves from the 'toxic ditty' of 'sort by day, burn by night' to the 'giving & giving & giving' of 'pollution, dodged?' in order to stage both the spatiality of disposal and its disjunctive and ongoing temporalities. Employing multilingualism and experiments with space and lineation, Wong adjusts the pace of the poem in order to enact both the quick and the slow. In so doing, her toxic forms seek to expose the long dyings engendered by electronic waste.

Afterlives

What does all this mean for the death of the phone and its material and conceptual remains? And in what ways might the phone also operate according to a toxic stickiness? For many, the rapid obsolescence of the mobile phone – and the toxic practices of manufacture and disposal that structure its lifecycle – is the symbol par excellence of the slow violence of electronic waste. But to think more precisely about the role of the telephone in literary depictions of Guiyu, I wish to return to *Waste Tide* to pick up on Chen's handling of the smartphone and its possible futures. What is particularly notable here is that despite the novel's futuristic setting – where prosthetic limbs obey mental directions and squid extract has been adapted to translate brain signals to electronic currents – the telephones of *Waste Tide* have changed relatively little from their current form and function. Like smartphone use in the present day, the characters of *Waste Tide* employ handheld devices to make calls, share pictures, check their location, and light the way in the dark. And although the phone in the novel can also be used to placate chipped dogs and scan for electromagnetic emissions, its overt materiality is a stubborn reminder of its future remains. On first encountering the mecha on Tide Gazing beach, for instance, Kaizong 'took out his ruggedized mobile phone and wiped off the condensation. The screen emitted a pale glow'.[103] Later, when Scott is handed a video phone, the chunkiness of the apparatus is uncanny in the midst of other digital advances: 'The space shuttle-shaped satellite phone rang in Scott's hand, a rather unusual series of Jamaican-style electronic beeps.'[104] In fact, Scott resents the materiality and errancy of the phone call: '[he] couldn't get through to Kaizong's phone no matter how many times he tried; he really despised these devices designed for communication under restricted bitrate'.[105] Scott is referring here to the fact that Silicon Isle is a restricted bitrate zone with limited access to remote databases. But the phone's bulky hardware does more than simply illustrate the digital poverty of the region; it also appears to offer a connecting line between the futurism of the novel and the interminable material effects of current telephoning practices. Moreover, the anachronism of this shuttle-shaped video phone reflects the temporal disjunction inherent in the lifecycle of electronic goods; in other words, the telephone in *Waste Tide* operates according to the oscillation between the quick and the slow – between what Wong terms the 'toxic rollercoaster' and the 'slow release traffic jam' of contaminants. Chen's decision to arrest the development of the phone in the face of so many other futuristic technologies thus points not only to the persistence of the phone in the cultural imaginary but also to its absolute refusal to give up the ghost.

At once critical to the narrative and largely obscured, the ambivalent status of the telephone in *Waste Tide* is embodied by Mimi. According to Healey, the character known in English as Mimi is named Xiao Mi in the original Chinese version of the novel.[106] Xiao Mi translates as China's staple 'millet', with 'xiao' denoting 'little', conveying her rural upbringing. But, as Healey notes, Xiao Mi is also contained in the name 'Xiaomi Keji', a Chinese electronics company founded in 2010, which rose to prominence as a popular Chinese smartphone brand in the years surrounding *The Waste Tide*'s 2013 publication'.[107] Healey argues:

> More smartphones mean more e-waste, so Xiao Mi's name, her very identity, is tied to her position as a cog in the machine of the e-waste processing industry. Furthermore, Xiaomi phones are notable for their low cost (particularly compared to the iPhone) and online flash sales, making smartphones available to a broad segment of the Chinese population.[108]

For Healey, Mimi's name is associated with the 'democratization of smartphone ownership', but Mimi's fate also reinforces the contribution of the phone to the 'ongoingness' of digital rubbish.[109] On the one hand, the treatment of Mimi as a 'waste girl' by the village clans mirrors the planned obsolescence of the smartphone – a device that is designed to have an ever-shorter life span, boosting the need for upgrades at regular intervals. On the other hand, however, Mimi's unresolved fate at the end of the novel speaks to the ways in which electronic waste frustrates the possibility of what Hetherington calls a 'final state of rubbishing' and instead returns in unexpected ways and forms.[110] In the novel's concluding scenes, Mimi 0, weakened by the efforts of Mimi 1 to stop Scott's heart, begs Kaizong to turn the gun on her, despite the taunts and threats issued by her cyborg double: 'The voices stopped. [...] He had finally pulled the trigger.'[111] But Mimi doesn't die as a result of Kaizong's bullet. Kaizong learns: 'As the electromagnetic pulse penetrated her brain, the heat had instantaneously incinerated the neural tissue around the metal particles. However, as the pulse had lasted only a few milliseconds, the damage wasn't life-threatening.'[112] The damage, however, is horribly cruel: devoid of emotion and logic, Mimi is left with the cognitive capacity of a three-year-old, and when Kaizong visits her in hospital for the last time, she stares back at him 'as though looking at a lifeless thing. Something had been wiped from her gaze forever, leaving her a soulless shell. She opened her mouth, but no voice came out. Her face was expressionless, like a machine that had been restored to factory defaults'.[113] If Mimi's Chinese name Xiao Mi recalls the mobile phone, then she is ultimately rendered a broken handset, her memory wiped and her capacity for communication destroyed. Although for Kaizong the survival of Mimi represents an 'impossible hope', her unresolved fate at the novel's end continues to haunt the text.[114] Returning awkwardly as the novel's unexpected remainder, she thwarts narrative closure with her own sticky remains.

The final pages of Chen's novel hover between presenting a revised poetics of waste that holds open the hope that it may still be possible to slow environmental damage if we work together to combat global injustice and the fear that the site of damage has merely shifted elsewhere. The novel's epilogue explains that TerraGreen Recycling has signed an agreement to build a new recycling facility, and has also established a foundation to support migrant workers whose health has been damaged as a result of their labour. Resigning from his post and turning away from his work as a historian, Kaizong embarks on a new journey with the environment protection organization Coltsfoot Blossom, where his job is to track the 'giant floating islands' that have formed as a result of the 'hundreds and millions of tons of unprocessed trash' that have been dumped in the world's oceans.[115] Something peculiar is taking place on these trash islands, Kaizong is told, leading him to believe that they are '*not as desolate as Mars*'.[116] Yet while chasing these trash islands and their uncertain life forms, Kaizong cannot help but recall Mimi's last words: '*I'm only a beginning.*'[117] As a beginning – even at the end of the novel – Mimi speaks both to Karen Thornber's notion of 'ecoambiguity' and to Chen's own statement that *Waste Tide* cannot be 'simply reduced to black and white, good and bad'.[118] Not only do Mimi's final worlds '*I'm only a beginning*' function as a disturbing reminder of the slow violence inflicted on the planet by electronic waste and the capitalist structures that enable it, but they also overturn Kaizong's understanding of historical progress by interrupting the future with its own remains. Indeed, Mimi, as a strange human telephone, keeps on calling. In so doing, her position as a beginning at the novel's end speaks to the telephone's refusal to disappear as well as to the ways in which its material remains haunt the afterlife of the text. The telephone, in other words, always leaves a trace.

The telephone as trace returns us to the inaugural object in Station Eleven. The founding exhibit in Clark's 'Museum of Civilization', the iPhone serves to remind the survivors of a time when you could lift the receiver and speak to anyone anywhere and leave your rubbish on the curb for it to be placed elsewhere. But at the end of Mandel's novel, Clark shows Kirsten what he can see through the telescope: 'In the distance, pinpricks of light arranged into a grid. There, plainly visible on the side of the hill some miles distant; a town, or a village, whose streets were lit up with electricity.'[119] And while Clark stays at the airport 'dusting his beloved objects' in the museum, Kirsten is 'beside herself with impatience to see the far southern town with the electrical grid'.[120] This pattern of movement and retreat points to our ambivalent relationship with technology and its after-effects. It is a pattern evident in the work of Chen, Mao and Wong, too, where varying modes of generic hybridity enact trans-corporeality while also exposing both the spatial and temporal displacements embedded in current disposal practices.

Challenging technological determinism while avoiding a straightforward antimaterialist stance, these writers prompt new engagements with the ways in which waste and its afterlives persist in geological time. For Gabrys, the earth itself operates as an archive or 'garbage museum' – a museum that 'at once preserves remainders but also generates new possibilities for material transformation'.[121] Exploring the possibilities of corrosive forms, toxic poetics and both sticky and leaky language, these texts are defined by their own resistant materiality; by showing us that the end of the telephone is always the beginning, they invite us to read the smartphone's non-linguistic traces and to consider the ways in which its materiality remains stored in a geological archive. In unexpected ways, the afterlife of the telephone, its enduring material effects and its spectral traces continue to resound. Speaking beyond itself, then, the literary telephone calls urgently for a more ethical response to our planetary connections.

Notes

1 Emily St John Mandel, *Station Eleven* (London: Picador, 2015), 160.
2 Ibid., 234–5.
3 Ibid., 254.
4 Ibid., 254–5.
5 Ibid., 258.
6 Ibid., 202, 203.
7 Jennifer Gabrys, *Digital Rubbish: A Natural History of Electronics* (Ann Arbor, MI: University of Michigan Press, 2011), 132.
8 Rob Nixon, *Slow Violence and the Environmentalism of the Poor* (Cambridge, MA: Harvard University Press, 2011).
9 Robert Hertz, *Death and The Right Hand*, trans. Rodney and Claudia Needham (Glencoe, IL: The Free Press, 1960); Marcel Mauss, *The Gift: Forms and Functions of Exchange in Archaic Societies*, trans. Ian Cunnison (London: Cohen & West, 1966); Mary Douglas, *Purity and Danger: An Analysis of Concepts of Pollution and Taboo* (London: Routledge, 2002); Michael Thompson, *Rubbish Theory: The Creation and Destruction of Value* (London: Pluto Press, 2017).
10 Brian Neville and Johanne Villeneuve, 'Introduction: In Lieu of Waste', in *Waste-Site Stories: The Recycling of Memory*, ed. Brian Neville and Johanne Villeneuve (New York: SUNY Press, 2002), 1–25 (2).
11 Gabrys, *Digital Rubbish*, 2.
12 Ibid.

13 Zygmunt Bauman, *Wasted Lives: Modernity and Its Outcasts* (Cambridge: Polity, 2004), 5–6.
14 It is estimated that e-waste processing began in Guiyu in 1996. See Michael Standaert, 'China's Notorious E-Waste Village Disappears Almost Overnight', *Basel Action Network* (17 December 2015), available at: https://www.ban.org/news-new/2015/12/17/chinas-notorious-e-waste-village-disappears-almost-overnight (accessed 2 April 2022).
15 The Basel Convention and the United Nations Environment Programme, *The Basel Convention on the Control of Transboundary Movements of Hazardous Wastes and Their Disposal* (22 March 1989; texts and annexes revised 2019), available at: http://www.basel.int/TheConvention/Overview/tabid/1271/Default.aspx (accessed 2 April 2022); see also Feng Wang, Ruediger Kuehr, Daniel Ahlquist and Jinhui Li, 'E-Waste in China: A Country Report', *StEP: Solving the E-Waste Problem Green Paper Series* (5 April 2013), 54, available at: https://www.step-initiative.org/step-papers-copy.html (accessed 2 April 2022).
16 The Basel Action Network (BAN) and Silicon Valley Toxics Coalition (SVTC), 'Exporting Harm: The High-Tech Trashing of Asia' (25 February 2002), 1, available at: https://issuu.com/greenpeace_eastasia/docs/exporting-harm-the-high-tech-trashing-asia (accessed 2 April 2022).
17 Wang et al., 'E-Waste in China', 54. See, for instance, Yan Guo, Changjiang Huang, Hong Zhang and Qiaoxiang Dong, 'Heavy Metal Contamination from Electronic Waste Recycling at Guiyu, Southeast China', *Journal of Environmental Quality*, 38.4 (2009), 1617–26.
18 World Trade Organization, 'Notification: Committee on Technical Barriers to Trade' (18 July 2017), available at: https://docs.wto.org/dol2fe/Pages/SS/directdoc.aspx?filename=q:/G/TBTN17/CHN1211.pdf&Open=True (accessed 2 April 2022). See also World Trade Organization, 'China's Import Ban on Solid Waste Queried at Import Licensing Meeting' (3 October 2017), available at: https://www.wto.org/english/news_e/news17_e/impl_03oct17_e.htm (accessed 2 April 2022).
19 Visiting in 2018, Davor Mujezinovic notes: 'Guiyu is relatively clean and well developed, and the spaces previously occupied by recycling workshops have been rented out to other businesses. There is little sign of e-waste except for the occasional litter and the bags outside the few remaining workshops' (Davor Mujezinovic, 'Electronic Waste in Guiyu: A City under Change?', *Arcadia*, 29 (2019), available at: https://www.environmentandsociety.org/arcadia/electronic-waste-guiyu-city-under-change (accessed 2 April 2022)).
20 See Zhuang Pingui, 'China's most notorious e-waste dumping ground now cleaner but poorer', *South China Morning Post* (22 September 2017), available at: https://www.scmp.com/news/china/society/article/2112226/chinas-most-notorious-e-

waste-dumping-ground-now-cleaner-poorer (accessed 2 April 2022); Mujezinovic, 'Electronic Waste in Guiyu'.
21 See Laura Parker, 'China's Ban on Trash Imports Shifts Waste Crisis to Southeast Asia', *National Geographic* (16 November 2018), available at: https://www.nationalgeographic.com/environment/article/china-ban-plastic-trash-imports-shifts-waste-crisis-southeast-asia-malaysia (accessed 2 April 2022). Pure Earth's Toxic Sites Identification Program (TSIP) – a global database of sites contaminated with toxic chemicals – has to date identified nearly 5,000 toxic sites in over fifty low- and middle-income countries. This represents a health risk to more than 80 million poor people around the world. See Pure Earth, 'Toxic Site Identification Program', available at: https://www.pureearth.org/our-projects/toxic-site-identification-program-tsip/ (accessed 2 April 2022).
22 Mengtian Sun, 'Imagining Globalization in Paolo Bacigalupi's *The Windup Girl* and Chen Qiufan's *The Waste Tide*', *Science Fiction Studies*, 46.2 (2019), 289–306 (294).
23 Giles Slade, *Made to Break: Technology and Obsolescence in America* (Cambridge, MA: Harvard University Press, 2007), 263–4. Noting that in addition to increasing numbers of new users, existing consumers are replacing phones more rapidly, as well as purchasing more than one phone, Slade suggests that 'such a pattern renders the term "obsolescence" itself obsolete. It makes no sense to call a discarded but working phone obsolete when the same make and model is still available for purchase and continues to provide excellent service to its owners' (264).
24 See Waste Electrical and Electronic Equipment Recycling Forum, 'International E-Waste Day: 57.4M Tonnes Expected in 2021' (n.d.), available at: https://weee-forum.org/ws_news/international-e-waste-day-2021/ (accessed 2 April 2022). Despite the ongoing global rise in mobile phone ownership, researchers note that efforts to recycle mobile phones remain unpopular. See, for instance, Mahmud et al., who note that although the average cell phone is expected to last five years, most Americans replace their mobile phone every twelve months, and of the estimated 141 million phones discarded in 2009, only 8 per cent were recycled (Nadim Mahmud, Isaac Holeman, Kenny Puk, Regina Lam and Damian Lee, 'The Cell Phone Problem/Solution', *Journal of Environmental Health*, 76.6 (2014), 140–5 (140)).
25 Slade, *Made to Break*, 262, 276.
26 Ibid.
27 Mahmud et al., 'The Cell Phone Problem/Solution', 140.
28 Although this chapter focuses on the afterlife of electronics, this is not to deny the phone's ecological impact throughout its lifecycle, including the effects of its modes of production, its participation in global financial markets, and the generation and storage of vast quantities of data. For an analysis of electronic waste from manufacture to disposal, and across a number of cultural sites, see Gabrys, *Digital Rubbish*.

29 For readings of the fictional Guiyu, see Martha Swift, 'How Recycling Ruined the World: A Review of Chen Qiufan's Waste Tide', *It's Freezing in LA* (12 October 2020), available at: https://itsfreezinginla.com/articles/how-recycling-ruined-the-world (accessed 2 April 2022); Yuanyuan Hua, 'The Dual Alienation in *Waste Tide*', *Comparative Literature Studies*, 57.4 (2020), 670–85 (671).

30 See Chen's own account of the name 'Guiyi' in Chen Qiufan, 'Electronic Waste: Can We Really Turn the Tide?', trans. Emily Jin (16 April 2019), available at: https://www.tor.com/2019/04/16/electronic-waste-can-we-really-turn-the-tide/ (accessed 2 April 2022)). My thanks to Pei Liu for her translation support.

31 Chen Qiufan, *Waste Tide*, trans. Ken Liu (London: Tor, 2019), 16, 164.

32 Ibid., 16.

33 Ibid.

34 Ibid., 30.

35 Ibid., 18–19.

36 'junk, n.3', *OED Online* (Oxford University Press, March 2022), available at: https://www.oed.com/view/Entry/102091?rskey=Les5r6&result=3&isAdvanced=false#eid (accessed 2 April 2022).

37 Chen, *Waste Tide*, 19.

38 Iona B. Jucan, 'Introduction: Remain x Remain(s)', in *Remain: In Search of Media*, by Iona B. Jucan, Jussi Parikka and Rebecca Schnieder (Lüneburg: Meson Press, 2018), ix–xx (ix).

39 Although museum culture is centred on notions of 'physical permanence', Rudi Colloredo-Mansfeld proposes that we need to move beyond our preoccupation with fixed forms and durable matter towards the 'disintegration/release/circulation' of matter as both social and material practice (Rudi Colloredo-Mansfeld, 'Introduction: Matter Unbound', *Journal of Material Culture* 8.3 (2003), 245–54 (246, 248)). For further discussion of the museum's role in the storage and display of waste, see for instance Brian Neville and Johanne Villeneuve (eds), *Waste-Site Stories: The Recycling of Memory* (New York: SUNY Press, 2002).

40 Chen, *Waste Tide*, 164.

41 Gabrys, *Digital Rubbish*, 96.

42 Douglas, *Purity and Danger*, 44.

43 Ibid.

44 Kevin Hetherington, 'Secondhandedness: Consumption, Disposal, and Absent Presence', *Environment and Planning D: Society and Space*, 22 (2004), 157–73 (159).

45 Ibid., 160.

46 Stacy Alaimo, *Bodily Natures: Science, Environment, and the Material Self* (Bloomington, IN: Indiana University Press, 2010), 28–9. See also Richard Hofrichter, 'Introduction', in *Toxic Struggles: The Theory and Practice of Environmental Justice*, ed. Richard Hofrichter (Philadelphia, PA: New Society Publishers, 1993), 1–11; Dorceta E. Taylor, *Toxic Communities: Environmental*

Racism, Industrial Pollution, and Residential Mobility (New York: New York University Press, 2014).
47 Chen, *Waste Tide*, 27, 29.
48 Ibid., 4, 53.
49 Ibid., 203.
50 Bauman, *Wasted Lives*, 5, 59. See also Gabrys, *Digital Rubbish*, 95.
51 Bauman, *Wasted Lives*, 60.
52 Chen, *Waste Tide*, 27.
53 Douglas, *Purity and Danger*, 2.
54 See Swift, 'How Recycling Ruined the World'. Existing studies of *Waste Tide* largely focus on Mimi's cyborg hybridity and the parallels between the violence inflicted on the female body and the land. See, for instance, Cara Healey, 'Estranging Realism in Chinese Science Fiction: Hybridity and Environmentalism in Chen Qiufan's "The Waste Tide"', *Modern Chinese Literature and Culture*, 29.2 (Fall 2017), 1–33; Yuqin Jiang, 'Echotech, Alienation, and Science Realism in the Chinese Cyborg Novel *Waste Tide*', *Comparative Literature Studies* 57 no. 4 (2020), 665–69; Christine Xiong, 'Rethinking the Cyborg in Chen Qiufan's *Waste Tide*', *Foundation*, 50.139 (2021), 75–89.
55 Alaimo, *Bodily Natures*, 2.
56 Ibid., 18. See also Lawrence Buell for a discussion of the anxiety of toxic discourse (Lawrence Buell, 'Toxic Discourse', *Critical Inquiry*, 24.3 (1998), 639–65)).
57 Contemporary Chinese science fiction has witnessed a rapid rise with critics noting that it provides writers with a mode of reconfiguring modernity and the notion of historical progress. For a discussion of the growing popularity of Chinese science fiction, see Healey, 'Estranging Realism in Chinese Science Fiction' and Mingwei Song, 'Representations of the Invisible: Chinese Science Fiction in the Twenty-First Century', in *The Oxford Handbook of Modern Chinese Literatures*, ed. Carlos Rojas and Andrea Bachner (Oxford: Oxford University Press, 2016), 546–65.
58 Peter Vermeulen, *Literature and the Anthropocene* (London: Routledge, 2020), 30.
59 Ibid.
60 Healey, 'Estranging Realism in Chinese Science Fiction', 5.
61 Sally Wen Mao, 'Electronic Necropolis', in *Oculus* (Minneapolis, MN: Graywolf Press, 2019), 54–5; Rita Wong, 'sort by day, burn by night', in *Forage* (Gibsons, BC: Nightwood Editions, 2007), 46–7.
62 Mao, 'Electronic Necropolis', 54.
63 Ibid.
64 Ibid.
65 Ibid.
66 Ibid.
67 Ocean Vuong, 'Introduction: Sally Wen Mao', *The Massachusetts Review*, 59.4 (2018), 804–5 (804).
68 Mao, 'Electronic Necropolis', 54, 55.

69 Ibid.
70 David Farrier, *Anthropocene Poetics: Deep Time, Sacrifice Zones, and Extinction* (Minneapolis, MN: University of Minnesota Press, 2019), 9.
71 Mao, 'Electronic Necropolis', 54.
72 Hetherington, 'Secondhandedness', 162.
73 Ibid., 157.
74 Ibid., 159.
75 Ibid., 170.
76 Gabrys, *Digital Rubbish*, v.
77 Jonathan Sterne, 'Out with the Trash: On the Future of New Media', in *Residual Media*, ed. Charles Ackland (Minneapolis, MN: University of Minnesota Press, 2007), 16–31 (17).
78 Ibid. See also Jonathan Sterne, *MP3: The Meaning of a Format* (Durham, NC: Duke University Press, 2012), 6–7.
79 Hetherington, 'Secondhandedness', 162.
80 'skin, v.' and 'skinned, adj', *OED Online* (Oxford University Press, March 2022), available at: https://www.oed.com/view/Entry/180946?rskey=pVQJUz&result=2&is Advanced=false#eid (accessed 2 April 2022).
81 Samantha Walton, 'Body Burdens: The Materiality of Work in Rita Wong's *Forage*', in *Poetry and Work: Work in Modern and Contemporary Anglophone Poetry*, ed. Jo Lindsay Walton and Ed Luker (Basingstoke: Palgrave Macmillan, 2019), 263–90 (283). See also Matthew Zantingh, who draws on Bruno Latour's actor network theory (ANT) alongside Bill Brown's thing theory to argue that Wong 'asks us to consider how the material objects of everyday life emerge from networks that connect disparate places and peoples together' (Matthew Zantingh, 'When Things Act Up: Thing Theory, Actor-Network Theory, and Toxic Discourse in Rita Wong's Poetry', *Interdisciplinary Studies in Literature and Environment*, 20.3 (2013), 622–46 (624)).
82 Rita Wong, 'sort by day, burn by night', 46–7. See Basel Action Network, *Exporting Harm: The High-Tech Trashing of Asia*, dir. Jim Puckett (2002), available at: https://www.ban.org/watch-films/ (accessed 2 April 2022).
83 Rita Wong, 'sort by day, burn by night', 46.
84 Ibid.
85 Jussi Parikka, 'Remain(s) Scattered', *Remain: In Search of Media* by Iona B. Jucan, Jussi Parikka and Rebecca Schneider (Lüneburg: Meson Press, 2018), 1–48 (34).
86 Jussi Parikka, *The Anthrobscene* (Minneapolis, MN: University of Minnesota Press, 2014), 41.
87 Jucan, 'Introduction: Remain x Remain(s)', xix.
88 Rita Wong, 'sort by day, burn by night', 47.
89 Ibid. Walton points out that Wong's poem 'urges an awareness that the text itself has been produced on the computers and devices which poison Guiyu's workers' (Walton, 'Body Burdens', 283).

90 See Walt Whitman, 'One's Self I Sing', in *The Complete Poems* (London: Penguin, 2004), 37; Wong, 'sort by day, burn by night', 46.
91 Walton, 'Body Burdens', 285. See Farrier, *Anthropocene Poetics*, 5–6.
92 Ibid. See also Harriet Tarlo, 'Open Field: Reading Field as Place and Poetics', in *Placing Poetry*, ed. Ian Davidson and Zoë Skoulding (Amsterdam: Brill, 2013), 113–48.
93 Rita Wong, 'pollution dodged?' in *undercurrent* (Gibsons, BC: Nightwood Editions, 2015), 68–70 (69).
94 Ibid.
95 Ibid., 68.
96 Ibid., 70.
97 Ibid., 69. Will Steffen, Paul J. Crutzen and John R. McNeill, 'The Anthropocene: Are Humans Now Overwhelming the Great Forces of Nature?' *Ambio* 36.8 (2007), 614–27 (617–18). See also Nixon, *Slow Violence*, 11, 12.
98 Wong, 'pollution dodged?', 69.
99 Nixon, *Slow Violence*, 2.
100 Ibid.
101 Ibid., 3, 10.
102 Gabrys, *Digital Rubbish*, 88.
103 Chen, *Waste Tide*, 118.
104 Ibid., 163.
105 Ibid., 273.
106 Healey, 'Estranging Realism in Chinese Science Fiction', 22.
107 Ibid.
108 Ibid.
109 Ibid.
110 Hetherington, 'Secondhandedness', 159.
111 Chen, *Waste Tide*, 328.
112 Ibid., 332.
113 Ibid., 331.
114 Ibid., 332.
115 Ibid., 334.
116 Ibid.
117 Ibid.
118 Karen Thornber writes: 'Environmental ambiguity manifests itself in multiple, intertwined ways, including ambivalent attitudes towards nature; confusion about the actual condition of the nonhuman, often a consequence of ambiguous information; contradictory human behaviors towards ecosystems; and discrepancies among attitudes, conditions, and behaviors that lead to actively downplaying and acquiescing to nonhuman degradation, as well as to

inadvertently harming the very environments one is attempting to protect' (Karen Thornber, *Ecoambiguity: Environmental Crises and East Asian Literatures* (Ann Arbor, MI: University of Michigan Press, 2012), 6); Chen, 'Electronic Waste: Can We Really Turn the Tide'. See also Healey, 'Estranging Realism', 8.
119 Mandel, *Station Eleven*, 311.
120 Ibid., 331.
121 Gabrys, *Digital Rubbish*, 131.

Coda

A long goodbye

The Happy Corpse in Leonora Carrington's eponymous story relays the fate of his father to a young man:

> My father died of a heart attack during a telephone conversation, and then of course he went to Hell. Now he is in Telephone Hell, where everyone has these apparatuses constantly glued to their lips or ears. This causes great anguish. My father will be with his telephone for nine hundred and ninety-nine billion aeons before he gets rid of it.[1]

The notion of being stuck on the line for 'nine hundred and ninety-nine billion aeons' – or at times for even one minute longer – is no doubt a disturbing one, and it is one that perhaps contributes to our reluctance to even pick up the receiver in the first place. Despite the fear of being forever on hold, it can also be, as Avital Ronell admits in *The Telephone Book*, 'difficult to hang up'.[2] She relates this difficulty to claims made by Thomas Watson regarding the telephone's initial developments:

> In the early days of telephony[,] average users, explains Watson, often forgot to hang up. They drew a blank on throwing the bell back after using the telephone. No calls could come through. 'I tried several devices to remedy this trouble and finally designed the automatic switch operated by the weight of the telephone' [...]. The weight of the telephone has taught us to hang up, he writes.[3]

Although the design of an automatic switch made things easier, the telephone call remains haunted by the weight of the terminal exchange – in other words, when and how it is best to say goodbye. This is an anxiety that plagues the literary exchange too, as Nicholas Royle suggests: 'At what point stop the citation, hang up on the text?'[4] Royle is discussing the role of the telephone in Raymond Chandler's *The Little Sister*, a text about which he claims 'everything [...] depends on the telephone'.[5] But he also remarks that 'people are repeatedly hanging up in Chandler's texts'.[6] Relating this to the suspense created through the figure of aposiopesis, he insists: 'It recurs relentlessly in Chandler's texts, as if punctuating, and puncturing, time itself: the violence of silence'.[7] This is the case in *The Long Goodbye* too, the 1953 novel in which Chandler's detective Philip Marlowe reflects: 'There is something compulsive about a telephone. The gadget-ridden man of our age loves it, loathes it, and is afraid of it. But he always treats it with respect, even when he is drunk. The telephone is a fetish.'[8] *The Long Goodbye* is filled with iterations of the terminal exchange, including the deadly telephone call during which Roger Wade cuts the connection (or it is cut for him):

> He didn't answer. There was a crashing sound, then a dead silence, then in a short while a kind of banging around. I yelled something into the phone without getting any answer. Time passed. Finally the light click of the receiver being replaced and the buzz of an open line.[9]

Elsewhere in the novel, Marlowe grapples for control over the violence of the ending, attempting on one occasion to say goodbye to Sergeant Green, who won't allow it: 'I started to say goodbye but he chopped me off. "What did Mr. Money want with you?"'[10] Green isn't the only police officer to deny Marlowe the goodbye. Bernie leaves him without saying farewell and Marlowe muses: 'Cops never say goodbye. They're always hoping to see you again in the line-up.'[11] And although he gets the chance to say an extra goodbye to Linda, it leaves him knowing that 'to say goodbye is to die a little'.[12] But it is his troubled relationship with the missing Terry Lennox that most frustrates his parting call. Admitting, 'I've never really said goodbye to him', the novel resists closure until eventually he defers the end of the exchange: 'So long, amigo. I won't say goodbye. I said it to you when it meant something. I said it when it was sad and lonely and final.'[13] In this way, Marlowe's final goodbye is forever withheld.

This is also true of this volume, where to continue to defer closure risks leaving things up in the air. But, of course, suspension is a concept that runs throughout my analysis – from the secret to the atomic missile to the slow violence of the telephone's afterlife. It is an idea that also taps into a wider interest in verticality that has emerged during the course of this research, connecting clouds of unknowing and other foggy forms to birds in flight and satellites and stars. But there are many other connections too, from the grounded to the unearthly: questions of dispatch and destinerrance, of response and responsibility, of place and displacement, and of materiality and spectrality, not to mention a whole chorus of sounds and calls and rings and cries. These calling points were not all necessarily part of the plan, and they have sometimes made themselves known as a kind of noise in the discussion – a productive glitch or signifying static on the line. But despite its interest in the linguistic, technical, political and conceptual disruptions of the literary telephone, this book remains concerned above all with the poetic, political and spatial possibilities of the exchange, and to the new connections and renewed energies that the telephone enables us to call up.

In Chandler's novel, ways of saying goodbye are varied: Sylvia Lennox says, 'Good night'; Eileen Wade entreats Marlowe to 'call me at anytime, no matter how late it is'; Sergeant Green tells him to 'Go to Hell' before hanging up in his ear; and Candy says, 'Hasta la vista, amigo.'[14] More often than not, however, the characters don't say goodbye at all but simply put down the receiver. Why not end this exchange in a similar way? Returning to my discussion in the preface of Dennis Overbye's discovery of the instructions contained within a New Haven telephone directory dated November 1878, perhaps I should end with the instructions contained therein: 'That is all.'[15] But, of course, it never is and there is always more to say. So, despite the risks associated with leaving things up in the air, I end by pointing to the much larger conversations of which this book is a part, with the hope that these calling points continue to prompt new questions regarding the relationship between literature and the telephone, and the different ways that telephoning practices might open up the possibilities of reading, writing, talking and thinking across cultures.

Notes

1 Leonora Carrington, 'The Happy Corpse Story', in *The Seventh Horse and Other Tales*, trans. Kathrine Talbot and Anthony Kerrigan (New York: E. P. Dutton, 1988), 176–80 (179).
2 Avital Ronell, *The Telephone Book: Technology, Schizophrenia, Electric Speech* (Lincoln, NE: University of Nebraska Press, 1989), 274.
3 Thomas A. Watson, *Exploring Life: The Autobiography of Thomas A. Watson* (New York: D. Appleton and Company, 1926), 131, cited in Ronell, *The Telephone Book*, 274.
4 Nicholas Royle, *Telepathy and Literature: Essays on the Reading Mind* (Oxford: Basil Blackwell, 1990), 167.
5 Ibid., 163.
6 Ibid., 167.
7 Ibid.
8 Raymond Chandler, *The Long Goodbye* (New York: Vintage, 1992), 200.

9   Ibid., 189.
10 Ibid., 241.
11 Ibid., 338.
12 Ibid., 365.
13 Ibid., 331, 378.
14 Ibid., 16, 139, 241, 318.
15 Dennis Overbye, 'Among Scientific Treasures, a Gem', *New York Times* (10 June 2008), F3, available at: https://www.nytimes.com/2008/06/10/science/10auct.html (accessed 19 April 2022).

Bibliography

Abba, Tom, Jonathan Dovey and Kate Pullinger (eds). *Ambient Literature: Towards a New Poetics of Situated Writing and Reading Practices*. Basingstoke: Palgrave Macmillan, 2021.
Aciman, Alexander and Emmett Rensin. *Twitterature: The World's Greatest Books Retold Through Twitter*. London: Penguin, 2009.
Agamben, Giorgio. *Homo Sacer: Sovereign Power and Bare Life*, trans. Daniel Heller-Roazen. Stanford, CA: Stanford University Press, 1998.
Ahmed, Sara. *Queer Phenomenology: Orientations, Objects, Others*. Durham, NC: Duke University Press, 2006.
Aiken, F. B. 'Abraham '59 – a Nuclear Fantasy'. *Dissent* 6 (1959): 18–24.
Alaimo, Stacy. *Bodily Natures: Science, Environment, and the Material Self*. Bloomington, IN: Indiana University Press, 2010.
Al-Kasim, Mohammad. 'Palestinians Eagerly Await Arrival of 4G Cellular Service'. *Jerusalem Post*, 31 August 2021. Available online: https://www.jpost.com/middle-east/palestinians-eagerly-await-arrival-of-4g-cellular-service-678301 (accessed 2 February 2022).
Allen, Edward. *Modernist Inventions: Media Technology and American Poetry*. Cambridge: Cambridge University Press, 2007.
Allen, Edward. 'Romancing the Phone: Woolf's First Media Age'. *Critical Quarterly* 61 no. 4 (2019): 100–15.
Allen, John. 'Topological Twists: Power's Shifting Geographies'. *Dialogues in Human Geography* 1 no. 3 (2011): 283–98.
'"Allo!" "Hello!" and "Hullo!"'. *The National Telephone Journal*, 1 May 1906, 29.
Amis, Martin. *Einstein's Monsters*. New York: Harmony Books, 1987.
Andén-Papadoulous, Kari. 'Media Witnessing and the "Crowd-Sourced Video Revolution"'. *Visual Communication* 12 no. 3 (2013): 341–57.
Andersen, Tore Rye. 'Staggered Transmissions: Twitter and the Return of Serialized Literature'. *Convergence* 23 no. 1 (2017): 34–48.
Arac, Jonathan. 'History and Mystery: The Criticism of Frank Kermode'. *Salmagundi* 55 (1982): 135–55.
Auster, Paul. *The New York Trilogy*. London: Faber, 1987.
Auster, Paul and J. M. Coetzee. *Here and Now: Letters 2008–2011*. London: Vintage, 2014.
Awoonor, Kofi. *The Promise of Hope: New and Selected Poems 1964–2013*. Lincoln, NE: University of Nebraska Press, 2014.
Barghouti, Mourid. *I Saw Ramallah*, trans. Ahdaf Soueif. London: Bloomsbury, 2005.

Barghouti, Mourid. *I Was Born There, I Was Born Here*, trans. Humphrey Davies. London: Bloomsbury, 2012.
Barrell, John. 'Subject and Sentence: The Poetry of Tom Raworth'. *Critical Inquiry* 17 no. 2 (1991): 386–410.
Barthes, Roland. *A Lover's Discourse: Fragments*, trans. Richard Howard. London: Jonathan Cape, 1979.
Basel Action Network. *Exporting Harm: The High-Tech Trashing of Asia*, dir. Jim Puckett, 2002. Available online: https://www.ban.org/watch-films/ (accessed 2 April 2022).
Baudrillard, Jean. 'The Ecstasy of Communication', trans. John Johnston. In *The Anti-Aesthetic: Essays on Postmodern Culture*, ed. Hal Foster, 126–33. Port Townsend, WA: Bay Press, 1983.
Baudrillard, Jean. *Simulations*, trans. Paul Foss, Paul Patton and Philip Beitchmann. Cambridge, MA: Semiotext[e], 1983.
Bauman, Zygmunt. *Wasted Lives: Modernity and Its Outcasts*. Cambridge: Polity, 2004.
BBC. 'Lampedusa Boat Tragedy: Migrants Raped and Tortured', 8 November 2013. Available online: https://www.bbc.co.uk/news/world-europe-24866338 (accessed 18 January 2022).
Benjamin, Walter. 'A Berlin Chronicle'. In *Reflections: Essays, Aphorisms, Autobiographical Writings*, trans. Edmund Jephcott, ed. Peter Demetz, 3–60. New York: Schoken, 1986.
Bennett, Andrew. 'Elizabeth Bowen on the Telephone'. In *Elizabeth Bowen: Theory, Thought and Things*, ed. Jessica Gildersleeve and Patricia Juliana Smith, 182–98. Edinburgh: Edinburgh University Press, 2019.
Bennington, Geoffrey. 'Teleanalysis'. *Paragraph* 36 no. 2 (2013): 270–85.
Benstock, Shari. 'Afterword: The New Woman's Fiction'. In *Chick Lit: The New Woman's Fiction*, ed. Suzanne Ferris and Mallory Young, 253–6. London: Routledge, 2006.
Bergvall, Caroline. *Drift*. New York: Nightboat Books, 2014.
Bergvall, Caroline. 'Infra-materiality and Opaque Drifting'. In *Minding Borders: Resilient Divisions in Literature, the Body and the Academy*, ed. Nicola Gardini, Adriana X. Jacobs, Ben Morgan, Mohamed-Salah Omri and Matthew Reynolds, 67–75. Cambridge: Modern Humanities Research Association/Legenda, 2017.
Bernard, Anna. *Rhetorics of Belonging: Nation, Narration, and Israel/Palestine*. Liverpool: Liverpool University Press, 2013.
Bernard, Anna. 'Genres of Refugee Writing'. In *Refugee Imaginaries: Research across the Humanities*, ed. Emma Cox, Sam Durrant, David Farrier, Lyndsey Stonebridge and Agnes Woolley, 65–80. Edinburgh: Edinburgh University Press, 2020.
Bilston, Brian. *You Took the Last Bus Home*. London: Unbound, 2016.
Blanchot, Maurice. *The Space of Literature*, trans. Ann Smock. Lincoln, NE: University of Nebraska Press, 1982.
Boffey, Daniel. 'Russia Reasserts Right to Use Nuclear Weapons in Ukraine'. *The Guardian*, 26 March 2022. Available online: https://www.theguardian.com/

world/2022/mar/26/russia-reasserts-right-to-use-nuclear-weapons-in-ukraine-putin (accessed 29 April 2022).

Briathwaite, Oyinkan. *My Sister, The Serial Killer*. London: Atlantic, 2019.

Bridle, James. 'You Are Here'. In *Where You Are: A Book of Maps That Will Leave You Completely Lost*, ed. Chloe Aridjis et al., n.p. London: Visual Editions, 2013.

Brooks, John. 'The First and Only Century of Telephone Literature'. In *The Social Impact of the Telephone*, ed. Ithiel de Sola Pool, 208–24. Cambridge, MA: MIT Press, 1977.

Bryant, Peter. *Red Alert*. Las Vegas: Wolfpack, 2020.

Buell, Lawrence. 'Toxic Discourse'. *Critical Inquiry* 24 no. 3 (1998): 639–65.

Burdick, Eugene and Harvey Wheeler. *Fail-Safe*. New York: RosettaBooks, 2013.

Bureau of Arms Control, Verification, and Compliance. 'Treaty Banning Nuclear Weapon Tests in the Atmosphere, in Outer Space and under Water', signed Moscow 5 August 1963, entered into force 10 October 1963. Available online: https://2009-2017.state.gov/t/isn/4797.htm (accessed 2 March 2022).

Bureau of Arms Control, Verification, and Compliance. 'Comprehensive Nuclear Test Bay Treaty' (opened for signature 24 September 1996; not yet entered into force). Available online: https://2009-2017.state.gov/t/avc/c42328.htm (accessed 2 March 2022).

Butler, Judith. 'Critically Queer'. In *Playing with Fire: Queer Politics, Queer Theories*, ed. Shane Phelan, 11–30. London: Routledge, 1997.

Butler, Judith. *Frames of War: When Is Life Grievable?* London: Verso, 2016.

Butler, Judith and Athena Athanasiou. *Dispossession: The Performative in the Political*. Cambridge: Polity, 2013.

Caldicott, Helen. *Missile Envy: The Arms Race and Nuclear War*. New York: Bantam Books, 1986.

Calvino, Italo. *Under the Jaguar Sun*, trans. William Weaver. New York: Harcourt Brace, 1990.

Caputo, John. *The Prayers and Tears of Jacques Derrida: Religion without Religion*. Bloomington, IN: Indiana University Press, 1997.

Carrington, Leonora. 'The Happy Corpse Story'. In *The Seventh Horse and Other Tales*, trans. Kathrine Talbot and Anthony Kerrigan, 176–80. New York: E. P. Dutton, 1988.

Caruthers, Gerard. 'Muriel Spark as Catholic Novelist'. In *The Edinburgh Companion to Muriel Spark*, ed. Michael Gardiner and Willy Maley, 74–83. Edinburgh: Edinburgh University Press, 2010.

Chandler, Raymond. *The Long Goodbye*. New York: Vintage, 1992.

Chasar, Mike. *Poetry Unbound: Poems and New Media from the Magic Lantern to Instagram*. New York: Columbia University Press, 2020.

Chion, Michel. *Sound: An Acoulogical Treatise*, trans. James A. Steintrager. Durham, NC: Duke University Press, 2020.

Cixous, Hélène. *Reading with Clarice Lispector*, trans. Verena Andermatt Conley. Minneapolis, MN: University of Minnesota Press, 1990.

Cixous, Hélène. 'Writing Blind: Conversation with the Donkey', trans. Eric Prenowitz. In *Stigmata: Escaping Texts*, 184–203. London: Routledge, 2005.

Clarke, Susanne. *Cold Warriors: Manliness on Trial in the Rhetoric of the West*. Carbondale and Edwardsville, IL: Southern Illinois University Press, 2000.

Clarkson, Helen. *The Last Day*. New York: Torquil, 1959.

Clément, Catherine. *Syncope: The Philosophy of Rapture*, trans. Sally O'Driscoll and Deirdre M. Mahoney. Minneapolis, MN: University of Minnesota Press, 1994.

Colloredo-Mansfeld, Rudi. 'Introduction: Matter Unbound'. *Journal of Material Culture* 8 no. 3 (2003): 245–54.

Cordle, Daniel. 'Cultures of Terror: Nuclear Criticism during and since the Cold War'. *Literature Compass* 3 no. 6 (2006): 1186–99.

Cordle, Daniel. *States of Suspense: The Nuclear Age, Postmodernism and United States Fiction and Prose*. Manchester: Manchester University Press, 2008.

Cordle, Daniel. *Late Cold War Literature and Culture: The Nuclear 1980s*. Basingstoke: Palgrave Macmillan, 2017.

Couldry, Nick and Anna McCarthy (eds). *MediaSpace: Place, Scale and Culture in a Media Age*. London: Routledge, 2004.

Cripps, Charlotte. 'Twihaiku? Micropoetry? The Rise of Twitter Poetry'. *Independent*, 17 July 2013. Available online: https://www.independent.co.uk/arts-entertainment/books/features/twihaiku-micropoetry-the-rise-of-twitter-poetry-8711637.html (accessed 15 October 2021).

Danius, Sara. *The Senses of Modernism: Technology, Perception, and Aesthetics*. New York: Cornell University Press, 2002.

Darby, Andrew. *Flight Lines*. Crows Nest, NSW: Allen & Unwin, 2020.

Davidson, Guy and Monique Rooney. 'Introduction: Queer Objects'. In *Queer Objects*, ed. Guy Davidson and Monique Rooney, 3–5. London: Routledge, 2019.

Davies, Ben. 'Address, Temporality and Misdelivery: The Postal Effects of Ali Smith's Short Stories'. In *British Women Short Story Writers: The New Woman to Now*, ed. Emma Young and James Bailey, 163–78. Edinburgh: Edinburgh University Press, 2017.

Day, Angel. *The English Secretary*. London: Printed by Peter Short for C. Burbie, 1599.

Del Grande, Gabriele. *Fortress Europe*. Available online: http://fortresseurope.blogspot.com/ (accessed 18 January 2022).

DeLillo, Don. *The Silence*. New York: Simon & Schuster, 2020.

Derrida, Jacques. 'No Apocalypse, Not Now (Full Speed Ahead, Seven Missiles, Seven Missives)', trans. Catherine Porter and Philip Lewis. *Diacritics* 14 no. 2 (1984): 20–31.

Derrida, Jacques. *The Post Card: From Socrates to Freud and Beyond*, trans. Alan Bass. Chicago: University of Chicago Press, 1987.

Derrida, Jacques. 'Ulysses Gramophone: Hear Say Yes in Joyce', trans. Tina Kendall and Shari Benstock. In *Acts of Literature*, ed. Derek Attridge, 253–309. London: Routledge, 1992.

Derrida, Jacques. *Specters of Marx: The State of the Debt, the Work of Mourning, and the New International*, trans. Peggy Kamuf. London: Routledge, 1994.
Derrida, Jacques. 'Telepathy', trans. Nicholas Royle. In *Deconstruction: A Reader*, ed. Martin McQuillan, 496–526. Edinburgh: Edinburgh University Press, 2000.
Derrida, Jacques. 'Am I in Jerusalem?' In Catherine Malabou and Jacques Derrida, *Counterpath: Traveling with Jacques Derrida*, trans. David Wills, 120–1. Stanford, CA: Stanford University Press, 2004.
Derrida, Jacques. *On Touching – Jean-Luc Nancy*, trans. Christine Irizarry. Stanford, CA: Stanford University Press, 2005.
Derrida, Jacques. *H.C. For Life, That Is to Say ...*, trans. Laurent Milesi and Stefan Herbrechter. Stanford, CA: Stanford University Press, 2006.
Derrida, Jacques. *The Beast and the Sovereign*, vol. 1, trans. Geoffrey Bennington. Chicago: University of Chicago Press, 2008.
Derrida, Jacques. *The Gift of Death and Literature in Secret*, trans. David Wills. Chicago: University of Chicago Press, 2008.
Derrida, Jacques. 'Avowing – the Impossible: "Returns," Repentance, and Reconciliation', trans. Gil Anidjar. In *Living Together: Jacques Derrida's Communities of Violence and Peace*, ed. Elisabeth Weber, 18–41. New York: Fordham University Press, 2012.
Derrida, Jacques and Élisabeth Roudinesco. *For What Tomorrow... A Dialogue*, trans. Jeff Fort. Stanford, CA: Stanford University Press, 2004.
Dicken, Peter and James S. Ormrod. *Cosmic Society: Towards a Sociology of the Universe*. London: Routledge, 2007.
Dharker, Imtiaz. *The Terrorist at My Table*. Northumberland: Bloodaxe, 2006.
Dolar, Mladen. *A Voice and Nothing More*. Cambridge, MA: MIT Press, 2005.
Douglas, Mary. *Purity and Danger: An Analysis of Concepts of Pollution and Taboo*. London: Routledge, 2002.
Doyle, Roddy. *Two Pints*. London: Jonathan Cape, 2012.
Duffy, Carol Ann. 'Poems Are a Form of Texting'. *The Guardian*, 5 September 2011. Available online: https://www.theguardian.com/education/2011/sep/05/carol-ann-duffy-poetry-texting-competition (accessed 12 November 2021).
El-Rifae, Yasmin. 'Where Does Palestine Begin?' In *This Is Not a Border: Reportage and Reflection from the Palestine Festival of Literature*, ed. Ahdaf Soueif and Omar Robert Hamilton, 11–15. London: Bloomsbury, 2017.
Emerson, Lori. *Reading Writing Interfaces: From the Digital to the Bookbound*. Minneapolis, MN: University of Minnesota Press, 2014.
Falk, Richard. 'How to Live Together Well: Interrogating the Israel/Palestine Conflict'. In *Living Together: Jacques Derrida's Communities of Violence and Peace*, ed. Elisabeth Weber, 275–92. New York: Fordham University Press, 2012.
Farman, Jason. 'Site-Specificity, Pervasive Computing, and the Reading Interface'. In *The Mobile Story: Narrative Practices with Locative Technologies*, ed. Jason Farman, 3–16. London: Routledge, 2015.

Farrier, David. *Anthropocene Poetics: Deep Time, Sacrifice Zones, and Extinction*. Minneapolis, MN: University of Minnesota Press, 2019.

Ferguson, Frances. 'The Nuclear Sublime'. *Diacritics* 14 no. 2 (1984): 4–10.

Ferraris, Maurizio. *Where Are You? An Ontology of the Cell Phone*, trans. Sarah De Sanctis. New York: Fordham University Press, 2014.

Forensic Architecture. 'The Left-to-Die Boat', 11 April 2012. Available online: https://forensic-architecture.org/investigation/the-left-to-die-boat (accessed 18 January 2022).

Forensic Architecture. *Forensis: The Architecture of Public Truth*. London: Sternberg Press, 2014.

Foucault, Michel. *Discipline and Punish: The Birth of the Prison*, trans. Alan Sheridan. London: Vintage, 1979.

Foucault, Michel. 'The Confession of the Flesh'. In *In Power/Knowledge: Selected Interviews and Other Writings*, trans. Colin Gordon, Leo Marshall, John Mepham and Kate Soper, ed. Colin Gordon, 194–228. New York: Pantheon, 1981.

Foundation for Middle East Peace. 'Sharon's New Map'. *Report on Israeli Settlement in the Occupied Territories* 12 no. 3 (2002): 1–6.

Frank, Pat. *Alas, Babylon!* New York: Bantam Spectra, 1976.

Freud, Sigmund. 'Recommendations to Physicians Practising Psycho-Analysis'. In *Standard Edition*, vol. 12, trans. James Strachey, 109–20. London: Vintage, 2001.

Funkhouser, Christopher T. *Prehistoric Digital Poetry: An Archaeology of Forms, 1959–1995*. Tuscaloosa, AL: University of Alabama Press, 2007.

Funkhouser, Christopher T. *New Directions in Digital Poetry*. London: Continuum, 2012.

Gabrys, Jennifer. *Digital Rubbish: A Natural History of Electronics*. Ann Arbor, MI: University of Michigan Press, 2011.

Gaedtke, Andrew. *Modernism and the Machinery of Madness: Psychosis, Technology, and Narrative Worlds*. Cambridge: Cambridge University Press, 2017.

Gatrell, Peter. 'Refugees in Modern World History'. In *Refugee Imaginaries: Research across the Humanities*, ed. Emma Cox, Sam Durrant, David Farrier, Lyndsey Stonebridge and Agnes Woolley, 18–35. Edinburgh: Edinburgh University Press, 2020.

Gay, Peter. *Freud: A Life for Our Time*. London: MAX, 2006.

Gessen, Masha. 'To Be, or Not to Be'. *New York Review of Books*, 8 February 2018. Available online: https://www.nybooks.com/articles/2018/02/08/to-be-or-not-to-be/ (accessed 18 January 2022).

Giddens, Anthony. *Beyond Left and Right: The Future of Radical Politics*. Cambridge: Polity Press, 1994.

Gillespie, Marie, Lawrence Ampofo, Margaret Cheesman, Becky Faith, Evgenia Iliadou, Ali Issa, Souad Osseiran and Dimitris Skleparis. *Mapping Refugee Media Journeys: Smartphones and Social Media Networks*. Milton Keynes: The Open University / France Médias Monde, 2016.

Gillespie, Marie, Souad Osseiran and Margie Cheesman. 'Syrian Refugees and the Digital Passage to Europe: Smartphone Infrastructure and Affordances'. *Social Media and Society* 4 no. 1 (2018): 1–12.

Ginsberg, Allen. 'Abstraction in Poetry'. *It Is* 3 (Winter–Spring 1959): 73–5.

GISTI. 'Le Gisti va déposer plainte contre l'OTAN, l'Union européenne et les pays de la coalition en opération en Libye', 9 June 2011. Available online: http://www.gisti.org/spip.php?article2304 (accessed 18 January 2022).

Goggin, Gerard. *Cell Phone Culture: Mobile Technology in Everyday Life*. London: Routledge, 2006.

Goggin, Gerard and Caroline Hamilton. 'Narrative Fiction and Mobile Media after the Text-Message Novel'. In *The Mobile Story: Narrative Practices with Locative Technologies*, ed. Jason Farman, 223–37. London: Routledge, 2014.

Goggin, Gerard and Larissa Hjorth (eds). *The Routledge Companion to Mobile Media*. London: Routledge, 2014.

Gordon, I. L. (ed). *The Seafarer*. London: Methuen, 1960.

Govrin, Michal. 'From Jerusalem to Jerusalem – a Dedication', trans. Atar Hadari. In *Living Together: Jacques Derrida's Communities of Violence and Peace*, ed. Elisabeth Weber, 259–74. New York: Fordham University Press, 2012.

Goytisolo, Juan. 'Palestinian Notebooks: First Notebook – From Netanya to Ramallah', trans. Peter Bush, n.d. Available online: http://www.mafhoum.com/press3/92Ca11.htm (accessed 6 June 2020).

Green, Venus. *Race on the Line: Gender, Labor, and Technology in the Bell System, 1880–1980*. Durham, NC: Duke University Press, 2001.

Gregory, Derek. 'Palestine and the "War on Terror"'. *Comparative Studies of South Asia, Africa and the Middle East* 24 no. 1 (2004): 183–95.

Guo, Yan, Changjiang Huang, Hong Zhang and Qiaoxiang Dong. 'Heavy Metal Contamination from Electronic Waste Recycling at Guiyu, Southeast China'. *Journal of Environmental Quality* 38 no. 4 (2009): 1617–26.

Hamilton, Patrick. *Hangover Square*. London: Abacus, 2016.

Hanke, Bob. 'McLuhan, Virilio and Speed'. In *Transforming McLuhan: Cultural, Critical, and Postmodern Perspectives*, ed. Paul Grosswiler, 203–26. New York: Peter Lang, 2010.

Healey, Cara. 'Estranging Realism in Chinese Science Fiction: Hybridity and Environmentalism in Chen Qiufan's "The Waste Tide"'. *Modern Chinese Literature and Culture* 29 no. 2 (2017): 1–33.

Heidegger, Martin. 'The Question Concerning Technology'. In *Basic Writings*, ed. D. F. Krell, 311–41. New York: HarperCollins, 2008.

Heidegger, Martin. '"Only a God Can Save Us": The Spiegel Interview (1966)'. In *Heidegger: The Man and the Thinker*, ed. Thomas Sheehan, 45–68. London: Routledge, 2017.

Heller, Charles and Lorenzo Pezzani (dir). 'Liquid Traces', 2014. Available online: https://forensic-architecture.org/investigation/the-left-to-die-boat (accessed 18 January 2022).

Heller, Charles, Lorenzo Pezzani and Situ Studio. *Report on the 'Left-to-Die Boat'*. Goldsmiths, University of London: Forensic Oceanography, 2012. Available online: https://forensic-architecture.org/investigation/the-left-to-die-boat (accessed 18 January 2022).

Hennessey, Michael S. 'Poetry by Phone and Phonograph: Tracing the Influence of Giorno Poetry Systems'. In *Audiobooks, Literature, and Sound Studies*, ed. Matthew Rubery, 76–91. London: Routledge, 2011.

Herbert, W. N. *Cabaret McGonagall*. Northumberland: Bloodaxe, 1996.

Herd, David. *Enthusiast! Essays on Modern American Literature*. Manchester: Manchester University Press, 2007.

Herrera, Yuri. *Signs Preceding the End of the World*, trans. Lisa Dillman. Sheffield: And Other Stories, 2015.

Hertz, Robert. *Death and the Right Hand*, trans. Rodney and Claudia Needham. Glencoe, IL: The Free Press, 1960.

Hetherington, Kevin. 'Secondhandedness: Consumption, Disposal, and Absent Presence'. *Environment and Planning D: Society and Space* 22 (2004): 157–73.

Hight, Jeremy. 'Locative Narrative, Literature and Form'. In *Beyond the Screen: Transformations of Literary Structures, Interfaces and Genres*, ed. Jörgen Schäffer and Peter Gendolia, 317–30. New Brunswick, NJ: Transition, 2010.

Hirsch, Edward. *The Making of a Sonnet: A Norton Anthology*, ed. Edward Hirsch and Eavan Boland. New York: Norton, 2009.

Hjorth, Larissa, Jean Burgess and Ingrid Richardson (eds). *Studying Mobile Media: Cultural Technologies, Mobile Communication, and the iPhone*. London: Routledge, 2012.

Hofrichter, Richard. 'Introduction'. In *Toxic Struggles: The Theory and Practice of Environmental Justice*, ed. Richard Hofrichter, 1–11. Philadelphia, PA: New Society Publishers, 1993.

Hook, Sidney. *The Fail-Safe Fallacy*. New York: Stein and Day, 1963.

Horn, Eva. 'The Apocalyptic Fiction: Shaping the Future in the Cold War'. In *Understanding the Imaginary War: Culture, Thought and Nuclear Conflict, 1945–90*, ed. Matthew Grant and Benjamin Ziemann, 30–50. Manchester: Manchester University Press, 2016.

Hua, Yuanyuan. 'The Dual Alienation in *Waste Tide*'. *Comparative Literature Studies* 57 no. 4 (2020): 670–85.

Human Rights Watch. 'NATO: Investigate Fatal Boat Episode', 10 May 2011. Available online: https://www.hrw.org/news/2011/05/10/nato-investigate-fatal-boat-episode (accessed 18 January 2022).

International Maritime Organization. *International Convention for the Safety of Life at Sea*, 1 November 1974. Available online: https://www.imo.org/About/Conventions/ListOfConventions/Pages/International-Convention-for-the-Safety-of-Life-at-Sea-(SOLAS),-1974.aspx (accessed 18 January 2022).

International Maritime Organization. *International Convention on Maritime Search and Rescue (SAR Convention)*, adopted 27 April 1979, entered into force 22 June 1985. Available online: https://www.imo.org/en/About/Conventions/Pages/International-

Convention-on-Maritime-Search-and-Rescue-(SAR).aspx (accessed 18 January 2022).
International Organization for Migration. 'Rising Migrant Deaths Top 4,400 This Year: IOM Records More Than 45,000 since 2014', 10 December 2021. Available online: https://www.iom.int/news/rising-migrant-deaths-top-4400-year-iom-records-more-45000-2014 (accessed 18 January 2022).
Izenberg, Oren. *Being Numerous: Poetry and the Ground of Social Life*. Princeton, NJ: Princeton University Press, 2011.
Jackson, Michael. *The Politics of Storytelling: Variations on a Theme by Hannah Arendt*. Copenhagen: Museum Tusculanum Press, 2013.
Jackson, Sarah. 'Derrida on the Line'. *Derrida Today* 10 no. 2 (2017): 142–59.
Jackson, Sarah. 'Calling without Calling: Barghouti, Derrida and "The International Day of Telephones"'. *Textual Practice* 36 no. 9 (2022): 1393–412.
Jarrett, Kylie and Janeen Naji. 'What Would Media Studies Do? Social Media Shakespeare as a Technosocial Process'. *Borrowers and Lenders: The Journal of Shakespeare and Appropriation* 10 no. 1 (2016): 1–18.
Jiang, Yuqin. 'Echotech, Alienation, and Science Realism in the Chinese Cyborg Novel *Waste Tide*'. *Comparative Literature Studies* 57 no. 4 (2020): 655–69.
Jones, Nathan. 'Glitch Poetics: The Posthumanities of Error'. In *The Bloomsbury Handbook of Electronic Literature*, ed. Joseph Tabbi, 237–52. London: Bloomsbury, 2017.
Joudah, Fady. *Textu*. Washington: Copper Canyon Press, 2014.
Joudah, Fady. 'Interview with Kaveh Akbar', 2 February 2015. Available online: https://www.divedapper.com/interview/fady-joudah/ (accessed 15 March 2019).
Jucan, Ioana B. 'Introduction: Remain x Remain(s)'. In *Remain: In Search of Media*, by Iona B. Jucan, Jussi Parikka and Rebecca Schneider, ix–xx. Lüneberg: Meson Press, 2018.
Jung, Carl G. 'Analysis of a Case of Paranoid Dementia as a Paradigm'. In *The Psychology of Dementia Praecox*, trans. R. F. C. Hull, 99–152. Princeton, NJ: Princeton University Press, 1974.
Kafka, Franz. *Letters to Felice*, ed. Erich Heller and Jürgen Born, trans. James Stem and Elisabeth Duckworth. New York: Schocken, 1973.
Kahn, Herman. *Thinking the Unthinkable*. New York: Horizon Press, 1962.
Kaplan, Caren. 'Precision Targets: GPS and the Militarization of U.S. Consumer Identity'. *American Quarterly* 58 no. 3 (2006): 693–713.
Kaplan, Edward. *To Kill Nations: American Strategy in the Air-Atomic Age and the Rise of Mutually Assured Destruction*. Ithaca, NY: Cornell University Press, 2015.
Kassabova, Kapka. *Borders: A Journey to the Edge of Europe*. Minneapolis, MN: Graywolf Press, 2017.
Kaufmann, David. 'Drift: Book Review'. *Asymptote*, October 2014. Available online: https://www.asymptotejournal.com/criticism/caroline-bergvall-drift/ (accessed 18 January 2022).

Kaur, Rupi. *Milk and Honey*. Kansas City, MO: Andrew McMeel, 2015.
Kerckhove, Derrick de. 'On Nuclear Communication'. *Diacritics* 14 no. 2 (1984): 71–81.
Kermode, Frank. 'To the Girls of Slender Means'. *New Statesman* 66, September 1964, 397–8. Reprinted in *Critical Essays on Muriel Spark*, ed. Joseph Hynes, 174–8. New York: G. K. Hall & Co., 1992.
Kermode, Frank. *The Genesis of Secrecy: On the Interpretation of Narrative*. Cambridge, MA: Harvard University Press, 1979.
Kermode, Frank. 'Secrets and Narrative Sequence'. *Critical Inquiry* 7 no. 1 (1980): 83–101.
Kern, Stephen. *Culture of Time and Space, 1880–1918*. Cambridge, MA: Harvard University Press, 1983.
Keyser, Barbara Y. 'Muriel Spark, Watergate, and the Mass Media'. *The Arizona Quarterly* 32 no. 2 (1976): 146–53.
Kircher, Althanasius. *Musurgia Universalis*. Rome: Francesco Corbelletti, 1650.
Kittler, Friedrich A. *Gramophone, Film, Typewriter*, trans. Geoffrey Winthrop-Young and Michael Wutz. Stanford, CA: Stanford University Press, 1999.
Klepp, Silja. 'A Double Bind: Malta and the Rescue of Unwanted Migrants at Sea, a Legal Anthropological Perspective on the Humanitarian Law of the Sea'. *International Journal of Refugee Law* 23 no. 3 (2011): 538–57.
Koenigsberg, Allen. 'The First "Hello!" Thomas Edison, the Phonograph and the Telephone'. *Antique Phonograph Monthly* 8 no. 6 (October 1987): 1, 3, 6–9.
Kubrick, Stanley (dir.). *Dr. Strangelove or: How I Learned to Stop Worrying and Love the Bomb*. Culver City, CA: Hawk Films/Columbia Pictures, 1964.
Laing, R. D. *The Divided Self*. London: Penguin, 2010.
Lake, Carol. *Switchboard Operators*. London: Bloomsbury, 1994.
LaRue, Frank. 'Report of the Special Rapporteur on the Promotion and Protection of the Right to Freedom of Opinion and Expression'. In *United Nations General Assembly, Human Rights Council*. Geneva: UN Printing Office, 2011. Available online: https://digitallibrary.un.org/record/706200?ln=en (accessed 18 January 2022).
Latour, Bruno. *We Have Never Been Modern*, trans. Catherine Porter. Cambridge, MA: Harvard University Press, 1993.
Lawson, Dominic. 'Smartphones Are the Secret Weapon Fuelling the Great Migrant Invasion'. *Daily Mail*, 28 September 2015. Available online: https://www.dailymail.co.uk/debate/article-3251475/DOMINIC-LAWSON-Smartphones-secret-weapon-fuelling-great-migrant-invasion.html (accessed 18 January 2022).
Lea, Daniel. *Twenty-First-Century Fiction: Contemporary British Voices*. Manchester: Manchester University Press, 2017.
Leighton, Angela. *Hearing Things: The Work of Sound in Literature*. Cambridge, MA: Harvard University Press, 2018.
Leonard, Philip. *Orbital Poetics: Literature, Theory, World*. London: Bloomsbury, 2019.

Levinson, Chaim. 'Israel's Supreme Court Orders State to Dismantle Largest West Bank Outpost'. *Haaretz*, 2 August 2011. Available online: https://www.haaretz.com/1.5039235 (accessed 6 June 2020).

Lewis Hood, Kate. 'Clouding Knowledge in the Anthropocene: Lisa Robertson's *The Weather* and Caroline Bergvall's *Drift*'. *Green Letters* 22 no. 2 (2018): 181–96.

Lindley, Dan. 'What I Learned since I Stopped Worrying and Studied the Movie: A Teaching Guide to Stanley Kubrick's *Dr. Strangelove*'. *PS: Political Science and Politics* 34 no. 3 (2001): 663–7.

Lispector, Clarice. 'Correct Assumptions' (15 January 1972). In *Discovering the World*, trans. Giovanni Pontiero, 525–6. Manchester: Carcanet, 1992.

Lispector, Clarice. *Água Viva*, trans. Stefan Tobler. New York: New Directions, 2012.

Lopez, Beatriz. 'Muriel Spark and the Scrambler Telephone'. *Telepoetics Symposium*, 27 May 2020. Available online: https://crossedlines.co.uk/conversation2 (accessed 12 January 2022).

Lynch, Claire. *Cyber Ireland: Text, Image, Culture*. Basingstoke: Palgrave Macmillan, 2014.

MacCabe, Colin. 'Dissolving the Voice: Tom Raworth's Writing'. *Times Literary Supplement*, 30 December 1983. Reprinted in *Critical Quarterly* 59 no. 2 (2017): 83–6.

MacKay, Marina. 'Muriel Spark and the Meaning of Treason'. In *Muriel Spark: Twenty-First-Century Perspectives*, ed. David Herman, 94–111. Baltimore, MD: Johns Hopkins University Press, 2010.

MacLeod, Lewis. 'Matters of Care and Control: Surveillance, Omniscience, and Narrative Power in *The Abbess of Crewe* and *Loitering with Intent*'. *Modern Fiction Studies* 54 no. 3 (2008): 574–94.

Mahmud, Nadim, Isaac Holeman, Kenny Puk, Regina Lam and Damian Lee. 'The Cell Phone Problem/Solution'. *Journal of Environmental Health* 76 no. 6 (2014): 140–5.

Malkki, Liisa H. 'Speechless Emissaries: Refugees, Humanitarianism and Dehistoricization'. *Cultural Anthropology* 11 no. 3 (1996): 377–404.

Maloney, Sean M. *Deconstructing Dr. Strangelove: The Secret History of Nuclear War Films*. Lincoln, NE: Potomac Books, 2020.

Mandel, Emily St John. *Station Eleven*. London: Picador, 2015.

Mao, Sally Wen. *Oculus*. Minneapolis, MN: Graywolf Press, 2019.

Marks, Peter. *Imagining Surveillance: Eutopian and Dystopian Literature and Film*. Edinburgh: Edinburgh University Press, 2015.

Marx, Karl. *Capital: A Critique of Political Economy*, vol. 1, trans. Ben Fowkes. London: Penguin, 1976.

Masco, Joseph. *The Nuclear Borderlands: The Manhattan Project in Post-Cold War New Mexico*. Princeton, NJ: Princeton University Press, 2006.

Mauss, Marcel. *The Gift: Forms and Functions of Exchange in Archaic Societies*, trans. Ian Cunnison. London: Cohen & West, 1966.

Mbembe, Achille. 'Necropolitics', trans. Libby Meintjes. *Public Culture* 15 no. 1 (2003): 11–40.

McCaffery, Steve. 'From Phonic to Sonic: The Emergence of the Audio-Poem'. In *Sound States: Innovative Poetics and Acoustical Technologies*, ed. Adelaide Morris, 149–68. Chapel Hill, NC: University of North Carolina Press, 1998.

McCanles, Michael. 'Machiavelli and the Paradoxes of Deterrence'. *Diacritics* 14 no. 2 (1984): 11–19.

McCarren, Felicia. '*Téléphone Arabe*: From Child's Play to Terrorism – The Poetics and Politics of Postcolonial Telecommunication'. *Journal of Postcolonial Writing* 44 no. 3 (2008): 289–305.

McClure, James Baird. *Edison and His Inventions*. Chicago: Rhodes and McClure, 1879.

McLoughlin, Kate. 'Interruption Overload: Telephones in Ford Madox Ford's "4692 Padd", *A Call* and *A Man Could Stand Up –*'. *Journal of Modern Literature* 36 no. 3 (2013): 50–68.

McLuhan, Marshall. *Understanding Media: The Extensions of Man*. London: Routledge, 2001.

McMurtry, Áine. 'Sea Journeys to Fortress Europe: Lyric Deterritorializations in Texts by Caroline Bergvall and José F. A. Oliver'. *The Modern Language Review* 113 no. 4 (October 2018): 811–45.

McNeil, Horace J. and Clarence Stratton (eds). *Poems for a Machine Age*. New York: McGraw-Hill, 1941.

McQuillan, Martin. 'Introduction – "I Don't Know Anything about Freud": Muriel Spark Meets Contemporary Criticism'. In *Theorising Muriel Spark: Gender, Race, Deconstruction*, ed. Martin McQuillan, 1–31. Basingstoke: Palgrave Macmillan, 2001.

McQuillan, Martin. 'Clarity and Doubt: Derrida among the Palestinians'. *Paragraph* 39 no. 2 (2016): 220–37.

McQuillan, Martin and Muriel Spark. 'The Same Informed Air'. In *Theorising Muriel Spark: Gender, Race, Deconstruction*, ed. Martin McQuillan, 210–29. Basingstoke: Palgrave MacMillan, 2001.

Menke, Richard. *Literature, Print Culture, and Media Technologies, 1880–1900*. Cambridge: Cambridge University Press, 2019.

Menkman, Rosa. *The Glitch Moment(um)*. Amsterdam: Institute of Network Cultures, 2011.

Meyer, Robinson. 'On Top of Everything Else, Nuclear War Would Be a Climate Problem'. *The Atlantic*, 9 March 2022. Available online: https://www.theatlantic.com/science/archive/2022/03/nuclear-war-would-ravage-the-planets-climate/627005/ (accessed 29 April 2022).

Meyrowitz, Joshua. *No Sense of Place: The Impact of Electronic Media on Social Behaviour*. Oxford: Oxford University Press, 1985.

Meyrowitz, Joshua. 'The Rise of Glocality: New Sense of Place and Identity in the Global Village'. In *A Sense of Place: The Global and the Local in Mobile Communication*, ed. Kristóf Nyíri, 21–30. Vienna: Passagen Verlag, 2005.

Miller, Michael F. 'Why Hate the Internet?: Contemporary Fiction, Digital Culture, and the Politics of Social Media'. *Arizona Quarterly: A Journal of American Literature, Culture, and Theory* 75 no. 3 (2019): 59–85.

Miller, Steven E. 'Nuclear Hotlines: Origins, Evolution, Applications'. *Journal for Peace and Nuclear Disarmament* 4 no. 1 (2021): 176–91.

Milner, Greg. *Pinpoint: How GPS Is Changing Our World*. London: Granta, 2016.

Minges, Michael. 'Overview'. In *Information and Communications for Development 2012: Maximizing Mobile*, ed. World Bank, 11–30. Washington: World Bank Publication, 2012.

Mir, Salam. 'Mourid Barghouti: The Blessings of Exile'. *Arab Studies Quarterly* 37 no. 4 (2015): 311–33.

Moore, Gerald and Ulli Beier (eds). *Modern Poetry from Africa*. London: Penguin, 1963.

Morris, Adelaide. 'Sound Technologies and the Modernist Epic: H.D. On the Air'. In *Sound States: Innovative Poetics and Acoustical Technologies*, ed. Adelaide Morris, 32–55. Chapel Hill, NC: University of North Carolina Press, 1998.

Morris, Adelaide. 'Forensic Listening: NourbeSe Philip's *Zong!*, Caroline Bergvall's *Drift*, and the Contemporary Long Poem'. *Dibur Literary Journal* 4 (2017): 77–87.

Morris, Adelaide and Thomas Swiss. *New Media Poetics*. Cambridge, MA: MIT Press, 2006.

Moten, Fred. *In the Break: The Aesthetics of the Black Radical Tradition*. Minneapolis, MN: University of Minnesota Press, 2003.

Moysaenko, Daniel. 'Syncope: A Review'. *Harvard Review Online*, 3 March 2020. Available online: https://harvardreview.org/book-review/syncope/ (accessed 18 January 2022).

Mujezinovic, Davor. 'Electronic Waste in Guiyu: A City under Change?' *Arcadia* 29 (2019). Available online: https://www.environmentandsociety.org/arcadia/electronic-waste-guiyu-city-under-change(accessed 2 April 2022).

Murakami, Haruki. *Sputnik Sweetheart*, trans. Philip Gabriel. London: Vintage, 2001.

Nabokov, Vladimir. *Speak, Memory: An Autobiography Revisited*. New York: Vintage, 1989.

Naji, Janeen. *Digital Poetry*. Basingstoke: Palgrave Macmillan, 2021.

Nancy, Jean-Luc. *Listening*, trans. Charlotte Mandell. New York: Fordham University Press, 2007.

Nanz, Tobias. 'Communication in Crisis: The "Red Phone" and the "Hotline"'. *Behemoth: A Journal on Civilization* 2 (2010): 71–83.

Nanz, Tobias. 'The Red Telephone: A Hybrid Object of the Cold War', trans. Gregory Simms. In *Disruption in the Arts: Textual, Visual, and Performative Strategies for Analyzing Societal Self-Descriptions*, ed. Lars Koch, Tobias Nanz and Johannes Pause, 275–89. Berlin: De Gruyter, 2018.

Nasser, Tahia Abdel. 'Between Exile and Elegy, Palestine and Egypt: Mourid Barghouti's Poetry and Memoirs'. *Journal of Arabic Literature* 45 no. 2/3 (2014): 244–64.
Neville, Brian and Johanne Villeneuve (eds). *Waste-Site Stories: The Recycling of Memory*. New York: SUNY Press, 2002.
Nixon, Rob. *Slow Violence and the Environmentalism of the Poor*. Cambridge, MA: Harvard University Press, 2011.
Noland, Carrie. *Poetry at Stake: Lyric Aesthetics and the Challenge of Technology*. Princeton, NJ: Princeton University Press, 1999.
O'Hara, Frank. *The Collected Poems of Frank O'Hara*, ed. Donald Allen. Berkeley: University of California Press, 1995.
Oliver, Jessica Eve. '*The Raft, the Ladder, the Transitional Space, the Moratorium …*': *Digital Interventions in Twenty-First-Century Private and Public Lives*. PhD Thesis, University of Sussex, June 2018.
Ong, Walter. *Orality and Literacy: The Technologizing of the Word*. London: Methuen, 1982.
Overbye, Dennis. 'Among Scientific Treasures, a Gem'. *New York Times*, 10 June 2008, F3. Available online: https://www.nytimes.com/2008/06/10/science/10auct.html (accessed 19 April 2022).
Oxford English Dictionary Online, Oxford: Oxford University Press, 2022. Available online: https://www.oed.com/ (accessed 12 May 2022).
Palladino, Mariangela and Agnes Woolley. 'Migration, Humanitarianism, and the Politics of Salvation'. *LIT: Literature Interpretation Theory* 29 no. 2 (2018): 129–44.
Papanicolopulu, Irini. 'The Duty to Rescue at Sea, in Peacetime and in War: A General Overview'. *International Review of the Red Cross* 92 no. 2 (2016): 491–514.
Parikka, Jussi. *The Anthrobscene*. Minneapolis, MN: University of Minnesota Press, 2014.
Parikka, Jussi. 'Remain(s) Scattered'. In *Remain: In Search of Media*, by Iona B. Jucan, Jussi Parikka and Rebecca Schneider, 1–48. Lüneburg: Meson Press, 2018.
Parker, Laura. 'China's Ban on Trash Imports Shifts Waste Crisis to Southeast Asia'. *National Geographic*, 16 November 2018. Available online: https://www.nationalgeographic.com/environment/article/china-ban-plastic-trash-imports-shifts-waste-crisis-southeast-asia-malaysia (accessed 2 April 2022).
Parks, Lisa. *Cultures in Orbit: Satellites and the Televisual*. Durham, NC: Duke University Press, 2005.
Parks, Lisa and James Schwoch. 'Introduction'. In *Down to Earth: Satellite Technologies, Industries, and Cultures*, ed. Lisa Parks and James Schwoch, 1–16. New Brunswick, NJ: Rutgers University Press, 2012.
Parliamentary Assembly of the Council of Europe. '"The Left-to-Die Boat": There Should Be No Gaps in the Division of Responsibility for Search and Rescue', 16 December 2011. Available online: https://pace.coe.int/en/news/3759?__cf_chl_jschl_tk__=7uVel6GXYly6BgKFV9ekJgS6zV1yonhcoNPdm1Xpfos-1643104672-0-gaNycGzNCJE (accessed 18 January 2022).

Peace Agreements & Related. *Israeli-Palestinian Interim Agreement on the West Bank and the Gaza Strip* (Oslo II)', 28 September 1995. Available online: https://www.refworld.org/docid/3de5ebbc0.html (accessed 20 March 2020).

Perloff, Marjorie. 'Frank O'Hara and the Aesthetics of Attention'. *boundary 2* 4 no. 3 (1976): 779–806.

Perloff, Marjorie. *Frank O'Hara: Poet among Painters*. Chicago: University of Chicago Press, 1977.

Perloff, Marjorie. 'The Word as Such: L=A=N=G=U=A=G=E Poetry in the Eighties'. *The American Poetry Review* 13 no. 3 (1984): 15–22.

Perloff, Marjorie. *Radical Artifice: Writing Poetry in the Age of Media*. Chicago: University of Chicago Press, 1991.

Perloff, Marjorie. 'Filling the Space with Trace: Tom Raworth's "Letters from Yaddo"'. In *Removed for Further Study*, ed. Nate Dorward. *The Gig* 13/14 (2003): 130–44.

Perloff, Marjorie. *Unoriginal Genius: Poetry by Other Means in the New Century*. Chicago: University of Chicago Press, 2010.

Perloff, Marjorie and Craig Dworkin. 'The Sound of Poetry/The Poetry of Sound: The 2006 MLA Presidential Forum'. *PMLA* 123 no. 3 (2008): 749–61.

Perlow, Seth. *The Poem Electric: Technology and the American Lyric*. Minneapolis, MN: University of Minnesota Press, 2018.

Perril, Simon. '"What Rhymes with Cow / and Starts with an N": Tom Raworth's Time and Motion Studies'. In *Removed for Further Study*, ed. Nate Dorward. *The Gig* 13/14 (2003): 108–29.

Pessl, Marisha. *Night Film*. New York: Random House, 2013.

Phelps, Elizabeth Stuart. 'The Chief Operator'. In *The Oath of Allegiance and Other Stories*, 353–74. Boston: Houghton Mifflin, 1909.

Pingui, Zhuang. 'China's most notorious e-waste dumping ground now cleaner but poorer'. South China Morning Post, 22 September 2017. Available online: https://www.scmp.com/news/china/society/article/2112226/chinas-most-notorious-e-waste-dumping-ground-now-cleaner-poorer (accessed 2 April 2022).

'Points from Publishers: Speed'. *The Bookseller*, 22 January 1966, 210–11.

Prenowitz, Eric. 'Crossing Lines: Jacques Derrida and Hélène Cixous on the Phone'. *Discourse* 30 no. 1–2 (2008): 123–56.

Prochnau, William. *Trinity's Child*. New York: G. P. Putnam's Sons, 1983.

'Proposal for a Diacritics Colloquium on Nuclear Criticism'. *Diacritics* 14 no. 2 (1984): 2–3.

Pullinger, Kate. *Breathe*. London: Editions at Play/Visual Editions, 2018. Available online: https://www.breathe-story.com/ (accessed 13 November 2020).

Pure Earth. 'Toxic Site Identification Program'. Available online: https://www.pureearth.org/our-projects/toxic-site-identification-program-tsip/ (accessed 2 April 2022).

Qiufan, Chen. 'Electronic Waste: Can We Really Turn the Tide?', trans. Emily Jin, 16 April 2019. Available online: https://www.tor.com/2019/04/16/electronic-waste-can-we-really-turn-the-tide/ (accessed 2 April 2022).

Qiufan, Chen. *Waste Tide*, trans. Ken Liu. London: Tor, 2019.
Raley, Rita. 'Walk This Way'. In *Beyond the Screen: Transformations of Literary Structures, Interfaces and Genres*, ed. Jörgen Schäffer and Peter Gendolia, 299–316. New Brunswick, NJ: Transition, 2010.
Rambuss, Richard. 'The Secretary's Study: The Secret Designs of the Shepeardes Calendar'. *ELH* 59 no. 2 (1992): 313–35.
Rankin, Ian. 'Introduction'. In *The Hothouse by the East River*, by Muriel Spark, ix–xvi. Edinburgh: Polygon, 2018.
Raworth, Tom. *The Relation Ship*. London: Goliard Press, 1967.
Raworth, Tom. *The Big Green Day*. London: Trigram, 1968.
Raworth, Tom. *Eternal Sections*. Los Angeles: Sun & Moon Press, 1993.
Raworth, Tom. *Collected Poems*. Manchester: Carcanet, 2003.
Raworth, Tom. *Writing*, Rockdrill #5. Contemporary Poetics Research Centre, Optic Nerve for Birkbeck College, 2004. Available online: https://media.sas.upenn.edu/pennsound/authors/Raworth/Rockdrill-5/Raworth-Tom_01_Writing_Writing_Rockdrill-5_2004.mp3 (accessed 15 March 2019).
Raworth, Tom. *Earn Your Milk: Collected Prose*. Cambridge: Salt, 2009.
Raworth, Tom. 'Curriculum Vitae', last updated 1 August 2016. Available online: https://web.archive.org/web/20161110063408/http://tomraworth.com/cvweb.html (accessed 18 March 2022).
Raworth, Tom, Bill Griffiths and Tom Leonard. *Etruscan Reader V*. Wilkes-Barre, PA: Etruscan Books, 1997.
Reed, Brian M. *Phenomenal Reading: Essays on Modern and Contemporary Poetics*. Tuscaloosa, AL: University of Alabama Press, 2012.
Reines, Ariana. *Telephone*. New York: Wonder, 2018.
Reizbaum, Marilyn. 'The Stranger Spark'. In *The Edinburgh Companion to Muriel Spark*, ed. Michael Gardiner and Willy Maley, 40–51. Edinburgh: Edinburgh University Press, 2010.
Richtel, Matt. 'Introducing the Twiller'. *New York Times*, 29 August 2008. Available online: https://bits.blogs.nytimes.com/2008/08/29/introducing-the-twiller/ (accessed 15 March 2021).
Ronell, Avital. *The Telephone Book: Technology, Schizophrenia, Electric Speech*. Lincoln, NE: University of Nebraska Press, 1989.
Rooney, Caroline. 'Derrida and Said: Ships That Pass in the Night'. In *Edward Said and the Literary, Social and Political World*, ed. R. Ghosh, 36–52. London and New York: Routledge, 2009.
Roshwald, Mordecai. *Level 7*. Madison, WI: University of Wisconsin Press, 2004.
Rosi, Gianfranco (dir.). *Fuocoammare*. Rome: Stemal Entertainment, 2016.
Royle, Nicholas. *Telepathy and Literature: Essays on the Reading Mind*. Oxford: Basil Blackwell, 1990.
Royle, Nicholas. 'Memento Mori'. In *Theorising Muriel Spark: Gender, Race, Deconstruction*, ed. Martin McQuillan, 189–203. Basingstoke: Palgrave Macmillan, 2001.

Ruddick, Nicholas. 'Adapting the Absurd Apocalypse: Eugene Burdick's and Harvey Wheeler's *Fail-Safe* and Its Cinematic Progeny'. In *Future Wars: The Anticipations and the Fears*, ed. David Seed, 161–79. Liverpool: Liverpool University Press, 2012.

Rudin, Michael. 'From Hemingway to Twitterature: The Short and Shorter of It'. *The Journal of Electronic Publishing* 14 no. 2 (2011): n.p.

Salinger, J. D. *The Catcher in the Rye*. London: Penguin, 1994.

Saucier, P. Khalil and Tryon P. Woods. 'Ex Aqua: The Mediterranean Basin, Africans on the Move, and the Politics of Policing'. *Theoria: A Journal of Social and Political Theory* 61 no. 141 (2014): 55–75.

Saussure, Ferdinand de. *Course in General Linguistics*, trans. Wade Baskin. New York: Columbia University Press, 2011.

Sawafta, Ali. 'Palestinians Get 3G Mobile Services in West Bank'. *Reuters*, 24 January 2018. Available online: https://www.reuters.com/article/israel-palestinians-telecom/palestinians-get-3g-mobile-services-in-west-bank-idUSL8N1PJ3FW (accessed 6 June 2020).

Schafer, R. Murray. *The Soundscape: Our Sonic Environment and the Tuning of the World*. Rochester VT: Destiny Books, 1994.

Schantz, Ned. *Gossip, Letters, Phones: The Scandal of Female Networks in Film and Literature*. Oxford: Oxford University Press, 2008.

Schelling, Thomas C. 'Meteors, Mischief, and War'. *Bulletin of the Atomic Scientists* 16 no. 7 (September 1960): 293–300.

Schelling, Thomas C. *Arms and Influence*. New Haven, CT: Yale University Press, 1966.

Scherman, David E. 'The Doomsday Lawsuit'. *Life Magazine*, 8 March 1963, 49–50.

Schmidt di Friedberg, Marcella. *Geographies of Disorientation*. London: Routledge, 2019.

Schuerewegen, Franc. 'A Telephone Conversation: Fragments', trans. Marvin N. Richards, *Diacritics* 24 no. 4 (1994): 30–40.

Schwartz, Claire. 'An Interview with Rita Dove'. *The Virginia Quarterly Review* 92 no. 1 (2016): 164–71.

Schwartz, Mattathias. 'The Anchor'. *The New Yorker*, 21 April 2014. Available online: https://www.newyorker.com/magazine/2014/04/21/the-anchor (accessed 18 January 2022).

Sconce, Jeffrey. *The Technical Delusion: Electronics, Power, Insanity*. Durham, NC: Duke University Press, 2019.

Sedgwick, Eve Kosofsky. *Tendencies*. Durham, NC: Duke University Press, 1993.

Seed, David. *Under the Shadow: The Atomic Bomb and Cold War Narratives*. Kent, OH: Kent State University Press, 2013, 188.

Selerie, Gavin. 'A Letter from London'. *North Dakota Quarterly*, 11 May 1985, 115–34.

Self, Will. *Phone*. London: Penguin, 2017.

Serres, Michel with Bruno Latour. *Conversations on Science, Culture, and Time*, trans. Roxanne Lapidus. Ann Arbor, MI: University of Michigan Press, 1995.

Shannon, Claude E. and Warren Weaver. *The Mathematical Theory of Communication*. Urbana, IL: University of Illinois Press, 1964.

Sharpe, Christina. *In the Wake: On Blackness and Being*. Durham, NC: Duke University Press, 2016.

Shea, Ammon. *The Phone Book: The Curious History of the Book That Everyone Uses but No One Reads*. New York: Penguin, 2010.

Shenker, Jack and Giles Tremlett. 'Migrant Boat Disaster: Spain Challenges NATO over Distress Call Claim'. *The Guardian*, 29 March 2012. Available online: https://www.theguardian.com/world/2012/mar/29/migrant-boat-disaster-spain-nato (accessed 18 January 2022).

Sheppard, Robert. *The Poetry of Saying: British Poetry and Its Discontents, 1950–2000*. Liverpool: Liverpool University Press, 2005.

Slade, Giles. *Made to Break: Technology and Obsolescence in America*. Cambridge, MA: Harvard University Press, 2007.

Smith, Ali. *Free Love and Other Stories*. London: Virago, 1998.

Smith, Ali. *Other Stories and Other Stories*. London: Penguin, 2004.

Smith, Ali. *There but for The*. London: Penguin, 2012.

Smith, Ali. *How to Be Both*. London: Penguin, 2014.

Smith, Ali. *Autumn*. London: Penguin, 2017.

Smith, Ali. *Winter*. London: Penguin, 2018.

Smith, Ali. *Spring*. London: Penguin, 2020.

Smith, Ali. *Summer*. London: Penguin, 2021.

Smith, Ali and Gillian Beer. 'Gillian Beer Interviews Ali Smith'. In *Ali Smith: Contemporary Critical Perspectives*, ed. Monica Germanà and Emily Horton, 137–53. London: Bloomsbury, 2013.

Smith, Hazel. *Hyperscapes in the Poetry of Frank O'Hara: Difference, Homosexuality, Topography*. Liverpool: Liverpool University Press, 2000.

Solnit, Rebecca. *A Field Guide to Getting Lost*. Edinburgh: Canongate, 2009.

Song, Mingwei. 'Representations of the Invisible: Chinese Science Fiction in the Twenty-First Century'. In *The Oxford Handbook of Modern Chinese Literatures*, ed. Carlos Rojas and Andrea Bachner, 546–65. Oxford: Oxford University Press, 2016.

Souza e Silva, Adriana de. 'Mobile Narratives: Reading and Writing Urban Space with Location-Based Technologies'. In *Comparative Textual Media: Transforming the Humanities in the Postprint Era*, ed. N. Katherine Hayles and Jessica Pressman, 33–52. Minneapolis, MN: University of Minnesota Press, 2013.

Spark, Muriel. *Curriculum Vitae*. London: Penguin, 1993.

Spark, Muriel. *The French Window and The Small Telephone*. London: Colophon Press, 1993.

Spark, Muriel. *The Abbess of the Crewe*. New York: New Directions, 1995.

Spark, Muriel. *Memento Mori*. New York: New Directions, 2000.

Spark, Muriel. *The Comforters*. London: Virago, 2009.

Spark, Muriel. *The Prime of Miss Jean Brodie*. London: Penguin, 2012.

Spark, Muriel. *The Girls of Slender Means*. London: Penguin, 2013.

Spark, Muriel. *Mary Shelley: A Biography*. Manchester: Carcanet, 2013.

Spark, Muriel. *The Hothouse by the East River*. Edinburgh: Polygon, 2018.

Standaert, Michael. 'China's Notorious E-Waste Village Disappears Almost Overnight'. *Basel Action Network*, 17 December 2015. Available online: https://www.ban.org/news-new/2015/12/17/chinas-notorious-e-waste-village-disappears-almost-overnight (accessed 2 April 2022).

Stanford Arms Control Group. *International Arms Control: Issues and Agreements*, 2nd edition, ed. Coit D. Blacker and Gloria Duffy. Stanford, CA: Stanford University Press, 1984.

Stannard, Martin. *Muriel Spark: The Biography*. London: Weidenfeld & Nicolson, 2009.

Stefans, Brian Kim. *Word Toys: Poetry and Technics*. Tuscaloosa, AL: University of Alabama Press, 2017.

Steffen, Will, Paul J. Crutzen and John R. McNeill. 'The Anthropocene: Are Humans Now Overwhelming the Great Forces of Nature?' *Ambio* 36 (2007): 614–27.

Stephen, Paul. *The Poetics of Information Overload: From Gertrude Stein to Conceptual Writing*. Minneapolis, MN: University of Minnesota Press, 2015.

Sterne, Jonathan. 'Out with the Trash: On the Future of New Media'. In *Residual Media*, ed. Charles Ackland, 16–31. Minneapolis, MN: University of Minnesota Press, 2007.

Sterne, Jonathan. *MP3: The Meaning of a Format*. Durham, NC: Duke University Press, 2012.

Stevenson, Sheryl. '"Poetry Deleted," Parody Added: Watergate, Spark's Style, and Bakhtin's Stylistics'. *Ariel* 24 no. 4 (1993): 71–85.

Stewart, Garrett. *Reading Voices: Literature and the Phonotext*. Berkeley: University of California Press, 1990.

Stiegler, Bernard. *Technics and Time 1: The Fault of Epimetheus*, trans. Richard Beardsworth and George Collins. Stanford, CA: Stanford University Press, 1998.

Stiegler, Bernard. *Technics and Time 2: Disorientation*, trans. Stephen Barker. Stanford, CA: Stanford University Press, 2009.

Stillman, Sarah. 'Lampedusa's Migrant Tragedy, and Ours'. *The New Yorker*, 10 October 2013. Available online: https://www.newyorker.com/news/daily-comment/lampedusas-migrant-tragedy-and-ours (accessed 18 January 2022).

Strieber, Whitley and James Kunetka. *Warday*. New York: Holt, Rinehart and Winston, 1984.

Sun, Mengtian. 'Imagining Globalization in Paolo Bacigalupi's *The Windup Girl* and Chen Qiufan's *The Waste Tide*'. *Science Fiction Studies* 46 no. 2 (2019): 289–306.

Swift, Martha. 'How Recycling Ruined the World: A Review of Chen Qiufan's *Waste Tide*'. *It's Freezing in LA*, 12 October 2020. Available online: https://itsfreezinginla.com/articles/how-recycling-ruined-the-world (accessed 2 April 2022).

Swinburne, Henry. *Travels in Two Sicilies, in the Years 1777, 1778, 1779, and 1780*. London: T. Cadell & P. Elmsky, 1790.

Szasz, Ferenc Morton. *The Day the Sun Rose Twice: The Story of the Trinity Site Nuclear Explosion, July 16, 1945*. Albuquerque, NM: University of New Mexico Press, 1984.

Szendy, Peter. *All Ears: The Aesthetics of Espionage*, trans. Roland Végső. New York: Fordham University Press, 2017.

Szilard, Leo. 'The Mined Cities'. *Bulletin of the Atomic Scientists* 17 no. 10 (1961): 407–12.

Takatsu, *Secondhand Memories*. Hermitage, PA: Sakura, 2015.

Tarlo, Harriet. 'Open Field: Reading Field as Place and Poetics'. In *Placing Poetry*, ed. Ian Davidson and Zoë Skoulding, 113–48. Amsterdam: Brill, 2013.

Tawil-Souri, Helga. 'Networking Palestine: The Development and Limitations of Television and Telecommunications since 1993'. In *The Oslo Accords 1993–2013: A Critical Assessment*, ed. Petter Bauck and Mohammed Omer, 217–29. Cairo: American University in Cairo Press, 2013.

Tawil-Souri, Helga. 'Cellular Borders: Dis/Connecting Phone Calls in Israel-Palestine'. In *Signal Traffic: Critical Studies of Media Infrastructures*, ed. Lisa Parks and Nicole Starosielski, 157–80. Champaign, IL: University of Illinois Press, 2015.

Taylor, Dorceta E. *Toxic Communities: Environmental Racism, Industrial Pollution, and Residential Mobility*. New York: New York University Press, 2014.

'Terrors of the Telephone'. *Daily Graphic*, 15 March 1877, 1.

The Basel Action Network (BAN) and Silicon Valley Toxics Coalition (SVTC). 'Exporting Harm: The High-Tech Trashing of Asia', 25 February 2002. Available online: https://issuu.com/greenpeace_eastasia/docs/exporting-harm-the-high-tech-trashing-asia (accessed 2 April 2022).

The Basel Convention and the United Nations Environment Programme. *The Basel Convention on the Control of Transboundary Movements of Hazardous Wastes and Their Disposal*, 22 March 1989, texts and annexes revised 2019. Available online: http://www.basel.int/TheConvention/Overview/tabid/1271/Default.aspx (accessed 2 April 2022).

'The Red Phone that Was Not on the Hotline'. *Electrospaces*, 30 August 2013, updated 5 March 2016. Available online: https://www.electrospaces.net/2013/08/the-red-phone-that-was-not-on-hotline.html (accessed 8 May 2022).

Thomas, Bronwen. '140 Characters in Search of a Story: Twitter Fiction as an Emerging Narrative Form'. In *Analysing Digital Fiction*, ed. Alice Bell, Astrid Ensslin and Hans Rustad, 94–108. London: Routledge, 2014.

Thomas, Bronwen. *Literature and Social Media*. London: Routledge, 2020.

Thompson, Michael. *Rubbish Theory: The Creation and Destruction of Value*. London: Pluto Press, 2017.

Thornber, Karen. *Ecoambiguity: Environmental Crises and East Asian Literatures*. Ann Arbor, MI: University of Michigan Press, 2012.

Thurschwell, Pamela. *Literature, Technology and Magical Thinking, 1880–1920*. Cambridge: Cambridge University Press, 2009.

Tietchen, Todd. 'Frank O'Hara and the Poetics of the Digital'. *Criticism* 56 no. 1 (2014): 45–62.

Tietchen, Todd. *Technomodern Poetics: The American Literary Avant-Garde at the Start of the Information Age*. Iowa, IA: University of Iowa Press, 2018.

Trotter, David. *Literature in the First Media Age: Britain Between the Wars*. Cambridge, MA: Harvard University Press, 2013.

Trotter, David. *The Literature of Connection: Signal, Medium, Interface, 1850–1950*. Oxford: Oxford University Press, 2020.
United Nations High Commissioner for Refugees (UNHCR). 'UNHCR calls on States to uphold principles of rescue-at-sea and Burden Sharing', Press Release, 8 April 2011. Available online: https://www.unhcr.org/uk/news/press/2011/4/4d9f1f7e6/unhcr-calls-states-uphold-principles-rescue-at-sea-burden-sharing.html (accessed 18 January 2022).
United Nations High Commissioner for Refugees (UNHCR). 'Mediterranean Takes Record as Most Deadly Stretch of Water for Refugees and Migrants in 2011', Briefing Notes, 31 January 2012. Available online: http://www.unhcr.org/4f27e01f9.html (accessed 18 January 2022).
United Nations Oceans and Law of the Sea. *United Nations Convention on the Law of the Sea (UNCLOS)*, 10 December 1982. Available online: https://www.un.org/depts/los/convention_agreements/convention_overview_convention.htm (accessed 18 January 2022).
Vermeulen, Peter. *Literature and the Anthropocene*. London: Routledge, 2020.
Very, Jones. *The Complete Poems*, ed. Helen R. Deese. Athens, GA: University of Georgia Press, 1993.
Virilio, Paul. *Speed and Politics*, trans. Marc Polizzotti. Los Angeles: Semiotext(e), 2007.
Vogl, Joseph. 'Becoming-Media: Galileo's Telescope', trans. Brian Hanrahan. *Grey Room* 29 (2007): 14–25.
Vuong, Ocean. 'Introduction: Sally Wen Mao'. *The Massachusetts Review* 59 no. 4 (2018): 804–5.
Wadud, Asiya. *Syncope*. New York: Ugly Duckling Presse, 2019.
Wadud, Asiya. 'Burnished, Etched, Emblazoned: Asiya Wadud Interviewed by Emily Skillings'. *BOMB Magazine*, 27 March 2020. Available online: https://bombmagazine.org/articles/asiya-wadud/ (accessed 2 February 2022).
Wallace, David Foster. *Infinite Jest*. London: Little, Brown and Company, 1996.
Walton, Samantha. 'Body Burdens: The Materiality of Work in Rita Wong's *Forage*'. In *Poetry and Work: Work in Modern and Contemporary Anglophone Poetry*, ed. Jo Lindsay Walton and Ed Luker, 263–90. Basingstoke: Palgrave Macmillan, 2019.
Wang, Feng, Ruediger Kuehr, Daniel Ahlquist and Jinhui Li. 'E-Waste in China: A Country Report'. *StEP: Solving the E-Waste Problem Green Paper Series*, 5 April 2013. Available online: https://collections.unu.edu/eserv/UNU:1624/ewaste-in-china.pdf (accessed 2 February 2022).
Waste Electrical and Electronic Equipment Recycling Forum. 'International E-Waste Day: 57.4M Tonnes Expected in 2021', n.d. Available online: https://weee-forum.org/ws_news/international-e-waste-day-2021/ (accessed 2 April 2022).
Watson, Thomas A. *Exploring Life: The Autobiography of Thomas A. Watson*. New York: D. Appleton and Company, 1926.
Waugh, Patricia. 'Muriel Spark's "Informed Air": The Auditory Imagination and the Voices of Fiction'. *Textual Practice*, 32 no. 9 (2018): 1633–58.

Weber, Elisabeth. 'Vectorizing Our Thoughts toward "Current Events": For Avital Ronell'. In *Reading Ronell*, ed. Diane Davis, 222–40. Champaign, IL: University of Illinois Press, 2009.

Weber, Samuel. *Mass Mediauras*. Stanford, CA: Stanford University Press, 1996.

Weigel, Anna. 'New Reading Strategies in the Twenty-First Century: Transmedia Storytelling via App in Marisha Pessl's Night Film'. In *Reading Today*, ed. Arnoldo Hax, Lionel Olavarría, Heta Pyrhönen and Janna Kantola, 73–86. London: UCL Press, 2018.

Weizman, Eyal. *Hollow Land: Israel's Architecture of Occupation*. London: Verso, 2007.

Whitman, Walt. *The Complete Poems*. London: Penguin, 2004.

Wiffen, Declan. *Deconstruction and the Question of Palestine: Bearing Witness to the Undeniable*. PhD thesis, University of Kent, July, 2014.

Williams, William Carlos. *Selected Essays of William Carlos Williams*. New York: New Directions, 1954.

Wills, David. 'Post/Card/Match/Book/Envois/Derrida'. *SubStance* 43 (1984): 19–38.

Wilson, Emma. 'Telephone Calls in Gianfranco Rosi's Fire at Sea (Fuocoammare, 2016)'. *Alphaville: Journal of Film and Screen Media* 17 (2019): 12–23.

Wise, Christopher. 'Deconstruction and Zionism: Jacques Derrida's "Specters of Marx"'. *Diacritics* 31 no. 1 (2001): 55–72.

Wong, Rita. *Forage*. Gibsons, BC: Nightwood Editions, 2007.

Wong, Rita. *Undercurrent*. Gibsons, BC: Nightwood Editions, 2015.

Woodbury-Tease, Amy. 'Call and Answer: Muriel Spark and Media Culture'. *Modern Fiction Studies* 62 no. 1 (2016): 70–91.

Woolf, Virginia. *The Diary of Virginia Woolf, Volume 4*, ed. Anne Olivier Bell and Andrew McNeillie. London: Hogarth Press, 1982.

Woolf, Virginia. 'How It Strikes a Contemporary'. *Times Literary Supplement*, 5 April 1923, reprinted in *Virginia Woolf: Selected Essays*, ed. David Bradshaw, 23–31. Oxford: Oxford University Press, 2009.

World Bank. *Economic Monitoring Report to the Ad Hoc Liaison Committee*. Washington, DC: World Bank Group, 2022. Available online: https://documents.worldbank.org/en/publication/documents-reports/documentdetail/099407305062233565/idu091fed1da019eb042d6090100a9320aa572de (accessed 7 August 2022).

World Trade Organization. 'Notification: Committee on Technical Barriers to Trade', 18 July 2017. Available online: https://docs.wto.org/dol2fe/Pages/SS/directdoc.aspx?filename=q:/G/TBTN17/CHN1211.pdf&Open=True (accessed 2 April 2022).

World Trade Organization. 'China's Import Ban on Solid Waste Queried at Import Licensing Meeting', 3 October 2017. Available online https://www.wto.org/english/news_e/news17_e/impl_03oct17_e.htm (accessed 2 March 2022).

Worley, Will. 'Syrian Woman Explains Why Refugees Need Smartphones'. *The Independent*, 12 May 2016. Available online: https://www.independent.co.uk/news/world/europe/why-do-refugees-have-smartphones-syrian-woman-explains-perfectly-refugee-crisis-a7025356.html (accessed 18 January 2022).

Xiong, Christine. 'Rethinking the Cyborg in Chen Qiufan's *Waste Tide*'. *Foundation* 50 no. 139 (2021): 75–89.
Yourgrau, Barry. 'Thumb Novels: Mobile Phone Fiction'. *Independent*, 29 July 2009. Available online: https://www.independent.co.uk/tech/thumb-novels-mobile-phone-fiction-1763849.html (accessed 15 October 2021).
Zantingh, Matthew. 'When Things Act Up: Thing Theory, Actor-Network Theory, and Toxic Discourse in Rita Wong's Poetry'. *Interdisciplinary Studies in Literature and Environment* 20 no. 3 (2013): 622–46.
Zeavin, Hannah. *The Distance Cure: A History of Teletherapy*. Cambridge, MA: MIT Press, 2021.

Index

'Abstraction in Poetry' (Ginsberg) 19
address vii, 11, 19, 22–4, 26, 32, 44, 50–1, 70–1. *See also* apostrophe
affect 75, 87, 124, 131, 136, 148, 180
afterlife 176, 182–3, 186–90, 200. *See also* spectrality
Agamben, Giorgio 142 n.76
Ahmed, Sara 10, 71, 74, 78, 81, 83, 125
Aiken, F. B. 150–2, 156, 168 n.32
airspace 95, 105–6
Akbar, Kaveh 31–4
Alaimo, Stacy 178, 180–1, 183–6, 189. *See also* 'trans-corporeality' (Alaimo)
Alas, Babylon! (Frank) 157–9, 161–2
Alexander, Elizabeth 33
All Ears: The Aesthetics of Espionage (Szendy) 56–7, 65 n.79
Allen, Donald 19
Allen, Edward 37 n.11
ambient literature 8
Andersen, Tore Rye 8
answerability 11–12, 120, 130–1. *See also* responsibility
Anthropocene 35, 180–1, 185–6
aporia 45, 48, 61, 136. *See also* impasse
aposiopesis 200
apostrophe 23–4. *See also* address
Arac, Jonathan 50
archive 12, 84, 119, 177, 190
atomic weapon 96, 145–8, 151, 154–5, 157–61, 164–5, 167–8 n.27, 169–70 n.60, 171 n.98. *See also* Cold War; Cuban Missile Crisis; nuclear war
atomization of language 12, 159–65
atomphone 163–5
Auster, Paul 1, 6
autocommunication 43, 51, 60
Awoonor, Kofi 120

Barghouti, Mourid 12, 95–107, 111, 112 n.24
  I Saw Ramallah 95, 97–100, 103–4
  I Was Born There, I Was Born Here 96, 98, 100–1, 105

Barrell, John 29
Barthes, Roland 4
Baudrillard, Jean 6, 84
Bauman, Zygmunt 174, 179
Bell, Alexander Graham vi, 1
Bell Telephone System 159
Bennington, Geoffrey vii
Benstock, Shari 8
Bentham, Jeremy 56, 66 n.85
Bergvall, Caroline 12, 36, 118–19, 122–9, 131–2, 134–6, 139 n.34
Bernard, Anna 97, 143 n.97
birds 80–1, 128–9, 162–3, 200
Blanchot, Maurice vii–viii
booth 3, 7, 77, 98
border 83, 95–6, 102, 104–5, 118, 122, 142 n.76, 163, 174
Bradbury Science Museum 145, 147, 151, 155, 165
Braithwaite, Oyinkan 7
breath 20, 29, 34, 121, 132–3, 135–6
Breathe (Pullinger) 8
Brooks, John 1–3, 12
Bryant, Peter 147–50, 158–60, 163, 168 n.41
Buell, Lawrence 194 n.56
Burdick, Eugene and Harvey Wheeler 148–9, 151–4, 156–63, 168 n.32
Butler, Judith 10–11, 89 n.28, 130–3, 135
  and Athanasiou 131–2, 136

Caldicott, Helen 158
'call and answer' (Woodbury-Tease) 11, 46, 49, 51. *See also* response
capitalism 32, 73, 84, 88, 159, 183, 185–6, 189
Carrington, Leonora 199
The Catcher in the Rye (Salinger) 3
cell phone novel 8. *See also* 'twitterature'
Chandler, Raymond 199–201
Chion, Michel 28
City of Glass (Auster) 6
Cixous, Hélène 2, 7

Clarkson, Helen 162–3
Clément, Catherine 132, 143 n.104
Coetzee, J. M. 1–2
Cold War 12, 53, 64 n.56, 83, 145–65, 167 n.21, 169–70 n.60, 172 n.103, 176. *See also* atomic weapon; Cuban Missile Crisis; nuclear war
Colloredo-Mansfeld, Rudi 193 n.39
comedy 58, 148, 167 n.21
Control of Electromagnetic Radiation (CONELRAD) service 157
Cordle, Daniel 155, 157, 163
crossed lines 5–7, 12, 26, 28–30, 36, 43, 95, 100, 106, 156
crying 1, 69, 82, 128, 136
Cuban Missile Crisis 12, 146–7, 151, 153, 165. *See also* atomic weapon; Cold War; nuclear war
cyborg 179–80, 188–9, 194 n.54

Darby, Andrew 128–9
Davies, Ben 70–1, 87
Day, Angel 63 n.32
dead line 162–3
death 7, 47, 50–1, 54, 69–72, 75, 85, 97, 99–101, 109, 112 n.24, 118–19, 122, 129, 137 n.10, 163, 182, 186
deferral 22, 24, 47, 49, 52, 108, 151–2, 165, 200
de Kerckhove, Derrick 146–7
Derrida, Jacques 2, 7, 11–12, 21, 45, 95, 106–11, 165
  'Am I in Jerusalem?' 107
  'Avowing – the Impossible' 108–10
  The Beast and the Sovereign 84
  For What Tomorrow ... A Dialogue 107–8
  The Gift of Death 107
  H.C. For Life, That Is to Say ... 2
  Literature in Secret 50–2
  'No Apocalypse, Not Now' 154–5, 160
  On Touching 95
  The Post Card 24, 70
  Specters of Marx 107
  'Telepathy' 2
  'Ulysses Gramophone' vii–viii
'destinerrance' (Derrida) 11, 21, 24–5, 29–30, 36, 44, 47, 70–1, 160, 200. *See also* errancy

Dharker, Imtiaz 7
digital culture 5, 8–9, 19–20, 29, 35, 62 n.28, 85, 114 n.49, 174–6, 181, 183, 185–7
Digital Rubbish (Gabrys) 173–4, 176–8, 183, 186, 190
Direct Communications Link (DCL) 149, 153
Discipline and Punish (Foucault) 56, 66 n.85
disorientation 12, 47, 71, 74–88, 119–21, 123, 134–5. *See also* global positioning system (GPS); locative technologies; maps; orientation
displacement 10, 12, 24, 49, 71, 79–83, 88, 95, 97–9, 102, 119, 142 n.76, 177, 184–5, 189, 200. *See also* exile; migration; refugee
disposal practices 146, 174–9, 182–6, 189. *See also* recycling
dispositif 154–5, 169 n.51, 169–70 n.60
distance 1–2, 4–5, 7, 9, 21–5, 27, 33, 47, 98–102, 109–11, 149, 153, 189
distress 127–8, 135, 141–2 n.72
  distress call 12, 119, 124–30, 132–3, 135–6, 141–2 n.72, 143 n.87
  distressed language 135–6
Doyle, Roddy 8
drift 117–18, 128, 134
  poetic drift 120–4
Drift (Bergvall) 118–19, 122–4, 126, 131, 134–5, 139 n.34
Duffy, Carol Ann 31

ears 31, 33–4, 36, 43–4, 59–60, 75, 100, 199
Earth 83–8, 105, 109–10. *See also* unearthly
echo 27–8, 33, 56–7, 128, 135
'The Ecstasy of Communication' (Baudrillard) 6
Edison, Thomas vi
electromagnetic pulse (EMP) 172 n.103, 188
electronic literature 8–9, 20, 41 n.84
'Electronic Necropolis' (Mao) 181–3
electronic waste 12, 35, 173–8, 180–6, 188–90, 191 n.14, 191 n.19, 192 n.24, 192 n.28

Eliot, T. S. 58
El-Rifae, Yasmin 104–5
embodiment 10, 25, 34, 179–81, 133, 179–81, 187, 194 n.54
Enhanced Group Call (EGC) 126
eroticism 70, 75, 158
errancy 11, 21, 24, 29, 33–6, 44, 176, 187. *See also* 'destinerrance' (Derrida)
espionage 52, 54, 56–8. *See also* hearing; intelligence networks; listening; surveillance
exile 95–9, 101, 105–6, 133, 149. *See also* displacement; migration; refugee
Exporting Harm (Basel Action Network) 174, 183–4

'fabulous textuality' (Derrida) 154–5
Facebook 8. *See also* social media; Twitter
Fail-Safe (Burdick and Wheeler) 148–9, 151–4, 156–63, 168 n.32
The Fail-Safe Fallacy (Hook) 168 n.41
Farrier, David 182, 185. *See also* time
fear of the phone 4, 199
Ferraris, Maurizio 32, 34–5, 77
fetish 73, 89 n.21, 158–9, 165, 200
flight 54, 81, 129, 150, 200
fog 134–5, 144 n.121, 200
Forensic Architecture 118–20, 122–7, 136 n.1, 137 n.5, 139–40 n.48. *See also* left-to-die boat
forensics 119, 123–4, 126, 139–40 n.48
Foucault, Michel 56, 66 n.85, 169 n.51. *See also* surveillance
Frames of War (Butler) 130–3
Frank, Pat 157–9, 161–2
Freud, Sigmund 4, 14 n.22, 14 n.23
Funkhouser, Christopher 20
future 2, 10, 12–13, 22, 44, 46, 60, 73, 107, 111, 149–50, 163, 176, 180, 183, 187, 189

Gabrys, Jennifer 11, 173–4, 176–8, 183, 186, 190
Gay, Peter 4
gender 3, 10, 18 n.66, 158, 165
genre 3, 11, 51, 149–50, 180
generic hybridity 123, 180–1, 189
Gillespie, Marie 101, 125
Ginsberg, Allen 19

glitch 35–6, 201
globalization 10–11, 83–5, 99, 101, 146, 178, 183–6
global positioning system (GPS) 32, 80–1, 83, 85–6, 91 n.70, 117, 125–7. *See also* disorientation; locative technologies; maps; orientation
Goggin, Gerard and Caroline Hamilton 30
gossip 21, 45
Govrin, Michal 109–11
Goytisolo, Juan 101
green telephone 53–4, 57
Guiyu 12, 174–9, 181, 183–4, 187, 191 n.14, 191 n.19

Hamilton, Patrick vii
Hanke, Bob 29
Healey, Cara 180, 187–8
hearing vi, 11, 23, 31, 33–4, 36, 54, 56–60, 65 n.82, 66–7 n.94, 70, 100, 128–30, 136, 152, 160–3, 171 n.98. *See also* listening
hearing voices 44, 58
mishearing 19, 47, 57, 70, 128–9
overhearing 11, 19, 22, 27, 44, 51–2, 54–5, 57–61. *See also* espionage; listening; surveillance
Heidegger, Martin 84, 130
Heller, Charles, Lorenzo Pezzani and Situ Studio. *See* Forensic Architecture
Hennessey, Michael 20
Herbert, W. N. vii
Herd, David 21
Herrera, Yuri 10
Hetherington, Kevin 176, 178, 182–3, 188
Hirsch, Edward 20
hoax call 50
Hollow Land (Weizman) 95–6, 105–6
Horn, Eva 150, 169–70 n.60, 170 n.66, 171 n.97
hospitality 119–21
hotline 147–58, 160, 167 n.26, 169 n.49, 170 n.64, 170 n.67. *See also* nuclear communication; red telephone
human-waste relations 176, 178–83
hybrid object 154, 156, 169 n.52
hyperconnectivity 84–5

immateriality 30, 35, 106, 175, 182–3, 185–6
immediacy 5, 20, 30, 32, 35–6, 83, 102, 148–9, 186, 188
impasse 23, 48, 54. *See also* aporia
indeterminability vii, 6, 11, 24, 33, 47, 49–52, 50, 67 n.100, 77–8, 86–8, 160
intelligence networks 52–7, 59, 158. *See also* espionage; surveillance
interception 3, 53, 70
International Convention for the Safety of Life at Sea (SOLAS) 127, 141 n.72
International Convention on Maritime Search and Rescue (SAR) 127, 141 n.70
In the Break (Moten) 132–3, 144 n.108
intimacy 4, 19, 22–4, 33, 36, 77, 149–50, 181
Israeli-Palestinian conflict 12, 95–7, 100–11, 118. *See also* Oslo Accords; Palestine; Six-Day War
Izenberg, Oren 23

Jarrett, Kylie and Janeen Naji 8
Jimmy Carter Library and Museum 156, 170 n.64
Jones, Nathan 21, 35–6
Joudah, Fady 11, 21, 31–6
 'Bulb' 33
 'Iron Maiden' 33
 'Revolution 3' 32
 'Textu' 34–6
 Textu 31–6
Jung, Carl 4

Kafka, Franz 1
Kaplan, Caren 83–4
Kaplan, Edward 147
Kermode, Frank 11, 45, 49–50, 63 n.40
Kern, Stephen 9
Keyser, Barbara Y. 52, 55, 65 n.76
Kittler, Friedrich 4
Koenigsberg, Allen vi

Laing, R. D. 4
Lake, Carol vii
landline 30, 70, 77, 102–3
The Last Day (Clarkson) 162–3

Lea, Daniel 78, 86
left-to-die boat 12, 118–30, 132–6 n.1, 137 n.10, 138 n.15. *See also* Forensic Architecture
Leighton, Angela 21, 31, 33–6
Leonard, Philip 71, 83, 85, 87, 92 n.104
Lispector, Clarice 6–7
 Agua Viva 7
 'Correct Assumptions' 6–7
listening 4, 9, 13, 27–8, 30, 36, 44, 46, 52–61, 65 n.79, 65 n.82, 66–7 n.94, 118, 129–30, 136, 148. *See also* hearing; surveillance
Listening (Nancy) 57–8
Literature in the First Media Age (Trotter) 48
Literature of Connection (Trotter) 5–6
locative technologies 11, 77, 79–80, 83. *See also* disorientation; global positioning system; maps; orientation
long distance calling 21–2, 27, 98–9
The Long Goodbye (Chandler) 200
Lopez, Beatriz 53
Lynch, Claire 9

MacCabe, Colin 28
Mackay, Marina 52, 64 n.56
MacLeod, Lewis 52
Made to Break (Slade) 175
madness 4, 6, 58, 179
Maloney, Sean M. 155, 170 n.62
Mandel, Emily St John 173–4, 189
Mao, Sally Wen 12, 176, 181–3, 189
maps 76, 80–3, 87–8, 101, 118, 122, 176, 185. *See also* disorientation; global positioning system; locative technologies; orientation
Marks, Peter 65 n.79
Marx, Karl 89 n.21
Masco, Joseph 145–6, 161, 171 n.98
Mbembe, Achille 122
McCanles, Michael 147
McCarren, Felicia 100, 102
McLuhan, Marshall 1, 6, 10, 20, 160
McMurtry, Áine 123, 134–5, 142 n.76
McQuillan, Martin 44–5, 48–9, 62–3 n.28, 63 n.29, 67 n.100, 108
Menke, Richard 5

Meyrowitz, Joshua 9–10
migration 81, 98, 117–19, 125, 136 n.1 *See also* displacement; exile; refugee
Miller, Steven E. 153
missile 12, 145–7, 150, 152–5, 157–8, 163, 165, 200
Missile Envy (Caldicott) 158
missive 12, 153–5, 158, 163, 165
mobile phone 8–12, 20, 30–2, 34–6, 69–71, 73, 77–83, 85, 87, 91 n.70, 100, 102–6, 109–10, 124–6, 173, 175–6, 186–8, 192 n.23, 192 n.24. *See also* smartphone; text message
  and mobility 7–9, 11, 77, 95, 101, 104, 125
  reception vii, 14 n.22, 20, 54, 69–70, 105, 124, 135
  as writing machine 32, 34
modernism 4–5, 34, 62–3 n.28
more-than-human 28, 119, 128–30, 154, 179–82
Morris, Adelaide 34–5, 119, 124, 139–40 n.48
Moten, Fred 132–3, 144 n.108
Moysaenko, Daniel 121
Mujezinovic, Davor 191 n.19
multilingualism 134, 186
Murakami, Haruki 3
museum 177–8, 190, 193 n.39
Museum of Civilisation 173–4, 189
mutually assured destruction (MAD) 147, 150

Nabokov, Vladimir 133
Nancy, Jean-Luc 11, 45–6, 57–8, 60
Nanz, Tobias 150–1, 153–4, 156, 160–1, 167 n.26, 168 n.41, 169 n.49, 170 n.67
network 3, 6, 9–11, 22, 29, 34, 44, 52–7, 80, 97, 99, 102–3, 146, 151, 155–7, 159, 162
Night Film (Pessl) 8
Nixon, Rob 174, 176, 186, 189, 200
noise 10, 28–9, 36, 53–4, 59–61, 160–1, 201. *See also* Shannon and Weaver; sound
The Nuclear Borderlands (Masco) 145–6, 161, 171 n.98
nuclear communication 146–7, 157–9, 163. *See also* hotline; red telephone

Nuclear Test Ban Treaty 145
nuclear war 146, 148–9, 151–5, 158, 161, 163, 165, 168 n.41. *See also* atomic weapon; Cold War; Cuban Missile Crisis

obsolescence 1, 35, 174, 176, 186, 188, 192 n.23
O'Hara, Frank 3, 11, 19, 21–5, 36
  '3 Poems about Kenneth Koch' 21–2
  'A Sonnet for Jane Freilicher' 21
  'Metaphysical Poem' 22–3
  'Music' 21
  'Nocturne' 21, 23
  'Personism' 11, 19, 21–3, 25
  'Poem [Instant coffee with slightly sour cream]' 21
Olson, Charles 20
Ong, Walter 22
operator vii, 1, 10, 21, 26–7, 101, 104, 153
orbit 83, 85–8. *See also* stars; unearthly
orientation 12, 71, 75–6, 78, 81, 83–8, 134. *See also* disorientation; global positioning system; locative technologies; maps
Oslo Accords 96, 103–4. *See also* Israeli-Palestinian conflict; Palestine; Six-Day War
Overbye, Dennis vi, 201

Palestine 12, 31, 95–111, 118. *See also* Israeli-Palestinian conflict; Oslo Accords; Six-Day War
Perloff, Marjorie 19–22, 26–9, 33, 37 n.11
  and Craig Dworkin 29
Perlow, Seth 20–1, 23–4, 41 n.84
Perril, Simon 26
Pessl, Marisha 8
Political Warfare Executive (PWE) 44
pollution 85, 174–5, 178, 182, 185–6, 189. *See also* toxicity
postcolonial telephone 12, 85, 100
preservation 173, 177, 190
privacy 7, 20, 33, 37 n.11
Prochnau, William 158
prosthesis 109–10, 179, 187
proximity vii, 2, 7, 83, 107, 109–11
psychoanalysis 4–5, 14 n.22, 99
Pullinger, Kate 8

Qiufan, Chen 12, 176–81, 187–90
queer 71–80, 87–8, 89 n.28. *See also* twist
Queer Phenomenology (Ahmed) 74, 78, 125

racial politics 10, 18 n.66, 81–2, 144 n.108, 178, 182
Rambuss, Richard 63 n.32
Raworth, Tom 11, 21, 25–30, 34, 36, 39 n.49
 '7/8 of the Real' 30
 'Ace' 26
 'A Pressed Flower' 25
 'Beautiful Habit' 30
 'But I Don' *Love*' 25
 'Catacoustics' 27–8
 'Letters from Yaddo' 26–7
 'Nothing' 26
 'Patch Patch Patch' 25
 'Reverse in Through Driving' 25
 'There are Lime-Trees in Leaf on the Promenade' 25
 'The Wall' 25
 Writing 28–30
recycling 174–5, 177, 179, 181, 189, 191 n.19. *See also* disposal practices
Red Alert (Bryant) 147–50, 158–60, 163, 168 n.41
red telephone 155–60, 169 n.49, 170 n.62, 170 n.66, 170 n.67. *See also* hotline; nuclear communication
Reed, Brian 25
Reines, Ariana vii
refugee 96, 101, 117–29, 131–6, 136 n.1, 137 n.8, 142 n.76, 143 n.97. *See also* displacement; exile; migration
remainder 165, 176–7, 182–3, 185–90. *See also* trace
repetition 21–2, 33, 47, 74, 112 n.24, 121–3, 126–7, 132, 134, 144 n.121, 200
response vii–viii, 10–11, 49, 69, 82, 121, 124, 127–36, 151, 200. *See also* 'call and answer'
responsibility 12, 49, 86, 103, 118, 127–8, 130–1, 136, 136 n.4, 143 n.97, 146, 190, 200. *See also* answerability and responsibilization 131
rhythm 11, 25, 33–5, 120, 132–3
Ronell, Avital 2, 4, 7, 44, 46, 99, 130, 199

Roshwald, Mordecai 163–5, 172 n.112
Royle, Nicholas 2–3, 7, 51–2, 59, 199
Rubbish Theory (Thompson) 174
Rudin, Michael 31

Salinger, J. D. 3
satellite 83–6, 92 n.104, 109, 140 n.57, 200
 'satellization' 84, 95
satellite phone 117, 125–8, 187
Saucier, P. Khalil and Tryon Woods 129
Saussure, Ferdinand de 28
Schafer, R. Murray 33
Schantz, Ned 3, 5–6
Schmidt di Friedberg, Marcella 71, 81
Schwartz, Claire 33
Science-Based Stockpile Stewardship (SBSS) 145
scrambling 26–7, 31, 36, 53–4, 60
secrecy 11, 44–5, 47–56, 58, 60–1, 63 n.32, 63 n.40, 70–1, 200
Sedgwick, Eve Kosofsky 73
Seed, David 149, 158, 163, 167 n.21
Selerie, Gavin 26, 29
serialization 8
Serres, Michel 101
Shannon, Claude and Warren Weaver 28–9, 60, 160. *See also* noise
Sharpe, Christina 117
Shea, Ammon vi
Signs Preceding the End of the World (Herrera) 10
silence 10–11, 26, 31, 34, 43, 54, 134, 151–2, 158, 160–3, 165, 200
SIM cards 104
Six-Day War 96–7. *See also* Israeli-Palestinian conflict; Oslo Accords; Palestine
Slade, Giles 175, 192 n.23
'slow violence' (Nixon) 174, 186, 189, 200
smartphone 6, 8, 12, 31–2, 71, 73, 76, 79–80, 82–3, 101, 125, 173–5, 183, 186–8, 190. *See also* mobile phone; text message
Smith, Ali 12, 69–88
 Autumn 71
 'Being Quick' 69–71, 87
 'Blank Card' 70
 'The Book Club' 91 n.91

'Cold Iron' 70
How to Be Both 71–9, 85–6, 88, 88–9 n.16
Spring 71, 80–3
Summer 71, 79–81, 84, 86
There but for The 78
'The Unthinkable Happens to People Every Day' 70
Winter 71, 80–1, 84
Smith, Hazel 22, 28
social connectivity 21–4, 33
social media 8, 32–3, 80, 125. *See also* Facebook; Twitter
Solnit, Rebecca 77–8
sound 11, 14 n.22, 20, 27–31, 33–6, 56, 59–60, 69, 99, 120, 129, 134–6, 151–2, 156, 159–61, 164–5, 171 n.98, 200. *See also* noise
sovereignty 84, 86, 92 n.104, 96, 108, 122, 152
Soyinka, Wole 7
Spark, Muriel 11, 43–61, 62 n.12, 62–3 n.28, 64 n.53, 64 n.56, 67 n.100, 70, 77
    The Abbess of Crewe 54–7, 59–60, 63 n.29, 65 n.76
    The Comforters 52, 58
    Curriculum Vitae 44, 53, 58–9
    The Girls of Slender Means 45–50, 52, 57, 59
    The Hothouse by the East River 51–4, 57, 60, 64 n.53, 77
    Memento Mori 50–1
    The Prime of Miss Jean Brodie 52, 65 n.82
    'The Small Telephone' 43–4, 51, 60–1
Speak, Memory (Nabokov) 133
spectrality 52, 110, 112 n.24, 163, 182–3, 188–90, 200. *See also* afterlife
speech vii, 19, 24, 28, 32, 47, 59, 107–8, 118, 136, 165
    speechlessness 47, 137 n.8, 146
speed 29–31, 34–5, 43, 74, 79, 103, 148, 150, 183–7. *See also* time
Sputnik Sweetheart (Murakami) 3
Stannard, Martin 51, 58
stars 84–6, 129, 200. *See also* orbit; unearthly
Station Eleven (Mandel) 173–4, 189

Stevenson, Sheryl 52
Stewart, Garret 29, 36
Stiegler, Bernard 84–5
Stillman, Sarah 129
Strategic Air Command (SAC) 150–1, 158–9, 170 n.62
Sun, Mengtian 175
surveillance 11, 44, 53–7, 62–3 n.28, 66 n.85, 82, 85, 117, 118, 123, 126. *See also* espionage; hearing; intelligence networks; listening
    bugging 54–5
    and Christianity 65 n.79
    eavesdropping 19, 22, 54–5, 58–9
    intelligence 52–7, 59, 158
    listening-in 45, 52, 56, 58, 60. *See also* hearing, listening
    panacousticon 56–7
    panopticon 56, 66 n.85, 80, 84–5, 105. *See also* Foucault, Michel
    tapping 11, 29, 44–5, 55, 111, 200
suspension 20, 22, 45, 48–52, 54, 60–1, 69–70, 87, 105, 111 n.3, 122, 132, 152, 155, 157–8, 163, 165, 200–1
Swinburne, Henry 56
switchboard vii, 5, 10, 25–30, 62 n.19, 112 n.24
syncopation 120–1, 132–4, 143 n.104, 144 n.108
Syncope (Wadud) 118–22, 126–34, 136, 138 n.15
Szendy, Peter 56–7, 65 n.79, 66 n.88

tackiness 183, 186, 188, 190
Tawil-Souri, Helga 95, 102–4
technoaesthetics 145, 161
telecommunications infrastructure 12, 95, 97, 99, 101–4, 114 n.49, 146, 149
    antenna 105–6
    bandwidth 103–5
    cell phone tower 10, 104–5
    spectrum 104, 106, 114 n.49
telepathy 2–3, 44
'The Telephone' (Very) 19, 24
téléphone arabe 100
The Telephone Book: Technology, Schizophrenia, Electric Speech (Ronell) 2, 46, 99, 130, 199
telephone directory vi, viii n.1, 201

telephone greetings vi–viii, 7, 22, 69, 130
telephone hardware
   bell vi, 1, 6, 25, 27, 99–100, 156–7, 160
   cord 26, 99
   mouthpiece vii, 31
   receiver vii, 6, 14 n.22, 25–6, 31, 34, 43, 60, 70, 99, 151, 156, 170 n.67, 173, 188–9, 199–201
   screen 6, 30, 33, 69, 83, 85, 173, 185, 187
   wire vii, 1, 3, 7, 10–11, 21, 22, 24–6, 30, 43, 102, 152
television 28, 109
terminal exchange 57, 165, 199–201
text message 7–8, 30–6, 71, 73, 75–6, 127. *See also* mobile phone; smartphone; textspeak
textspeak 34–6. *See also* text message
Thomas, Bronwen 8
Thompson, Michael 174
Thornber, Karen 189, 196–7 n.118
Thuraya Telecommunications Company 125, 127, 140 n.57
Thurschwell, Pamela 2–5
Tietchen, Todd 20
time 8, 27–31, 74, 76, 86, 102, 109, 121, 123, 127, 134, 153, 175, 185–6, 200. *See also* speed
   'bomb time' (Bryant) 148
   deep time 180, 182, 185, 190
   real time 5, 29, 150
   'thick time' (Farrier) 182
toxicity 12, 20, 174–6, 178–90, 192 n.21, 194 n.56. *See also* pollution
trace 27, 35, 108, 124, 134–5, 139–40 n.48, 155, 189–90. *See also* remainder
'trans-corporeality' (Alaimo) 180, 183–6, 189
Trinity's Child (Prochnau) 158–9
Trotter, David 5–6, 48
twist 72–6, 78, 80, 85–8, 89 n.28, 101. *See also* queer
Twitter 32–3, 41 n.93, 80. *See also* Facebook; social media
'twitterature' 8. *See also* cell phone novel
Two Pints (Doyle) 8

unanswered calls 3, 6, 69–71, 128, 132–3, 136, 163

uncanny vii, 3, 44, 57, 77, 86, 112 n.24, 187
Understanding Media (McLuhan) 20
unearthly 83–8, 200. *See also* Earth; orbit; stars
United Nations Convention on the Law of the Sea (UNCLOS) 117, 127, 141 n.72

verticality 9, 95, 105–6, 200
Very, Jones 19, 24
videophone 7, 79, 125
Virilio, Paul 30, 34
virus 173, 179
voice vii–viii, 2–4, 6, 11–12, 22–4, 26–31, 33, 36, 51, 54, 59–60, 66–7 n.94, 96, 99, 110, 118, 120, 135, 148–9, 151–4, 159, 162, 164–5, 188
   marginalised voices 96, 118, 120, 125, 129, 131, 136
   multiple voices viii, 22, 26–8, 78, 120–1, 131, 134
   writing voice 58–9

Wadud, Asiya 118–22, 126–34, 136, 138 n.15
Wallace, David Foster 7
Walton, Samantha 183–5, 195 n.89
Waste Tide (Qiufan) 12, 176–81, 187–90
Watson, Thomas A. 1, 199
Waugh, Patricia 44–5, 53, 58–9
Weber, Elisabeth 77
Weber, Samuel 80
Weizman, Eyal 11–12, 95–6, 105–6
'Where Does Palestine Begin?' (El-Rifae) 104–5
Williams, William Carlos 20
Wills, David 24, 50
Wilson, Emma 130, 143 n.87
wireless 11, 19, 21, 70, 102, 109, 179
Wong, Rita 12, 176, 181, 183–7, 189
   'pollution dodged?' 185–7
   'sort by day, burn by night' 181, 183–5
Woodbury-Tease, Amy 44–7, 49, 51, 53, 62–3 n.28. *See also* 'call and answer'
Woolf, Virginia 1
World War II 5, 44, 51, 53–4, 64 n.56, 167 n.26

Zeavin, Hannah 4